P9-ASK-935

John Xántus:
The Fort Tejon Letters

John Xántus

John Xántus:
The Fort Tejon Letters
1857–1859

Ann Zwinger

The University of Arizona Press / Tucson

About the Author

Ann Zwinger, naturalist, author, and illustrator, was awarded the John Burroughs Memorial Association Gold Medal in 1976 for *Run, River, Run.* Earlier books include *Wind in the Rock* and *Beyond the Aspen Grove.* The natural history of the Cape region of Baja California is described in her 1984 publication, *A Desert Country Near the Sea.*

Frontispiece and portrait on page xvii reproduced from Xántus: Hungarian Naturalist in the Pioneer West, *by Henry Miller Madden, through the courtesy of William P. Wreden.*

Copyright © 1986 by Ann H. Zwinger
All Rights Reserved

THE UNIVERSITY OF ARIZONA PRESS

This book was set in Linotron 202 Meridien types.
Manufactured in the U.S.A.

Library of Congress Cataloging-in-Publication Data
Xántus, János, 1825–1894.
John Xántus, the Fort Tejon letters, 1857–1859.

Bibliography: p.
Includes index.
1. Xántus, Janos, 1825–1894—Correspondence.
2. Naturalists—United States—Correspondence.
I. Zwinger, Ann.   II. Title.
QH31.X3A35   1986   508.32'4   86-1908
ISBN 0-8165-0941-7 (alk. paper)

Contents

John Xántus
Fort Tejon, 1857–1859

John Xántus arrived at Fort Tejon on May 18, 1857, and left on January 14, 1859. Here, at this fort tucked into the southern Tehachapi Mountains of California, Xántus developed into one of Spencer Fullerton Baird's most prolific collectors.

Don Pedro Fages, on a reconnaissance trip from Mexico in 1772, first described Cañada des Uvas—Grapevine Canyon—where Fort Tejon would be located. He crossed what is now Tejon Pass and descended through groves of "white-oak and live-oaks" still characteristic of the countryside. Subsequently the area was held by the Church until the missions were secularized in 1834, whereupon Lieutenant Antonio del Valle received the land grant that became El Tejon. He supposedly named it when a badger—*tejon* in Spanish—confronted him at the mouth of a canyon.

El Tejon was still in Mexican hands when Lt. Edward Fitzgerald Beale acquired part of it for the Tejon Indian Reservation, having paid around five cents an acre. Beale, new Superintendent of Indian Affairs, established the reservation in 1853 about 15 miles northwest of the site where, two years later, Fort Tejon would be built, ostensibly as his headquarters. To the south, the Mexican Governor of California held another land grant, Rancho Castaic, of 22,178 acres. It was upon this land that Fort Tejon was eventually built.

The needs for a fort in this location were multiple. Although the Indians of the reservation were considered "friendly," wandering bands of other Indians freely attacked white settlers. Even worse were the marauding *bandidos* who plagued the few *ranchos* in the area. Since Tejon Pass was not only one of the main north-south passes between the

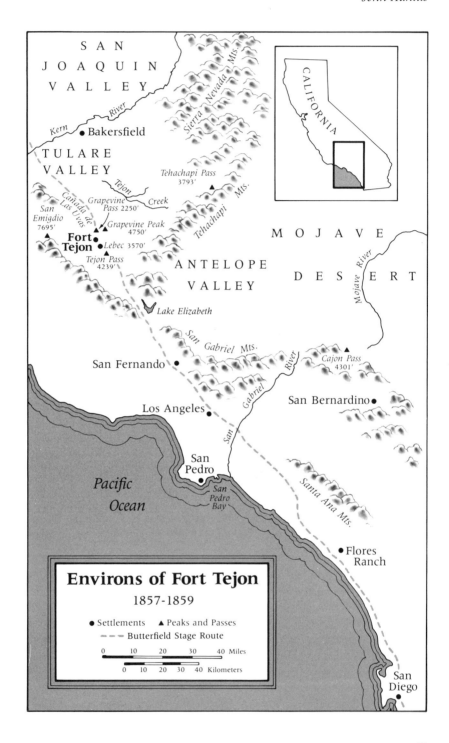

SAN
JOAQUIN
VALLEY

Sierra Nevada Mts.

Kern *River*

• Bakersfield

TULARE
VALLEY

Tejon

Tehachapi Pass
3793'

Cañada de Las Uvas

Grapevine Pass 2250'

Creek

San Emigdio 7695'

Grapevine Peak 4750'

Fort Tejon • *Lebec* 3570'

Tehachapi Mts.

Tejon Pass 4239'

ANTELOPE
VALLEY

MOJAVE

DESERT

Mojave River

Lake Elizabeth

San Gabriel Mts.

San Fernando •

Cajon Pass 4301'

River

Los Angeles •

San Gabriel

San Bernardino •

San

San Pedro •

Pacific Ocean

San Pedro Bay

Santa Ana Mts.

CALIFORNIA

• Flores Ranch

Environs of Fort Tejon
1857-1859

• Settlements ▲ Peaks and Passes
— — — Butterfield Stage Route

0	10	20	30	40 Miles
0	10	20	30	40 Kilometers

San Diego •

Mojave Desert and the San Joaquin Valley but one of the lowest, a fort would provide security for the westbound immigrants who crossed the Pass. To this end a fort was ordered established in June 1854, and the First Dragoons moved in two months later. The fort was officially completed in 1855.

To those parched immigrants who trudged up from the Mojave Desert, Grapevine Canyon must have looked like paradise, deeply green and well watered. General Joseph K. Mansfield, who made an inspection trip of the site the year before the fort was built, allowed that a fort would be "beautifully located among large oak trees near the mountains and with abundant water, wood, and grazing near."

The California segment of the Pacific Railroad Survey, under Lieutenant Robert Stockton Williamson, surveying for the most practical routes across California, also passed through the valley in 1853 and camped precisely where the fort's parade ground would lie. Williamson's geologist, William P. Blake, reported:

> The surface of the valley is covered with a luxuriant growth of grass, and a deep soil supports groves of magnificent oak trees, some of them eight feet in diameter. A small brook of pure and cold water was found here, and our camp was on its borders, under the branches of the large oaks, while those branches that had fallen, or been broken off by bears in gathering acorns, furnished fuel for the fires.

Fifty years later, Joseph Grinnell, the noted California ornithologist, found

> the most impressive feature of the Tejon valley to one entering from the dry barren plains on either side, are the magnificent oak groves, interspersed with green pastures. . . . Many springs contribute to a fair-sized brook, which, lined with immense willow and lofty maples, festooned with grapevines, takes its tumultuous way down the narrow gorge below the Fort to the San Joaquin Valley.

Because Fort Tejon lay at the joining of disparate environments—the mountains, the foothills, and the desert—the site was an ecotone and as such enjoyed rich populations of almost everything that crawled, flew, pounced, clawed, or fled across the countryside. To Spencer Fullerton Baird, sitting at the Assistant Secretary's desk at the Smithsonian Institution, building up an unparalleled natural-history collection for the National Museum, Fort Tejon was a tempting station from which to obtain specimens.

Baird was just beginning to put together his network of collectors and was continually looking for places where they might best be occupied. Two years after the establishment of the Fort Tejon, Baird wrote:

> There is no locality from which [specimens] would be more acceptable.
> We have a few things brought by Lt. Williamson from that vicinity, just enough for us to wish for more.

As if in answer to Baird's wish, into his purview came John Xántus.

《 》

Xántus, Hungarian immigrant, possessed many of the attributes of a good collector: he was ingenious and curious, productive despite a dearth of time and equipment, intelligent and acquisitive, able to prepare specimens properly, and quick to learn. He was also possessed of the hubris that comes from a glorified self-image unsupported by reality and intensified by the tenuousness of his personal circumstances, qualities that would try Baird's patience while rewarding his curator's eye. The route by which Xántus traveled to Fort Tejon is murky, for the only source of Xántus' early life is Xántus himself, and, typically, his glorified sense of self goaded him to rearrange facts and create a world in which he was hero.

In a letter from Fort Tejon dated November 16, 1858, he advised Baird that he had graduated from the Polytechnical School in Vienna and then entered the Royal Artillery; when the war broke out between Austria and Hungary in 1848, he attempted in vain to resign his commission but was instead entrusted with "an important mission" by the Hungarian Secretary of War. Meanwhile the Austrians accused him of desertion, seized his property, and "I found myself homeless & penniless trown out to Asia."

Henry Miller Madden, Xántus' biographer, documents that the only accurate statement in the above is that he was expelled from Austria. He fled to the United States (not Asia) and arrived in 1851. Here he found it impossible to make a living; "being a good piano player, and a tolerable draughtsmen, I procured a honorable support by teaching for a short time," but it was clearly not enough. No help was forthcoming from those whom he felt were in a position to help. The job market in the United States was poor, and there was undoubted prejudice against a foreign accent, especially when it was accompanied by Xántus' insufferable arrogance. His hypersensitivity, his jealousy and continual resentment of authority, must have made him difficult or impossible to hire or work with.

An inveterate name dropper, Xántus fantasized a meeting in New Orleans with the leading European naturalists of the day: Dr. Moritz Wagner and Karl Scherzer, Dr. Henrik Krøyer, Duke Paul Wilhelm of Württemberg, Louis Agassiz. He followed this with a tale of a spurious collecting expedition into northern Minnesota. Both trips are the product of an over-reaching imagination. Because the travels of the naturalists in question are well documented, it is impossible that Xántus could have been with all of them at the same time in New Orleans, although he did live there for about a year. As if reality were too troublesome to be bothered with, he wrote taradiddles home about his adventures, which his family would later have published as *Xántos János Levelei Éjszákamerikábol deli reszeiben*. To make his family proud of him was an admirable aim, but these letters, as well as those of the next few years, are characterized more by fraudulent adventures and plagiarism than by accuracy and actual accomplishment.

In August 1854, Xántus repaired to New Buda, a Hungarian settlement in Iowa, and remained there a year. New Buda had been established four years previously by a group of refugees who had taken up land under an Act of September 4, 1841, which gave special Congressional approval to Hungarian refugees wishing to homestead in the United States. Xántus claimed a parcel of land, the northeast and northwest quarters of Section 36, Township 70, Range 27, and undertook the required improvements with "my friend Madarass." Laszlo Madárasz was host to Xántus while he was there, but Xántus later was to accuse him of chicanery. Most of Xántus' compatriots considered him a fraud and he left under a cloud of acrimony; the bad feelings lasted so long that the group, hearing half a decade later of Xántus' exploits, checked out his stories and, finding them false, exposed him in the Hungarian newspapers.

At the close of the New Buda debacle, Xántus had no job prospects whatsoever. As a last resort he enlisted as a private in the U. S. Army in 1855. Joining the Army was so demeaning to him that he assumed a new name (a frequent practice in the mid-nineteenth century), Louis de Vésey, a deed which was to cause endless mischief and confusion. Despite his protestations to Baird to use his correct name, Xántus never signed a letter with it until he was discharged from the Army in January 1859.

Xántus' first Army station was hardly one to put joy into the heart of a city man: Fort Riley in the Kansas Territory. But at Fort Riley he found salvation. For Xántus, salvation came in the person of Dr. William A. Hammond, a remarkable man of intelligence and generosity. Hammond, an Army surgeon who would later become Surgeon General of the United States, was an amateur ornithologist and a friend of Baird's. As surgeon at Fort Riley, he heeded the exhortations of Spencer Baird to the military men who spread out over the unknown areas of North America to collect, collect, collect. Army surgeons were predisposed to handling zoological specimens, and many of them—Dr. Elliott Coues, Dr. James G. Cooper, Dr. William Hammond—became ornithologists, enchanted as much by the beauty of the birds as by the scientific challenge.

For men who were far from the comradeship of society, collecting was a diversion, something that pulled them out of themselves and the difficulties of their isolated existence, providing some instant satisfaction and a promise of tomorrow. Prestige was attached to collecting for someone else, especially the Smithsonian, and Baird was an enthusiastic visionary who inspired others. In addition, Army surgeons usually enjoyed considerable free time and, in remote areas, little place to spend it. Collecting must have been a godsend.

Such collectors always needed help and drew on the handy pool of enlisted men. In Xántus, Hammond found a willing and relatively sophisticated student. He taught Xántus something of ornithology and how to prepare specimens, and encouraged him to collect on his own. Xántus learned quickly and collected assiduously.

Soon Xántus was shipping specimens to both the Smithsonian and the Academy of Natural Sciences in Philadelphia. On the strength of his contributions, Xántus was honored by being elected to membership in the Academy in 1856, sponsored by two famous scientists, John Le Conte and Edward Hallowell, no small recognition. By this time, Xántus certainly must have discovered that collecting was infinitely preferable to other Army duties.

Hammond arranged for Xántus to be transferred to the medical department in January 1857 and raised him to the equivalent rank of sergeant. More important, Hammond introduced Xántus to Baird. In February of 1857 their seven-year correspondence began when Xántus wrote:

> So I take the opportunity now, to inform you sir, that I am willing, and am ready to send from time to time such contributions of Nat.

History to the S.I., as my poor abilities and my confined circumstances will allow.

Baird had connections (his father-in-law was Inspector General of the
Army, Brigadier General Sylvester Churchill) and he finagled Xántus'
transfer to Fort Tejon, California. But when Xántus arrived, the situation
turned out not to be what he anticipated. Baird's contact and surgeon
of the post, Dr. Gardiner, whom Baird assumed would be Xántus' patron at Fort Tejon, had been transferred elsewhere. His replacement and
Xántus' immediate superior was Dr. Peter G. S. Ten Broeck.

Ten Broeck quickly became Xántus' nemesis. He probably took reasonable exception to Xántus' predilection for hunting instead of running the dispensary; so Xántus made Ten Broeck his prime antagonist,
his stumbling block to greatness. Ten Broeck, according to Xántus, reported for roll call at the end of one month and the beginning of the
next and then absented himself to the fleshpots of Los Angeles, leaving
all the work on Xántus' shoulders. Actually, Ten Broeck's army records
indicate he was a commendable medical officer.

From Washington, Baird, the quintessential peacemaker, tried to
smooth Xántus' way. He wrote a cordial letter to Ten Broeck soon after
Xántus' arrival, as Xántus requested, recommending Xántus' past work
and its importance to the Smithsonian, and offering to send Ten Broeck
any of the government or Smithsonian publications that he might desire. He also subtly let it be known that, because of his position, he had
secured Xántus' assignment, a bit of power politics that probably did
not go unnoticed. Not only did Baird write to Ten Broeck, but he had
his father-in-law, Inspector General Churchill, write to Major Alexander
Hamilton Blake, commandant at Fort Tejon, which hardly could have
endeared either Baird or Xántus to the field officers. Baird, safely in
Washington, passed on Ten Broeck's promise of assistance in a letter to
Xántus on October 17, 1857:

> I had a very kind letter from Dr. Ten Broeck by the last mail in
> which he promises all assistance to you in his power. This I have no
> doubt he will do and I will write him again.

Irked by Xántus' insistence on special privilege, the field officers paid lip
service to Baird's requests and then proceeded not to honor them at all.
Xántus' popularity was scarcely enhanced when the grizzly bear cub he
kept as a pet ate the colonel's dog.

Although Xántus wrote Baird a month later that Dr. Ten Broeck had
been "very kind since some days towards me," the relationship soon

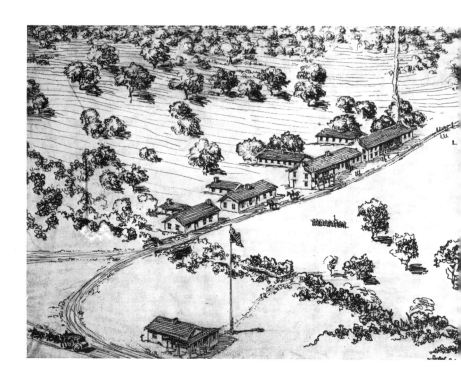

soured again and Ten Broeck put a lid on Xántus' collecting activities. Xántus found Ten Broeck beneath contempt and was not loath to say so—Xántus may simply have scotched the extra privileges by the abrasiveness of his own personality.

When Blake ordered that "no enlisted man is allowed to fire a gun within the limits of the garrison" and forbade enlisted men to leave their post duties and go off shooting birds, precisely what Xántus was doing, Xántus' letters blossomed into tantrums in print. Xántus was the only hospital steward and *did* have duties to perform, and it didn't take half an eye on the commandant's part to see that Xántus would ignore them and gallop off collecting on the instant. Baird was partly culpable, arranging Xántus' assignment in good collecting territory with little regard for the obligations implicit in the assignment.

Xántus, in fact, didn't get on with anyone while at Fort Tejon, such as officers who wanted Xántus to mount fancy birds in return for collecting privileges which never materialized. His reading of the enlisted men was not flattering; shortly after his arrival he complained:

> In F^t Riley not only Col. Cooke & Dr Hammond took interest in my pursuits, but I was assisted by *everybody*, citizens as well as soldiers.

Fort Tejon, California, as visualized by Clarence Cullimore, Old Adobes of Forgotten Fort Tejon; *the hospital building is the large building on the right, directly opposite Barracks #1 where Xántus bunked.*

They brought me in a great numbers of specimens from all parts around. But here everybody is a gambler and drunkard, they sit day & night in whisky shops, or gambling holes; and instead of supporting me they ridicule my sport and throw every obstacle in my way.

In retaliation, "I treat them of course with princely contempt"—not a prescription for friendly relations.

Within four months of his arrival at Fort Tejon, Xántus must have suspected (as well as fervently wished) that his Army days were numbered. Both he and Baird schemed to find another suitable post. When there were rumors that Ft. Tejon was going to be closed, scuttlebutt had it that there was going to be a post at San Gorgonio Pass, 70 miles southwest of San Bernadino. Xántus plumped for that, approaching Baird in precisely the right vein: there he could get more high-altitude specimens, adding to the variety of the Smithsonian's collections.

Baird, on his part, made inquiries about other stations and sent them to Xántus, who found them unacceptable. Fort Yuma? Too much sand, too much heat, no specimens. Go on one of the surveying expeditions in the Southwest? Xántus didn't like that either. Baird must have sighed. Xántus' first mention of an expedition to the Gulf of California and Baja California, which would be his next station, surfaced in February 1858. When Baird showed a spark of interest, Xántus pursued the idea of Lower California tenaciously. He delineated exactly what he wanted Baird to do and, when finished, went back and listed all the points all over again in case Baird missed them the first time, and repeated them still again in the next letter.

Baird was an experienced museum man and would not have sponsored Xántus had he not found him competent. The specimens that Xántus was sending back were apparently both sufficiently interesting and sufficiently well prepared for Baird to work with diligence to secure Xántus' release from the Army, his appointment as tide observer for the U. S. Coast Survey, and his orders to Cabo San Lucas.

Xántus, in anticipation, was packed up, ready to go, in mid-November. He heard nothing from Baird because of misdelivered mail. He fretted. In desperation he even agreed to go to Ft. Yuma.

His freedom from the Army reached him in January 1859, and in typical disarray he immediately left Fort Tejon for San Francisco. There he clashed head-on with Lt. George H. Elliot of the Coast Survey who was expecting a Mr. deVésey and not a John Xántus. Elliot proposed to bunk Xántus in with the enlisted men which Xántus would have none of, insisting upon the better quarters he felt appropriate for *his* station. At the Coast Survey station, Xántus insisted on completing only the minimal amount of training in operating the Coast Survey tide gauge, a move which would lead to disaster when he reached Cabo San Lucas.

Despite his irrascible encounter with Elliot, Xántus was taken in hand by Baird's West Coast agent, Alexander Forbes, who invited him to gatherings at his home, a reassuring recognition by his peers of Xántus' natural-history abilities. He dined with members of the United States Survey of the Forty-Ninth Parallel, with members of the new California Academy of Natural Sciences, and with residents of the city interested in natural-history collecting.

Xántus set sail from the sophisticated society of San Francisco early in March 1859. He arrived at Cabo San Lucas in April and remained in Baja California for 28 months, sending Baird back barrels and boxes, tanks and bottles, of priceless specimens.

Although Xántus' collections were outstanding, his tide gauge records were not. It took a year to achieve an accurate and acceptable record. As a result, his year's assignment was extended another year to compensate for the incorrect entries.

As at Ft. Tejon, Xántus was petitioning Baird for a change of station soon after he arrived. But when the tide gauge station was closed in August 1861, he had no new assignment, with the Coast Survey or anyone else. Once more his future was in doubt.

He returned to Hungary, thanks to financial help from Baird and his scientific friends. There he was unsuccessful in obtaining a position with the Hungarian National Museum, to which, at Xántus' request, the thorough Baird had sent many of Xántus' specimens.

In 1862 he returned to the United States for a brief time. Baird managed an appointment for Xántus as consul in Colima, Mexico, an area from which Baird was, as usual, desirous of specimens. In Colima, Xántus committed a diplomatic faux pas and was quickly sacked by the State Department. While there he had collected prodigiously, intending to sell his specimens to get passage home. Unable to let such gems out of his hands, Baird characteristically advanced Xántus the money to return to the United States in exchange for the collection for the Smithsonian.

Xántus went home to Hungary for the last time. There he married, fathered a child, divorced, remarried, and, from all evidence, spent the remainder of his life in the same disputatious mode—professional complainer, poseur, holder of grudges, irritant to almost everyone with whom he came in contact.

His correspondence with Baird continued a few years more; the last extant letter from Xántus was written in 1866, the last from Baird in 1875. Xántus died in 1894 at age 69, never having accomplished anything so noteworthy as being a collector for Spencer Baird and the Smithsonian Institution.

《 》

From today's perspective, it is difficult to imagine the dearth of solid natural-history information in the mid-nineteenth century. Plant and animal distributions were constantly being expanded as specimens poured into the leading museums. The torrent of specimens in plants alone was so great that John Torrey and Asa Gray, the two leading botanists of the day, had most of their time taken up with the classification of botanical specimens from the West. Specimens from Fort Tejon were useful not only to establish distribution patterns and extensions but to turn up new species.

Scientists of the period were bent on description and classification as well as engaged in the chauvinistic competition for discovering and naming new species. Ecological evaluations and understandings were yet to come. The number of "new species" that burgeoned in Xántus' time and are no longer considered valid species indicates the speed with which specimens poured into the Smithsonian and were catalogued, sometimes with more enthusiasm than with mature and meticulous research.

As far as the mechanics of collecting went, Xántus and Baird had rather loose arrangements about how Xántus was to proceed. They did not have the close personal connection Baird was to have with later collectors like Robert Kennicott and Elliott Coues. Baird was dealing with a volatile personality who would have to collect as an adjunct to his primary duties, not an authorized "naturalist" or "field ornithologist," or even an officer who could command the help of enlisted men. A minimum of six weeks was required for communications between coasts; there were no instant communications with which to work out problems as they arose. Baird, sitting in Washington, was often blissfully unaware of the logistical problems Xántus faced.

Xántus and Baird agreed to split shipping costs fifty-fifty. The Pacific Mail Steamship Company transported Smithsonian boxes to Washington gratis, but shipping had to be paid for from Fort Tejon to the port of San Pedro until Xántus was able to make arrangements with Phineas Banning, who agreed to freight free between the two points. The cost, which had to be paid up front (and Xántus was never one to leave an expense unnoted), was at times onerous for him.

Xántus promised to report to Baird every two weeks. This he did quite faithfully, his letters to the Smithsonian first going by steamer and then by the new overland route that was established in 1858. During his twenty months at Fort Tejon, Xántus wrote Baird 42 biweekly letters and sent him 24 boxes of skins, vials, skulls, and "botles of alcoholics." For his part, Baird communicated that

> The mail of this morning brings yours of Dec. 28, No. XVII. which I read with great pleasure and profit as I do all your epistles, and in accordance with my custom, proceed to answer as soon as possible so as to be in certain time for the mail.

Baird agreed to furnish him supplies, which was easier said than done. With up to two months' shipping time between Washington and California, supplies were not always promptly forthcoming. By the middle of September 1857, Xántus needed better traps, as well as alcohol and ammunition. It took months to get usable shot of suitable size.

Xántus had problems procuring alcohol. What Baird had sent him had been purloined by sharp-eyed compatriots who, Xántus suspected, probably drank it. He therefore procured alcohol on the open market, and was overcharged at $1.00 a gallon. Weaker than that needed to preserve his specimens, he liberated some hospital alcohol and replaced it with his weaker solutions, which were still adequate for hospital purposes. He was equally ingenious when he ran out of bullets. He made them out of brass filings until bullets of the proper caliber arrived.

There was naiveté on both Baird's and Xántus' part as to how much time Xántus could expect to give to collecting while still fulfilling his Army duties as hospital steward. Probably Xántus, with somewhat limited experience in preparation, did not realize beforehand the time necessary not only to obtain specimens but to skin and stuff birds, press plants, pin insects, keep a careful field notebook, and pack everything up for shipment. Taking care of hospital duties in the morning, acting as librarian and baker as well, hunting and collecting in the afternoon, skinning and preserving at night, required more hours in the day than Xántus had.

Other arrangements between Baird and Xántus were amorphous to non-existent. The disposal of what Xántus collected and the question of who was to write up the specimens quickly became thorny. Baird assumed that, since the Smithsonian provided Xántus with collecting materials and partly financed him, the Smithsonian had first call on all of Xántus' collections. Xántus insisted that excess specimens were *his* to sell. His constant need for money fueled his stubbornness. Baird's perception and tact are evident in his reassuring letter of October 17, 1857:

> Notwithstanding the uncertainty about making money from collections, I still think that it may be well to look a little forward to it. Even after kindly supplying the Smithsonian and Phila. Academy and the Hung. Nat. Mus. you will doubtless have duplicates which may be disposed of to your advantage. At least there will be no harm in looking forward to something of this kind. And of one thing I can assure you that though the birds of which you have most specimens are the most common, you get no species from S.

California, is as common but that it is wanted by collectors & all western specimens are in demand.

But when Baird suggested that Xántus "present" his extra specimens to European museums, Xántus flew into a royal indignation and asked with a certain logic (January 15, 1858),

> Now, dear sir, supposed I *present* my surplus specimens to the principal European Museums; what will I sell?
>
> And, supposed, I am through with presents, & still have some specimens on hand for sale, to whom shall I sell, if I already presented them to the *principal* Museums?

Baird, as a scientist, assumed he, or one of the scholars connected, directly or indirectly, with the Smithsonian, would write up Xántus' collections. Xántus held that since they were *his* specimens, he would do the scientific descriptions. The problem of writing up his discoveries was, on the surface, simply solved: Xántus' lack of in-depth scientific training limited him in writing proper descriptions. The problem was complicated by Xántus' ego, his reluctance to allow anyone else the credit, and his quickness to take offence at any suggestion that his scientific background was inadequate.

The scientific papers he did write in English are skeletal and lack distinction, demonstrated by "Descriptions of two new species of birds from the vicinity of Fort Tejon, California" and "Catalogue of birds collected in the vicinity of Fort Tejon, California, with a description of a new species of *Syrnium*," which were published in the 1858 and 1859 *Proceedings of the Academy of Natural Sciences of Philadelphia*.

Although Xántus gradually abandoned the idea of writing a "Memoir" of his collection, he still flared up when Baird let the ornithologist, George Lawrence, describe a new species of hummingbird Xántus found in Cabo San Lucas. He protested to Baird, "I told in my former letters, at your own suggestions, I will have the credit of describing *all* my new birds." His remarks were all the more petulant because Lawrence named the hummingbird *Amazilla* (now *Hylocharis*) *xantusii* (now *Hylocharis xanti*).

Because of Baird's forebearance and tact, Xántus eventually awarded Baird carte blanche to describe the specimens Baird wished to incorporate into his work in progress on birds, replying that he felt that Baird would act as "if our positions were just reversed." This was generosity indeed from a man so jealous of his meager prerogatives and so critical of his peers, and it speaks more of Baird's ability to handle a difficult man than of Xántus' capitulation.

《 》

Xántus' career as a professional collector began at Fort Riley and came to fruition at Fort Tejon. His apprenticeship under a patient mentor, Hammond, was over and he was on his own. He began at Fort Riley as a rank amateur, inept at identification and innocent of experience. To Xántus at Fort Riley, collecting may have begun as a means to an end, but at Fort Tejon he quickly took hold and developed into one of Baird's better field men and one of his most prolific collectors. He left Fort Tejon with some solid knowledge gained, skills sharpened, perceptions broadened, to become a collector who contributed substantially to the developing knowledge of the natural history of the western United States.

Xántus accomplished a considerable amount as a collector, and under formidable odds. A collector in Xántus' day had to know not only how to prepare specimens but how to pack and ship them for the sea journey to Washington. He learned quickly and well, despite a few setbacks. Soon all the scholars who received his specimens lauded his competence, and Baird, with his usual generosity of spirit, praised Xántus fully, as on June 16, 1858:

> By the way, all of your explorers, Dr. Hayden, Dr. Newberry, and all unhesitatingly concur you the first place as a collector, and are unanimous in saying that there is but one Xantus, unapproachable, and not to be equalled however much the second person may do.

Any good collector must be meticulous in record keeping, and here Xántus fell short, not only because of the practices of the day but the physical limitations. He was collecting in multiple fields, each of which had its own techniques and preparation. Xántus had no help of any kind—no graduate assistant, no typewriter or carbon paper, no copy machine, no computer. Everything had to be handwritten. To his credit, the preponderance of his work is meticulously penned. Nevertheless, by today's standards, information is minimal; whatever ecological observations he made were in his letters.

In addition, there are serious errors in record keeping. They came about not because of the physical problems of record keeping but because of Xántus' psychological need for recognition unballasted by a compunction for rigorous accuracy. His worst fault—carelessness (at best) or willful dishonesty (at worst)—was failure in correctly noting the provenance of some specimens. In Baja California he attributed shells brought him by sea captains from Pacific islands as found at Cabo San Lucas. Many of his California beetles have not been found since at Fort Tejon, suggesting that they came from elsewhere. There is some question whether Xántus found *Xantusia vigilis,* the Desert Night Lizard named after him, at Fort Tejon since its accepted habitat does not exist there.

Even when Xántus was confined to the post and felt he had cleaned out the area as far as specimens went, he still collected with a discipline and tenacity that, given the rest of his character, was as surprising as it was admirable.

Being a good collector involves a series of distinct and rather peculiar characteristics, many of which Xántus had. Collecting requires a certain acquisitiveness and concentration, a care and curiosity. Xántus proved to have these. He was a very good observer.

Preparing specimens requires dexterity. As was the practice of the day, he measured his birds carefully. He had the patience to maintain a General Register in which he made many detailed observations about individual birds with notations as to habitat and behavioral characteristics, which he also included in some of his letters. His watercolor and ink sketches are accurate and exquisite. With few exceptions, when Xántus described a bird, it could be, and still can be, identified.

A competent collector needs enough background to recognize good diagnostic characteristics, such as when "yellow legs" may or may not be an aid to identification. A neophyte collector often gets over-eager for new species, an excusable enthusiasm, something easy to do without sufficient knowledge of the local flora and fauna. It takes considerable background plus field experience to recognize how much variation in what species is normal, knowledge that Xántus had only in a limited way but worked hard to increase. What Xántus lacked in the beginning he made up for by eagerness to learn. He petitioned Baird for the current ornithology and mammology books. Judging from his letters, he studied them carefully—at the beginning of his tour he speaks of mammals in purely superficial terms, but three months later he writes about rodent molar counts as an aid to identification.

Birds labeled and numbered in the United States National Museum are evidence enough: there they lie, neatly tucked side by side, tagged and numbered, visual proof of the collector's effort and skill. According to the Smithsonian's own tally, Xántus sent from Fort Tejon 1,794 bird skins, 145 mammals, 229 containers of fishes and reptiles, 211 nests and 740 eggs, 107 bottles of insects; he prepared 140 skulls, pressed 14 bales of plants, and packed 17 packages of minerals.

《 》

Xántus, like Baird, was a prolific letter writer. He maintained a correspondence with family and friends, full of fanciful concoctions marred with self-delusion. He wrote to many members of the natural history community, many of them in Baird's collectors' network. These letters are often entertaining, witty, and revealing in a way that his more formal letters to Baird were not.

His letters to Baird, as his superior, are concerned with serious matters of collecting. But beyond that they tell of his difficulties, the imagined slights, his fears for the future, the basics of his life—where was he going next, how he was going to get there, what he was going to do when he got there, how he was going to survive. The prejudices of the period, the uncertainties of his life, his attempt to make his way in an alien place—all make his bombast and insistence upon his worth more understandable.

These letters are more than a handwritten tie between two disparate personalities. They also illuminate mid-nineteenth-century America and the personality of an expanding country in the halcyon years between the Mexican and Civil wars. His letters tell of Mormon problems and camels crossing the desert, of the world of hardtack and beans, when condors were "plentiful," of the avariciousness of filibusterers and the generosity of the natural history community, when there were Professors of Natural History rather than of separate disciplines, when unknown species piled up on laboratory tables faster than they could be named, and when there were more splitters than lumpers in the scientific community and variations and varieties proliferated into separately named species. These letters illumine the time when one man's vision, Baird's, could lay the foundation for a definitive natural-history collection for the United States.

Xántus was one of Baird's earliest "independent" collectors. Baird's network of surgeons consisted of, in a sense, ready-made vertebrate zoologists for whom collecting would always be secondary to their main concern of medicine. Xántus was representative of the nonscientifically trained collector who would, because of place and time and situation, contribute valuable series of specimens to the Smithsonian. Doubtless some of the misunderstandings that arose between Baird and Xántus are the result of working out a generic relationship that would best serve the Smithsonian.

In Xántus Baird found a good collector and an ambitious one, but also a man of volatile temperament. Dealing long-distance with Xántus must have required all of Baird's patience, but it also provided Baird with a useful practical insight into what he could expect from his collectors and what they could expect from him. Xántus' personality was a difficult one for Baird to cut his teeth on, but perhaps the very difficulty taught Baird early how to handle men in the field; he would be well rewarded.

In scouring the countryside around Fort Tejon for the creatures that defined a fauna, it mattered not whether Xántus was arrogant or humble, abrasive or amenable. What mattered is that he *was* there and he *did* collect, and to the best of his ability. What matters is that he had the collectors' irrepressible enthusiasm, curiosity, and optimism. What matters, as it always does in the perspective of time, is the work and the achievement.

For whatever reasons Xántus collected—for personal or scientific enrichment or both—he made a true contribution to the expanding natural history of mid-nineteenth-century North America. He wrote and sketched the joy of pursuit of all the crawlers and the flappers, the hoppers and the soarers, the bounders and the leapers, and penned a self-portrait of a man who at worst was deeply flawed and at best was lively, imaginative, flamboyant, and never dull.

Along the way, Xántus found for himself a kind of joyous immortality in the names of small California beetles, a centipede, a tiny lizard that haunts the Joshua Tree thatch, and flowers that retain an eternally fresh bouquet.

Transcriber's Note

Xántus wrote both his letters and General Register on thin 8¼ × 14″ paper folded to a 7 × 8¼″ page. Both are in the Archives of the Smithsonian Institution. His script is crisp, flowing, and generally easy to read. He wrote to the edge of the page and eschewed margins. He generally terminated a paragraph at the bottom of a page and began a new one on the following. His hyphenation falls where it may; words are separated where they abut against the end of the line, not by syllable. He frequently uses dashes to fill out the end of a line to the margin, as if he had an abomination of empty space.

Carry-overs from another language are evident: the first set of quote marks below the line, the second above; quixotic capitalization; the use of a slash after the salutation rather than a comma or colon; his misspellings. These are consistent and usually involve double consonants. He either omits one consonant: litle, midle, redish, later (for latter), apreciated, to (for too); or doubles the consonant or vowel: dupplicates, squirrell, labells, wagoons, galloons. He adds an extra "e" in departement and governement. His spelling of thausands, earthquaque, and menage (for manage) is phonetic and calls attention to the fact that he was transcribing what he heard rather than seeing it in writing. The *ei* digraph becomes truncated in fright (freight), hight (height). He consistently omits the apostrophe in "dont" and often forgets periods and closing parentheses.

In spite of misspellings, meaning is usually abundantly clear and therefore "[*sic*]" is seldom necessary. His vocabulary is literate and often sophisticated.

Baird's letterpress copies, now on microfilm, are also in the Smithsonian Institution Archives. The handwritten originals were slipped between the numbered and dampened onion-skin pages of a copybook which was then placed in a letterpress overnight. In the morning the originals were removed and mailed. Good copies are readable; bad copies, for whatever reason—too much ink, too much dampness, excessive blurring, lack of ink transfer—range from almost illegible to completely so. In addition, the thin paper is extremely delicate and some of it is already shredded into bits or gone.

The Letters

Fort Columbus, N. Y.[1]
April 4th 1857

Dear Sir/

In arriving here yesterday noon, I found the box already in charge of Lt. Churchill,[2] who delivered it to me, the key also.

This morning I had the pleasure of receiving your letter of the 2d inst; I will follow your advise concerning the outfit as well as future collection; and intend to inform you as often as necessary about my movements — when in California.

My trunks from Iowa and Ft Riley[3] will be sent — I hope — very soon to your care, please to forward me them the smaller articles, especially my shot gun,[4] and oblige

Your obt Sevt
XL deVésey[5]

---

1. Since there was no scheduled overland travel, Xántus went from Kansas to California via the East Coast. Fort Columbus, on Staten Island, was debarkation point for the *Illinois* which took him to Panama, where he disembarked and crossed the isthmus by train, then caught the steamer, *Golden Gate,* for San Francisco, a trip requiring almost a month.

2. Lt. Charles Courcell Churchill (1825–1908) was Baird's brother-in-law and evidently possessed Baird's same patience and tact; throughout his correspondence, there were only three people for whom Xántus consistently spoke with affection and respect: his two mentors, Hammond and Baird, and Churchill.

3. Fort Riley was established in May 1853 at the junction of the Republican and Smoky Hill rivers, a site chosen by Colonel Thomas T. Fauntleroy, First Dragoons (see June 5, 1857). Halfway between the Oregon and Santa Fe trails, it provided protection for travelers on both, and was originally called Camp Center because of its geographical proximity to the center of the United States. The name was soon changed to the present one to honor Colonel Bennett Riley and it became a permanent cavalry post, still in existence.

4. This concern for his personal articles, repeated throughout the next two years, was totally justified; despite promises and promises that they were on their way, Xántus never received them. Two years later, when he left Fort Tejon and they still had not arrived, he wrote Baird (January 21, 1859), "you know how much safety is in baggage — left behind, e.g. Brunswick & Fᵗ Riley."

5. Xántus' signature until the end of his sojourn at Fort Tejon was "deVésey," Louis deVésey being the name he assumed upon enlisting in the United States Army in 1855; see Henry Miller Madden's (1949a) definitive biography of Xántus. Xántus' conflicting explanations appear in letters to Baird, November 16, 1857, and December 2, 1858. When Xántus went to San Francisco after his service at Fort Tejon to learn how to operate the U. S. Coast Survey tide gauge, the double-name confusion came to a head; see January 23, 1859, note 1.

San Francisco, Ca.
May the 4ᵗʰ 1857

Dear Sir/

As the mail goes out tomorrow morning for the Atlantic States, I hasten to inform you of our safe arrival here on the 29ᵗʰ of last month.[1]

As the Steamship Co. at New York intended to charge the collecting box as fright (10 cts/pound), Lt. Churchill offered very kindly to take it out as his own personal baggage, and deliver it to me after our arrival in S. Francisco. Accordingly the box was labelled as his, and taken by the Co. as his baggage.

The number of Passengers (1476) was so large, and the baggage room in so immense confusion, that there was no possible an access to our baggage during the whole voyage. After our arrival in S. Francisco, amongst several other effects the collecting box was missing also, and although I and the Lieutenant, so Mʳ Forbes[2] used all efforts to find it out, we could not discover any traces of it. As Mʳ Forbes lost an other box also, entrusted to his care by you, and (I think) containing books; he promised me to use all his influence to find out the whereabouts of the boxes. But he has himself a very little hope only as to their recovery, he thinks they are lost, or taken. I saw the box the last time on the Pier at Aspinwall,[3] when the Illinois discharged her cargo; since that time never.[4]

You cannot imagine Sir, how much mortified I am, and how much disappointed; all my anticipations of a successful collection being so very nearly entirely destroyed. But amongst all I regret most the books!

M[r] Forbes bought for me; powder, shot, caps, alum saltpeter, wrapping & blotting paper, alcohol, and Rat traps, So [*sic*] Cotton, twine, and wire. The last two articles I considered indispensable, for making a seine, and nettings.

I don't know how to procure the other things? as my means are at present very limited, and on the other side I do not intend to intrude again on Mr Forbes. I will buy anyhow arsenic and such litle articles, as I mostly need, of my own pocket; and let rather suffer a litle my own comfort and wants.

Whatever you can replace sir of the articles, contained in the fatal box, please to do so, and oblige

yours
very ob[t] Sev[t]
L. X. de Vésey

P.S.

I hope my trunks from F[t] Riley & Iowa, so my guns, arrived in Washington until now. Please to send them out as soon as practicable. —— I shall start to morrow evening for San Pedro, from there via Los Angeles to F[t] Tejon; I am told, the Fort is connected with the above named port by a weekly hack line.[5]

I made—since here—several excursions, and amongst other things I collected of different nests with eggs, (two of them extremely interesting. But having no gun to my dispossing I of course could

not procure the birds themselves. The bay opposite
of the city (Oakland), is very interesting indeed; and
I am sure, there is much to be done yet in Nat. Hist.
but especially in Botany.

---

1. Mail also went by sea and land via the Pacific Mail Steamship Company which had been awarded a government contract. Mail delivery
between Baird and Xántus varied from three to six weeks. Baird (p. 41)
acknowledges the Pacific Mail Steamship Company as among the several companies "all of which transport Smithsonian packages free of
charge"; see also Kemble (1934).

2. Andrew Forbes (1824–1902) was partner from 1854 to 1862 in
Forbes & Babcock, agent for the Pacific Mail Steamship Company on
the West Coast. According to Bancroft (1884–90, vol. vii, p. 186),
Forbes arrived in San Francisco from New Jersey in 1849 as purser on
the *California* and was "always a public-spirited man, interested in the
welfare of the city." (William F. Babcock, an agent for a shipping company in Pennsylvania, was an Englishman who came to California in
1852.) Forbes also acted as Baird's agent, procured supplies for Xántus,
occasionally submitted specimens to the Smithsonian on his own, and
was in contact with the leading naturalists of the area as well as government survey teams. He is not to be confused with James Alexander
Forbes, British Vice-Consul during the conflict with Mexico.

3. Aspinwall (now Colon) was named for John Henry Aspinwall, one
of the owners of the Pacific Mail Steamship Company, who also built
the newly completed Panama Railway across the Isthmus. Five years in
the building at a cost of $8 million, the railway was completed in 1855
and greatly facilitated coast-to-coast traffic. See U. S. Secretary of the
Navy and the Postmaster-General, (1852).

4. Baird, June 1, 1857:

> I was very sorry to hear of your misfortune in losing the box and
> trust that it will be recovered. In a note from Lt. Churchill on the
> subject he thinks it possible that it may have gone on to Oregon &
> if so the returning voyage will bring it back.
>   I will endeavor to send you out another chest but may perhaps
> have to wait a few months until one comes in from the expeditions
> since out. This will not make much difference however as a station-
> ary you will be stationary at one point, and can collect alcoholic
> specimens in Tejon. This will give time to ascertain whether the box

will turn up or not. You need not be discouraged as the box and contents can easily be replaced.

Baird eventually did so; see November 2, 1878

5. Xántus wrote to his mother on this same date with his usual implication of grander plans (Madden 1949b, p. 130):

> Along the coast, steamships sail weekly up to the estuary of the Columbia River, and also to the south as far as San Diego. I intend to follow this way down to San Pedro, whence our party will continue its way on mules through Los Angeles to Tejon, into the Sierra Nevada.

The normal shipping route between San Francisco and San Diego made stops between, including San Pedro, a port named by the Spanish mariner, Sebastian Vizcaino, on his voyage up the coast of California in the sixteenth century. It was not a good port and freight was difficult to land there, but it was the only entryway to Los Angeles by sea; from San Pedro freight went overland the 25 miles to Los Angeles.

Fort Tejon, Cala.
June 5th, 1857[1]

Dear Professor/

    The 2d of last month I wrote to you from S. Francisco reporting the lamentable loss of the collecting box, I hope you received that letter. (?) —— Mr Forbes purchased everything for me, as I specified you in my last, & at my request asked the Southern Steamship Co.[2] to forward the boxes free to their destination; he said to me, that the Co. granted this favor but on arriving at San Pedro I had still to pay fright $5.50. From San Pedro I tried to transport the boxes as my own baggage, but the Quarter Master refused their transportation, so I was bound to give them to a forwarding house for transportation to Ft Tejon, and had to pay the regular transp. fee 10 cts per pound, i.e. $14.70.[3] —— My Oceanic expenses, to my long stay in San Francisco, & Los Angeles exhausted so much my means, that I was bound to sell my watch, to save the collecting apparatus. You cannot have Sir an adequate idea, how difficult and expensive is here in the Sierras, & their Cañons the travelling, and much more the forwarding of fright; and as the Governement does not keep her own teams, but transports everything by contractors at these Posts; and as the forwarders require always prepayment, you may suggest some means, how I shall send in from time to time my collections. —— Wells Fargo & Co.[4] the well known forwarding house has an agency in Los Angeles, which is only 125 miles from here; so I propose that you may make with this firm at your city some permanent agreement, and forward through them everything to me, so I to you; because unless you effect an arrangement something like this, I am entirely lost as to how to forward the specimens.[5]

Although I arrived here the 18th of last month, the boxes came in only the day before yesterday. Nothwithstanding this circumstance, after a preliminary reconnosance of the environs, I pitched in diligently, bought all the sutlers wrapping paper, some whisky etc and collected. At present I have on hand already some hundred plants,[6] several serpents,[7] toads,[8] frogs[9] hylas,[10] lizards etc. & about 50 birds & mammals, some skuls & skeletons also. The breading season was almost over as I made my appearance here, still I secured several interesting nests and eggs; I could procure more still, but never take the nest, unless I can take the bird also, or at least identify it. ——

Is a pity indeed, that my gun is not yet here, you may imagine yourself in my deplorable situation, when everything full with birds, and I have to start out with a rusty old dragoon carabine, but this is the fact.[12] I prey you send as quick as you can my gun, so books etc.

We have here grizlys in great abundance, they are really a nuisance, you cannot walk out half a mile, without meeting some of them, and as they just now have their clubs, they are extremely ferocious to, I was already twice driven on a tree, and close by to the fort.[13] —— Not very far on the plains, there are large herds of Antelopes,[14] we have some deers,[15] Elks,[16] 2 Wolves,[17] 2 Foxes,[18] the Panther,[19] wild cat,[20] immense quantity of Badgers,[21] & Others, the Porcupine,[22] Skunk,[23] flying squirrell,[24] Gopher,[25] Mole,[26] Bats,[27] and a ground Squirrel really in countless numbers, they dwell in holes & you can kill tausan in a day.[28] Everybody tells me there is no mouse here, but yesterday opening a large snake, I found 3 of them in her stomach. And so I was told there is no Rat; but some days ago on an excursion I noticed a nest on a tall Pine, I at once climbed it, hoping it to be the Maximilians Jays nest[29] (as there were many of them round), you may imagine my astonishment when looking into the nest, a—Rat jumped out, running up the three,—I of course after him, but he went on the highestmost top, where I could not follow him, but descended & brought him down with the old Carabine. He is a remarkable fellow, general colour slate gray, yellowish belly, & white feet, the hair is fine like that of the mush rats.[30] Length from nose to the base of tail 7"10 tail (not bushy) 5"2 —for feet 2"— hindfeet 2"10 moustache or whiskers 2"6—ear 1"2 high, and 1"2 broad, which makes him look like a Bat.[+31]

It is a singular circumstance, that I find here the three frogs invariably in Springs, & 2 species of snakes also in ice cold Springs![32]

I secured the other day a magnificent bird, splendend black, with longitudinal white lines on the wing, an inch long black crest on the head, and a long boat tail. Iris carmin red.[33]

[+]I use only a tape measure, divided in feet ('), inches ("), and lines ('''), the feet in 12 inches, and the inch also in 12 lines. You forgot the shell [? [scale, please send me one.

The Alcohol, procured by Mr Forbes is the worst
quality only 58°, and the traps good for nothing.
Here is a good blacksmith, he will make for me
some substancial traps after my own design, and I
will use the first rainy day to construct some wire
traps for smaller mammals, as I have with me
plenty wire.

To my great mortification Capt Gardiner[34] has left
before my arrival. The Cmdg officer of the Post is
Colonel Fauntleroy,[35] and the Asst. Surgeon Dr. P.S.
TenBroeck[36]; I am sorry that the last named gentleman dont takes any interest at all in NatHistory;
and having no sick man at present, I have scarcely
any intercourse with him. Should you know him
Prof. you could write him in the Interest of the Institution, to facilitate my explorations here, by al-
lowing me to leave some time the Post for the farther surrounding country.[37] Because here near is no
water with fish in but about 15 miles from the Post
there is a fine lake full with fish, turtles, & other
reptiles of all kind.[38] The evenings I use for making
a seine, I finished already 30 feet, my intention is to
make it 100 feet long, by 7' wide, & sweep the lake
with. I tried several pulls in the pools, & springs, but
safe some Cyprinas,[39] & Hydrophylos[40] caught nothing.

I dont forget Ostensacken,[41] I have already a botle
full of fine species of Diptera, and with my first
transport the Baron shall have them.

I noticed already two Phrynosomas, one already
known to me, but the other new, bright yellow
belly, 6 red spines on the head, 4 of them 8'" in
hight, Diameter 4"6, — found on almost inaccessible precipices, about 2000 feet above the post.[42]

There are 4 lizards, one beautifull small, with all
kind of brilliant colors,[43] the 3 others extremely
large reptiles, I secured one, which measured 3 feet
4" in length, has scales like an alligator and moves
very slowly forward.[44] The two other middle ones
on the contrary are very swift, they live on high &

big threes, and were by far smarter as I was.[45] For a couple days I could not secure any of them, at last took my resort to the old carabine, and now shot them in abundance.

Yesterday I noticed a very important thing. I climbed a three for a hawks nest & found amongst the young ones a Parrots head, feet, & scattered round long blue & red feathers; this circumstance gave me a hint, to hunt for the Parrott and procure him if possible, because to my knowledge there is only one Parrott in the U. S. until now known, and the remains in the nest, were decidedly of an other, quite different & larger species.[46]

I liked very much, if you would send me Professor Brewers Wilson,[47] or at least, his synopsis of the birds of America,[48] whatever shall cost is, I will remit you the amount with the first opportunity, it would facilitate very much my labors, by ascertaining the species. The woodpecker, figured in Cassin, (I think 1st or 2d plate of Birds of Cal. & Texas)[49] is here in immense flocks, but I dont know whether is worth or not to secure many of them. So is with the small red breasted *carduelis*,[50] & the Maximilians Jay.

There is an other *Picus*, very small, sulphur yellow vent, red crest, back as that of the *querulus*, not very common.[51] A third entirely slate color, as large as the *Auratus*,[52] with a dirty red spot on the top of the head, & black whiskers.[53] *Falconida* are numerous, in great variety. *Parus* are 3 species, all of them extremely beautifull.[54] *Trochylus* 2 only but none of them the *colubris*.[55] Plovers, Avocets, Cranes, Snipes, Terns are very abundant, I noticed the Ardea candidissima too.[56] With one word, the feathered world is here on a large scale represented; and it vexes me only the rusty carabine! else I had already 10 times as many, as I have actually.

With the next mail more.

sincerely yours
LX. de Vésey

Pray —— send my effects as soon, as you get them.

1. Fort Tejon appears as an historical site on the Grapevine and Frazier Mountain, California, 12.5-minute USGS Quadrangles. As Xántus (1859, p. 189) described it:

> It may be proper to state that Fort Tejon is a U. S. Military post, situated near the Tejon Pass, at the head of the Tulare Valley, between the cascade and coast mountain ranges of California, in about latitude 35° north, longitude 119° west. The height of the Post is about 4250 feet above the sea, and this altitude with the proximity of higher mountains, gives to it a peculiar Fauna, in many respects quite different from that of the low lands of the same parallel.

The land that was to become Fort Tejon was first described by Captain Pedro Fages on March 23, 1772, when he marched over what he called "Pass of Cortez" and down Grapevine Canyon — *Cañada de las Uvas* — where the fort was eventually situated. See Bolton (1931) and Treutlein (1972, p. 344):

> We ascended a pass over some low hills well-covered with grass, and descended the other side of the pass where we found a copious running stream. We went on through another very level valley well-grown with white-oaks and live-oaks.

Subsequently a great part of this area of California was controlled by Franciscan missions who were forced to relinquish it with the secularization of the Church in 1834. Lieutenant Don Antonio del Valle received some of these lands as a land grant in 1835 and, according to Cullimore (1949, p. 14), supposedly named the area *El Tejon* for a chance confrontation with a badger, in Spanish, *tejon*. Fort Tejon was built on the adjacent land grant South, the 22,178 acre Rancho Castaic, previously held by the Mexican Governor of California. The Fort lies north of Tejon Pass proper, on the west side of Grapevine Creek.

In 1850 Lieutenant George H. Derby explored the area and recommended the establishment of a fort there:

> The only point in the whole valley which struck me as at all suitable for a military post was the small portion of internal land contained by the five creeks of the river Frances. A position here would be central, being easy of communication with the Kings river to the north and with Kern river to the south, upon which two streams and their tributaries are situated the greater number of Indian rancherias in the valley. The land is excellent for cultivation, well timbered, and abundance of building material may be found in the vicinity, either stone or heavy pine or oak timber. A road leading through the Tejon pass from Los Angeles, and intersecting the emigrant trail through Walker's pass near Kern river, passes directly through this point to the northern mines of the San Joaquin valley. This road will undoubtedly be much travelled when brought into

notice, and the post being established at this point will contribute much to its safety and protection. (Farquhar 1932, p. 262)

The land grant was still in effect when Lieutenant Edward Fitzgerald Beale, as the new Superintendent of Indian Affairs, surveyed and acquired some 50,000 acres (for about five cents an acre) to establish the Tejon Indian Reservation in 1853.

By this time the pass was becoming well traveled; Lieutenant R. S. Williamson, surveying "Routes in California to Connect with Routes near the Thirty-fifth and Thirty-second Parallels," camped on the exact site, as recorded by his geologist, William P. Blake (1857, p. 47):

The surface of the valley is covered with a luxuriant growth of grass, and a deep soil supports groves of magnificent oak trees, some of them eight feet in diameter. A small brook of pure and cold water was found here, and our camp was on its borders, under the branches of the large oaks, while those branches that had fallen, or been broken off by bears in gathering acorns, furnished fuel for the fires. . . . One of the large oaks bears the following inscription, cut deeply into the hard wood: "Peter le Beck, killed by a bear, Oct. 17, 1837." A broad, flat surface was hewed upon the trunk, and well smoothed off before the letters were cut. It is a durable monument.

In twenty years, by the time Xántus was there, the tree had covered with bark the bare spot which held the inscription. A group called the Foxtail Rangers from Bakersfield removed the bark in the 1880–90s and found the inscription in reverse on its underside; the bark is now at Ranger Headquarters at the Park. They also exhumed Lebec's body and returned it to its grave.

When Colonel Joseph F. Mansfield tramped the same ground on an inspection trip prior to July 1854, he wrote to his commander:

The Tejon Pass, however, is nothing more than a road over the mountains. The pass into this valley from the south is that of Las Uvas thro' which the communication is kept up with Los Angeles, a city of 2,100 population, and with Los Angeles County, 7,000 population, about equally divided between the American and native Californian races. . . . Thus it seems that the principal population to be protected against the depredations of the wild Indians are the inhabitants of Los Angeles, Santa Barbara, and San Luis Obispo, and the friendly Indians on the reserve of Tejon . . . [who] will be protected by a force of one company of good troops stationed at the Tejon on the spot selected by Mr. Beale and Captain Jordan. (Frazer 1963, pp. 189–90)

Construction of the fort, the first military fort in interior California, began in the summer of 1854, 15 miles southwest of the Tejon Indian Reservation; the first contingent of Dragoons moved in that August. The

Episcopal bishop of California, the Right Reverend William Ingraham Kip, wrote three letters about Fort Tejon when he passed through while the site was under construction; he commented (Kip 1921):

> The barracks—handsome adobe buildings—are being erected around the sides of the parade ground. None of them are yet finished, and the soldiers are living in tents. . . . There are ordinarily about six officers and one hundred and twenty dragoons stationed here, besides the numerous civilians who are storekeepers and employees of the Post.

(This passage is quoted by Cullimore [1949, p. 49]; only 250 copies of Kip's book were published, by private subscription.)

No formal plans have ever been found, but the layout was standard, barracks and other buildings clustered around the parade ground (see map and reconstruction by Cullimore.). The hospital was on the northwest side of the parade ground, facing the barracks directly opposite. The buildings were well built of adobe bricks, probably made on the site, laid in two-foot-thick exterior walls; the millwork and carpentry were fine and precise; excellent diagrams of the construction are to be found in Cullimore (1949).

Clarence Cullimore, Jr. (personal communication, March 12, 1985), adds an interesting natural history note. His father grew some of the seeds encased in the adobe bricks; several of the grasses that appeared, and were therefore presumably common in Xántus' time, no longer grow in the area.

Fort Tejon, considered one of the best forts in the West, remained in use for ten years. When the reservation Indians were removed to the Tule River Reserve, the fort was abandoned to the weather, and it and much of the adjoining territory were purchased by Lt. Beale for his own use. Fifty years later, the noted California ornithologist, Joseph Grinnell, visited it to collect and observe the birds that Xántus had collected there. He wrote of it (Grinnell 1905, p. 10), when the adobe buildings were already disappearing, that

> the most impressive feature of the Tejon valley to one entering from the dry barren plains on either side, are the magnificent oak groves, interspersed with green pastures. . . . Many springs contribute to a fair-sized brook, which, lined with immense willows and lofty maples festooned with grapevines, takes its tumultuous way down the narrow gorge below the Fort to the San Joaquin Valley.

See Crowe (1957), Wilke and Lawton (n.d.), and Griffin and Woodward (1942).

According to Steve Lines, State Park Ranger stationed at Fort Tejon (personal comunication):

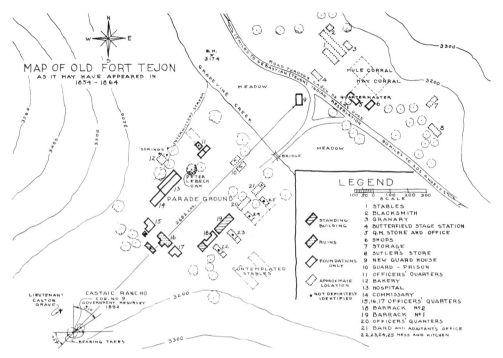

Map showing the arrangement of the buildings at Fort Tejon as reconstructed from remaining foundations. Xántus lived in Barrack No. 1 and worked in the Hospital directly across the Parade Ground. This drawing was made by Clarence Cullimore and published in his book on the fort, Forgotten Adobes of Old Fort Tejon.

Fort Tejon became part of the California State Park System in 1940, established on five acres donated by the Tejon Ranch Company. The Park bought an additional 200 acres in 1948. Today only two buildings stand at the site: Barracks #1 (in which Xántus lived) and the Officers' Quarters. The walls of the barracks are essentially the original ones; new floorboards, rafters, necessary woodwork, and roof were added to recreate the original construction (Barracks #2 fell in the 1957 earthquake). The Officers' Quarters were rebuilt after the same earthquake on the original foundations; small buildings to the back are the original walls with a new roof added. The hospital building was demolished around 1890 and is now only a heap of rubble, but pictures of it, taken in the 1880s, exist.

Despite the loss of buildings and the constant whine of traffic from a major highway, Fort Tejon's landscape looks much as it did in Xántus' day—the parade ground surrounded by big oaks, hillsides stained with orange poppies in the spring, and Grapevine Creek still bubbling down the hillside between grassy banks and overhanging willows.

2. According to Barsness (1967, p. 294), the normal shipping route between San Francisco and San Diego included several stops along the way, of which San Pedro was one; service was not notable for either comfort or speed. In 1853 the Southern Accomodation Line advertised weekly service between the two major cities on the *Southerner.*

3. The cost of freight service was so onerous that businessmen of Los Angeles requested that San Pedro be made a port of entry with its own customhouse to avoid the cost of all goods having to be processed through San Francisco. Cleland (1922, p. 310) quotes the merchants:

> The freight alone from San Francisco to San Pedro for the last two years has never been less than twice the amount of what is charged for conveying the same articles from New York to San Francisco . . . the average additional cost upon goods purchased at San Francisco is not less than 30 per cent upon their being landed at San Pedro.

4. Wells, Fargo, & Company was established in 1852 in New York to take advantage of business opportunities in California; it was a corporate enterprise as interested in banking as in transportation, and as such, was able to weather the difficult economic times of the mid-decade and to emerge as a dominant company in all kinds of transportation; see Jackson (1966).

*Xántus lived in Barrack Building No. 1 while he served at Fort Tejon; it was a two-story open building like other Army buildings of the period. Beds headed against the outside wall and a stove or stoves sat in the center. Clarence Cullimore (*Forgotten Adobes of Old Fort Tejon), *who did this drawing, remarks upon the fine detail work on windows and door jambs.*

5. Baird to Forbes, July 10, 1857, asking if there were any way to transport

> Mr. Vesey's collection between Los Angeles and San Francisco? He wrote a doleful account of his experiences to his post. In the way of freight the bill made him pay $8.50 freight from San Francisco & San Pedro on his "trap" to send them just from San Pedro to Fort Tejon. He had to sell his watch to secure the necessary funds. If it can be done it would be a great favor . . .

To Xántus, October 17, 1857:

> Mr. Forbes writes that the Cala. Mail [?] Co. from S. Francisco to San Pedro have agreed to make no charge on parcels, on by Wells Fargo . . . sent readily without prepaying. Mr. Forbes will refund cost from Tejon to Los Angeles.

6. Among the plants that Xántus sent from Fort Tejon were the new species, *Clarkia xantiana, Penstemon laetus,* and *Chorizanthe perfoliata* (Gray, 1859–61) and *Solanum xanti* (Gray, 1875–76).

7. Yarrow (1883) lists the following Xántus specimens from Fort Tejon with their accompanying United States National Museum number: #4254, *Crotalus lucifer* (now *viridis*), Northern Pacific Rattlesnake; *Rhinocheilus lecontei,* Long-nosed Snake; #4285, *Ophibolus* (now *Lampropeltis*) *getulus boyli,* Common Kingsnake; #4386, *Bascanium* (now *Masticophis*) *taeniatum laterale,* Striped Whipsnake (which occurs considerably east of Fort Tejon). The current printout from the USNM is not complete as to Xántus specimens and lists only two reptiles.

8. *Bufo halophilus* (now *boreas*), Western Toad, #4568, and *Eutaemia* (now *Scaphiopus*) *hammondi,* Western Spadefoot, #5496.

9. *Rana catesbiana,* Bullfrog, is to be expected but is not listed in Xántus' field notes.

10. *Hyla regilla,* Pacific Treefrog, #4568.

11. Yarrow (1883) lists #3063, *Xantusia vigilis,* Desert Night Lizard (type specimen); #4113, *Cnemidophorus tesselatus tigris,* Western Whiptail; #9364, *Gerrhonotus multicarinatus,* Southern Alligator Lizard; #9283, *Holbrokia maculata maculata,* Lesser Earless Lizard; #4359, *Sceloporus undulatus thayeri,* Eastern Fence Lizard; and #4587, *Phrynosoma coronata* (now *coronatum*), Coast Horned Lizard.

12. Mansfield (Frazer 1963, p. 149) reviewed the temporary detachment at Fort Tejon at the end of June 1854 and found that the "men were in the old uniform with swords and musketoons, but no pistols." Supplying the forts of the Far West was a constant problem, and guns were often in the shortest supply.

13. *"Ursus arctos"* (now *middendorfii*), Alaskan Brown Bear, does not range into California; Xántus' specimens, USNM #3537 and 3538, were doubtless the more common *Ursus americanus*, Black Bear.

Blake (1857, p. 47), encamped at the sight of Fort Tejon, noted:

> While we were encamped here an unusual number of grizzly bears were seen. They frequently came to the water to drink, in the evening, just after sunset.

See also Grinnell (1938), Merriam (1914), and Grinnell, Dixon, and Linsdale (1937).

14. *Antilocapra americana*, Pronghorn Antelope.

15. *Odocoileus hemionus*, Mule Deer, of which there are eight Xántus specimens in the USNM; "Blacktail" was another common name for Mule.

16. *Cervus elaphus* (now *canadensis*), NMNH #3539, 3544, 3551, 3552.

17. Probably coyotes, of which there were several USNM specimens.

18. *Urocyon cinereoargenteus*, Gray Fox, #3543 and 3545; there is no record of the other two foxes in central California, *Vulpes fulva*, Red Fox, and *V. macrotis*, Kit Fox.

19. *Felis concolor*, Mountain Lion, was also called Panther.

20. USNM credits Xántus with 6 specimens of *Lynx rufus*, Bobcat.

21. *Taxidea taxus*.

22. *Erethizon dorsatum*.

23. Neither *Spilogale putorius*, Spotted Skunk, nor *Mephitis mephitis*, Striped Skunk, appear on the USNM printout.

24. Baird, October 17, 1857, asked Xántus if he had seen any flying squirrels. See Xántus' letters of November 24, 1857, February 18, and October 18, 1858.

25. *Thomomys bottae*, Valley Pocket Gopher.

26. *Scapanus latimanus*, California Mole.

27. Of the 15-some bats that might be expected in this area of California, none appear in the USNM computer printout.

28. Xántus frequently mentions *Citellus beecheyi;* e.g., see September 15 and 30, 1857.

29. "Maximillian's jay," *Gymnorhinus cyanocephalus*, discovered by Alexander Philip Maximilian, Prince of Wied, who found it in 1833 in Montana, is now the Piñon Jay, so identified by Baird, November 10, 1857. Part of the confusion arose because, at the beginning of his Fort

Tejon sojourn, Xántus had only eastern bird books for reference; Baird, November 10, 1857:

> It is not surprising that you do not find many of your birds in Audubon: the Zoology of your part of California is very different from that of the rest of the United States. The descriptions of the Tejon birds are to be looked for in accounts of Western species.

30. *Ondatra zibethica,* Muskrat.

31. Baird, July 16, 1857:

> The rat I am not astonished at. It is a species of Neotoma, possibly N. mexicanus.

The Mexican Woodrat is not present in Southern California; from Xántus' measurements and description, this is *N. fuscipes,* Dusky-footed Woodrat.

32. Xántus' lack of field knowledge probably led to an over-generous estimate.

33. Baird misinterpreted Xántus' description of *Phainopepla nitens,* Phainopepla, as that of *Picus* (now *Campephilus*) *imperialis,* Imperial Woodpecker, commenting that if so, "this is a prize indeed—the male has a scarlet crest; on the female it is black," and requests an illustration. See Xántus, September 12, 1857; Baird, November 10, 1857:

> I do not believe Picus imperialis was ever found in N. America. Audubon describes a Mexican specimen on the ground that Townsend *thought* he saw a large woodpecker in Oregon which might have been the *P. pileatus* as much as P. imperialis.

34. Capt. John W. T. Gardiner (c. 1817–79) captained the First Dragoons, stationed at Fort Tejon in 1855; it was to his wife, an old friend, that Baird wrote about his interest in obtaining specimens from Fort Tejon.

35. Colonel Thomas Turner Fauntleroy (d. 1883) had been commandant of the First Dragoons since 1850 and acting commander of the Pacific Department of the U. S. Army until relieved by General Newman S. Clark (see December 2, 1858); he went on to command at Fort Union, New Mexico, during Ute problems there in the 1860s. He resigned his commission to serve as a brigadier general in the Confederate Army.

36. Dr. Peter Gerard Stuyvesant Ten Broeck (1822–67) was Assistant Surgeon at Fort Tejon, Xántus' immediate superior as well as the focus of his complaints. Despite Xántus' continual carping, Ten Broeck seems to have been an exemplary officer, and Mansfield reported (Frazer 1963, p. 160) that "The Medical Department [at Fort Reading] was well conducted under Assistant Surgeon Ten Broeck."

Clarence Cullimore's reconstruction of the Hospital Building at Fort Tejon also shows the famous Lebec Oak at the end of the Parade Ground; curiously, Xántus never mentions this landmark.

37. Baird to Ten Broeck, July 17, 1857:

I take the liberty of addressing a few lines to you for the purpose of respectfully commending Mr. Vesey, your new Hospital Steward, to your kind consideration. Mr. Vesey is a gentleman of intellect & education and for many years particularly devoted to the study of Natural History during which time he has devoted untiringly in South and Central America as well as in the United States. For a time before [posting?] to California he had been at Fort Riley, where in connections with Dr. W. A. Hammond he [made] many extremely interesting collections of animals and plants. In influencing his assignment to Fort Tejon through the kindness of the Surgeon General, my object was to secure Mr. Vesey's services in the development of the Natural History in what I know to be the most interesting of the unexplored portions of the United States. This was shown by the results of Dr. Newberry's labors while with Lt. Williamson, and abundantly confirmed by Mr. Vesey's experience and reports.

If therefore you could give Mr. Vesey any reasonable facilities in the persecution of his investigations, so far of course as they do not interfere with his regular duties, you would confer a very great favor on the Smithsonian as on science generally. In the present very extensive collection of North American Natural objects in the Smithsonian Institution we are in very great measure indebted to the officers of the Medical Corps of the Army. . . .

Can we do anything here for you in the way of furnishing public documents and Smithsonian publications? We always have a large supply of Presidents' messages, report of Coast Survey, Patent Office and some of which may be interesting to you. If you will let me know your interests in that respect, if will afford me much pleasure to do what is in our power to oblige you.

38. Probably Tulare Lake (see November 24, 1857, note 3).

39. Minnows.

40. Probably *Hydrophilus,* Water-scavenger Beetle.

41. Carl Robert Freiherr von Osten-Sacken (1828–1906), born in Russia, came to the United States as Secretary to the Russian Legation in Washington; an entomologist, he specialized in Diptera. His collections in this country are shared by the Museum of Comparative Zoology at Harvard and the American Entomological Society in Philadelphia.

42. Only *Phrynosoma coronatum* was in Xántus' area.

43. *Cnemidophorous tigris.*

44. There are no lizards of this size in the area. Baird, July 16, 1857:

I never heard of a lizard in N. Am. I feel conf. from your account however I should infer that it is a *Heloderma,* possibly *horridum.* You had better skin such large specimens and keep some skins dry; others in alcohol. It may also be well to secure a specimen or two of each and to send any healthy specimens as well. . . .

The only large lizard with an awkward gait is *Heloderma suspectum,* Gila Monster, today found in California only in a tiny area of the Clark Mountains.

45. *Gerrhontus multicarinatus.*

46. See Xántus' chagrined note about the parrot, November 24, 1857; one suspects the hawk that happened on somebody's pet.

47. Wilson (1853). Thomas M. Brewer (1814–80) was a Boston publisher who, as the leading oologist in the country, wrote "North American Oology" and, with Baird and Robert Ridgway, *North American Land Birds.*

48. John James Audubon, *A Synopsis of the Birds of North America.*

49. John Cassin (1813–69) became head of a large printing and lithography company in Philadelphia which produced the illustrations for many scientific and government publications. After he joined the

Academy of Natural Sciences of Philadelphia, in his non-business hours he catalogued the 26,000 birds that began the Academy's famous collection, publishing many papers in the Academy's *Proceedings* on taxonomy, synonomy, etc., in addition to *Illustrations of the Birds of California, Texas, Oregon, British, and Russian America*, covering the birds discovered since Audubon.

50. This turned out to be *Carpodacus mexicanus frontalis*, House Finch; see September 30, 1857.

51. From Xántus' description, possible *Picoides pubescens*, Downy Woodpecker.

52. *Colaptes auratus*, Yellow-shafted Flicker.

53. *Melanerpes formicivorus*, Acorn Woodpecker.

54. Chickadees.

55. Baird, July 16, 1857:

The XIX called *Trochylus colubris* is probably *T. alexandri*, a closely allied species. I wish you could send a pair of this species in a letter as I want to describe the alexandri and we have no specimens.

56. *Casmerodius albus*, Common Egret.

Fort Tejon, Cala
June 29th, 1857

Dear Sir,

Your letter of March 11th addressed to me to Ft Riley, reached me here the day before yesterday through kindness of Dr Hammond.[1] I am very much mortified, that this letter of yours did not come to hand, when I was at Ft Riley, because I had been fully able to fill all your "Requisitions" concerning the Fauna (chiefly living) of Kansas.

I try now to answer some of your questions, regarding the mammals of Kansas, as far as possible. I collected there the Vulpes fulvus,[2] & Macroutus[3] of yours.

    " Luppus pratensis,[4] Canis Latrans,[5] & Luppus Lobos.[6] (We have seen two specimens of L.

 Bachmanii[7] (black wolf) also, but could
 not secure any.
" Meles labradoria.[8]
" Ursus Americanus (only seen one)[9]
" Cervus virginiana[10]
" Putorius visor[11]
" Memphitis mesoleuca (Skunk)?[12]
" Spermophilus 13 lineatus[13]
" Tamias quadrivittatus[14]
" Pteronys volucella[15]
" Scirus magnicaudatus,[16] niger,[17] & the gray
 squirrell[18] (I forget his name) (the black is
 very abundant)
" Mustella wilsonii[19]
" Perognatus 2 species[20]
" Pseudostoma 2 species[21]
" 1 Neotoma,[22] 1 Cricetus,[23] & 3 Mus.
" 2 Vespertilis,[24] & 2 Rabbits, (the common Ar-
 temisia,[25] & a blue very small swamp Rab-
 bit.)[26]

There are very plenty Buffaloes,[27] and Antelopes
10–15 miles West of the Fort, in the delta of the Republican & Smoky rivers.[28] —— Otters,[29] & wild
cats,[30] so ground hogs are found some, but not
many. —— Beavers[31] & prairie dogs[32] are none in
the vicinity, they commence to appear only about
100 miles west on the Smoky fork. —— Coyotes
are so numerous, that we some time trapped 20–25
in one night, and the following morning used to let
them lose, & chase with dogs. —— I enclose you a
letter, to the Hospital Steward at F[t] Riley, he is not
very fond on making collections, but *for me* he will
certainly procure all living specimens, he can, or
you may desire. He studied medicine in Göttingen
(Germany), was driven out by the political movements from home, and is in *every respect* a well educated gentleman. Write to him.

 One of my scholars Henry Brandt[33] is a well-
educated young man to, at home he was a book-
seller, at present he is chief Bugler to Col. Cooke,[34]

2d Dragoons, stationed at Ft Leavenworth. Since my departure from Kansas he assisted Dr Hammond in making collections, and as the Dr writes me, he made up a very handsome collection. He is aquainted with all modes of collecting preserving etc and is indefatigable collector. His time of service expires November next (I think so), and he goes then to North Western Texas, where he secured some lands. I advise you to secure him anyhow, as he would be able and I presume willing to, to collect for the Smithsonian a very important series of the NW. Texan Nat. History.

Then I have an excellent correspondent in West Missouri, city of Brunswick, a Dr Crop.[35] He is an eminent Geologist & botanist, and quite a zeloures collector. As he is connected with the Missouri State Geological Survey, and so traverses in all directions the *litle yet known* west of Missouri, you can get a fine collection through him of that part of the Country, and he is willing to aid you in lieu of books on Nat. History. So he informs me.

I wrote you two letters since in California, the first from San Francisco May 1st, the last from here June the 8th, reporting you the loss of the collecting box, and my procedings in the field. I hope you received them both.

Since my last, I secured specimens of a delicate formed bluishgrey Rabbit, which I never yet seen in any collection, nor the description of it noticed.[36] The other day I killed to 2 Jakass hares (Lepus callotis),[37] and yesterday a beautifull specimen of Lynx rufus.[38] The white nacked & spotted ground Squirrells (of which I spoke already to you in my last) I secured in great numbers, skins & skulls of all ages & sexes. Birds skins I prepared many, already over 200 hundred. Alcoholic specimens are not so abundant as I anticipated, there are very few serpents. But I can fill still a keg of specimens on hand.

I closed the botanysing for the season; being everything dry, there are so few plants, that the

much trouble & loss of time cannot possible renu-
merative. Besides I came to late for Botany, the
rainy season being over. But notwithstanding I collected about 1000 species with their duplicates, and
hope some of them will turn out, as very interesting
& new, chiefly that of the very high altitudes, & of
Rocky vegetation.

Invertebrates, principally Coleoptera[39] I have several tausends.

Now I expect daily your letter, with instructions
as how to send in the specimens, and I will forward
at once several boxes to you.

I had an immense trouble with the boxing of
nests, eggs, labelling etc etc I had to make everything myself and lost much time with this manufac-
turing business. Lost much time I say, because I am
assisted by nobody here, I depend entirely and exclusively on myself. In F^t Riley not only Col. Cooke
& Dr Hammond took interest in my pursuits, but I
was assisted by *everybody,* citizens as well as soldiers.
They brought me in a great numbers of specimens
from all parts around. But here everybody is a gambler and drunkard, they sit day & night in whisky
shops, or gambling holes; and instead of supporting
me they ridicule my [sport?] and trow every obstacle in my way.[40]

I treat them of course with princely contempt,
and go on with doubled step in my path.

Pray—Have you not yet received my guns etc etc.
I am almost despiring!

Will you send an other collecting apparatus, instead of the last one? Do not forget some lecture. I
have no books whatever here.

Hoping to hear soon of you
I am, sir

Yours, very truly
LVésey

P.S. Would you be so kind, and send me out per
mail a couple dozen of glass eyes for birds. I will

mount a fancy birds & present here to *persons,* who
perhaps will assist me after this stratagem. Send
with yellow, & brown iris, for owls, herons, cranes,
ducks, etc.[42]

---

1. Dr. William Alexander Hammond (1828–1900) served in the West as
Assistant Surgeon, U. S. A., during which time he collected birds for
Baird and was an active member of the Academy of Natural Sciences of
Philadelphia. At Fort Riley he encouraged Xántus to collect and prepare
specimens; when Xántus showed promise he introduced him to Baird
and undoubtedly was influential in Xántus' election to the Philadelphia
Academy. In 1860 he resigned to teach at the University of Maryland
but rejoined the Army in 1861 at the beginning of the Civil War and
was quickly appointed surgeon general for his work in hospital sanita-
tion. He ran afoul of the personal animosity of Secretary of War Stanton
who brought charges of misconduct; Hammond demanded a court-
martial and was dismissed from the service in 1864. He went into successful private practice as well as a teaching career. In 1878 he was
exonerated of all charges.

Baird (1857, p. 52): "A collection of reptiles and birds from Fort Riley,
Kansas, was also received from Dr. Hammond."

2. Properly, *V. fulva,* Red Fox. "Donations to the Museum," *Proceedings
of the Academy of Natural Sciences of Philadelphia 1857,* p. iii, under the
entry of May 5, notes "Gray Fox, from Kansas. Presented by Dr. Hammond and Mr. L. de Vesey."

3. From context, Xántus probably meant *V. macrotis,* Kit Fox.

4. Now *Canis lupus,* Gray Wolf, surviving only in isolated pockets south
of Canada.

5. Coyote.

6. See note 4 above.

7. *Bachmani* is found in none of the synonomies; since Xántus lists it as
"*L. bachmani*" which would become *Sylvilagus bachmani,* Brush Rabbit.

8. Now *Taxidea taxus,* Badger.

9. Black Bear.

10. Now *Odocoileus virginianus,* White-tailed Deer.

11. Now *Spilogale putorius,* Spotted Skunk.

12. Now *Mephitis mephitis,* Striped Skunk.

13. *Citellus tridecemlineatus,* Thirteen-lined Ground Squirrel.

14. Now *Eustamias quadrivittatus,* Colorado Chipmunk.

15. *Glaucomys volans,* Southern Flying Squirrel, only in the eastern half of the United States.

16. Now *S. niger,* Eastern Fox Squirrel; only in the eastern part of the United States.

17. Same as note 16 above.

18. *Sciurus carolinensis,* Eastern Gray Squirrel.

19. *M. frenata,* Longtail Weasel.

20. Occurring in Kansas are *Perognathus flavus,* Silky Pocket Mouse; *P. flavescens,* Plains Pocket Mouse; and *P. hispidus,* Hispid Pocket Mouse.

21. *Thomomys talpoides,* Northern Pocket Gopher.

22. *N. floridana,* Eastern Woodrat.

23. Now *Oryzomys* sp., Rice Rats, only in southeastern United States.

24. Plainnose Bats.

25. No lagomorphs have the specific *artemisia;* the cottontails in Kansas are *Sylvilagus floridanus* and *S. auduboni.*

26. *Sylvilagus aquaticus* does not occur in Kansas.

27. *Bison bison.*

28. These two rivers near Fort Riley provided excellent collecting; Dr. Elliott Coues (1878, p. 529) enjoyed his "time very profitably in observing and collecting birds along the Republican Fork of the Kansas River ... [the time] was propitious, and the place proved to be a famous one for birds."

29. *Lutra canadensis.*

30. See Bobcat.

31. *Castor canadensis.*

32. *Cynomys* sp.

33. Neither a contemporary Brandt nor any variation in spelling appears in the U. S. Army registers of Francis B. Heitman (1903) or of Thomas H. S. Hamersly (1880), and none of the annual Army Registers list enlisted men.

Baird did contact him. Always on the lookout for new collectors, Baird followed suggestions from those already in the field; see Deiss (1980).

34. Philip St. George Cooke (d. 1895) commanded the Mormon Batallion in 1846 that traveled from Santa Fe to Tucson and continued across the desert to San Diego, establishing the first usable wagon route across

Arizona; he was brevetted a major general in the Civil War. He published two books describing his army experiences (Cooke 1857, 1878). See also December 28, 1857.

35. Dr. Flavius S. Croppe (b. 1825) was born and grew up in Virginia and migrated to Missouri in 1851, where he practiced medicine; during the Civil War he sided with the Confederates; he was still living in 1881, according to *The History of Carroll County* (1881, p. 574), kindly provided by the State Historical Society of Missouri, Columbia.

36. Either *Sylvilagus auduboni,* Desert Cottontail or *S. bachmani,* Brush Rabbit; *S. b. cinerascens* has a marginal record from "San Emigdio Canyon," and a specimen of *S. audubonii* is listed from the Tehachapi Mountains, dates coinciding with Xántus' tenure.

37. Now *L. californicus,* Blacktail Jackrabbit. A Baja California variety is named *L. c. xanti.*

38. Bobcat.

39. Beetles; this securing of "thousands" was somewhat suspect, for some have never been collected again in this area (see Davis 1932). February 20, 1860, Xántus wrote Baird from Cabo San Lucas:

> I can impossibly recollect now, whether the botle I sent to LeConte was from Tejon pass or not. I had certainly a botle from that locality, collected by Mr Feilner for me, and entirely different coleoptera of those from fort Tejon. I put apart the botle for LeCount in my trunk, but forgot to forward until I found it here again at my arrival, just when packing an instalment for the Smithsonian, & told to Mr. Berlandier [his assistant in Cabo San Lucas] to bladder it with the rest and pack up, and label. —— If the botle contains Mexican coleoptera, it has been exchanged probably with other. I will however recognize the botle anytime, as it contained all black Coleoptera, or of very dark color. . . .

John L. Le Conte listed Xántus' species in various issues of the *Proceedings of the Philadelphia Academy of Natural Sciences* (see Le Conte 1858, 1861, 1866).

40. Xántus' description, albeit negative, contains more than a grain of truth in it about Army life; see Rickey (1981).

41. A strategem that didn't work; see March 1 and May 15, 1858.

Fort Tejon Cala.
July 20th 1857

Dear Sir/

I had the pleasure of receiving your note of June 1st, and I feel extremely mortified, that I have to be without the box for several months yet. I do not care much for the coll. box itself, but for its contents, viz. labels, printed Registers, scale, Invoice, & especially the books & pamphlets. Now if you have no coll. box at hand, let it be; and send me in any box at hand—a steel scale, blanks for measurements, Invoices, printed labels, homeopathic vials, Cork sheets, Insect pins, dark lantern, & Strychnine (as much as you can, I intend to make an extensive slaughter at grizlys, wolves, panthers etc)—and send especially Pamphets on Calif. Nat. History. Sitgreaves,[1] Emorys,[2] Marcys,[3] & Stansbury[4] Reports would be very welcome. —— Could you not procure for me Emory former Report, at the same time.[5] (Military Reconnosane) and Simpson New Mexico Report (?)[6] —— Some substancial traps (steele, with pikes in) would do a great service, if you could procure them there, but they should be of at least 1 feet diameter, when set. My traps are entirely to small, they catch something every night, but always only the top of the nose, and I can get nothing else, in the morning, as some fragments of nose, hair, or mustache.

Dr Hammond wrote me, that the next week (May 25th) he is going to send my guns & effects, so from Iowa they inform me, that my things are already dispatched to your care. —— If this should be the case, and you have my effects already, so please send me out the gun, & trunk from Riley, and the other trunk from Iowa. But any other box or boxes from Iowa keep with you, as it or they contain my Minnesota collection. There are some enormous stuffed turtles, than ground hogs, badgers etc; I presume they are in good order, but still you will oblige

me greatly if looking after. One of the boxes contains some 30 tausen insects, please campher them
well up. And lastly a Demijohn filled with serpents
fish etc. take them out, and put in your collection, I
dont want them.

Since my last (Jun. 29) I secured again a fine
Lynx rufus, & several interesting birds. Amongst the
mammals I shot the other day a Tamias quadvivita-
tus, which I was surprised to find here. But he is
much darker as the Kansas specimens, nearly dark
red (snuff) color, and the fringes on the back entirely black.[7] —— I fired at an owl, whole plumage
white, and the size of a full grown turkey; but unfortunately missed.[8] I hope to fall in soon again
with an other one, and will take a better aim.

I have at present quite a menagerie; a fine grizzly
cub, & 5 badgers (he, she, & 3 young ones) besides
several ground Squirrels. I am sorry, that there is no
opportunity whatever to send them to you; more
yet because I am bound soon to kill the grizzly, he is
getting from day to day more mischivious, he kills
my hens as fast as possible, and tore to pieces already the Colonels dog.

I have great difficulty in preserving the alcoholic
specimens, the several severe Earthquaque shocks
broke almost everything here; what we can call a
mug, jar, or botle.[9] To pack them in the Keg is very
inconvenient as long, as there is no quantity
enough to fill a whole keg. I used until now Jars of
Cerastes,[10] water ketles, sauce pans etc, but the
specimens were much spoiled. I am really lost as
how to menage this branch of my collection. The
Philadelphia Academy has a very convenient kind
of tin Jars, with large screw mouths. They offered
me when there; but I declined to accept them, because I already offered to collect for the Smit. Institution. You could see by & by those Jars, (or rather
cans) and if you would send me out a box full,
filled with alcohol, they would be more valuable,
and handy (I think so) as anothers collecting ves-

sels, including Copper cans; because I could in the same cans return to you the specimens. ——
The mail goes out in some minutes, so for the present I remain

Yours truly
LVésey

---

1. Lorenzo Sitgreaves (1853), *Report of an Expedition down the Zuni and Colorado Rivers.*

2. William H. Emory (1811–87) was a West Point graduate who, 1846–47, was chief engineer on the expedition to New Mexico and California; as chief astronomer and Commissioner for the boundary survey, 1848–53, he wrote the three-volume *Report on the United States and Mexican Boundary*, the first scientific coverage of this unmapped area between the Rio Grande and Pacific Ocean. He resigned in 1861 and was reappointed a lieutenant colonel in the Civil War.

3. R. B. Marcy (1853), *Exploration of the Red River of Louisiana.*

4. Howard Stansbury's, publication (1852) *Exploration and Survey of the Valley of the Great Salt Lake of Utah, Including a Reconnaisance of a New Route through the Rocky Mountains* contained one of the first objective and empathetic accounts of Mormonism; it was "translated" by Xántus and published in Hungary in 1857. See December 10, 1857, note 1.

5. Probably Xántus refers to Emory's (1848) report, *Notes of a Military Reconnoissance, from Fort Leavenworth, in Missouri, to San Diego, in California, Including Parts of the Arkansas, Del Norte, and Gila Rivers.*

6. J. H. Simpson (1850), *Report of the Secretary of War, Communicating the Report of Lieutenant J. H. Simpson of an Expedition into the Navajo Country in 1849.*

7. *Eutamius quadrivitattus*, Colorado Chipmunk, not in the Tejon area; his description suggests *Citellus lateralis*, Golden-mantled Ground Squirrel, which superficially resembles this chipmunk and which is common in southern California.

8. *Nyctea scandiaca*, Snowy Owl.

9. Xántus missed the earthquake of January 9, 1857, which had a magnitude of 8.25 on the Richter scale, the same as the San Francisco earthquake of 1906. Both were caused by the rupture of the San Andreas fault, a "vertical right lateral strike-slip" fault. One of the remarkable features of earthquakes on the San Andreas is the limited depth of the

disturbance, which causes large surface waves. Yozo Fujino and Alfred H-S. Ang, (1891, pp. 23–42) studied the 1857 Tejon earthquake as a "prototype event" for the "potential great earthquake" liable to occur on the southern portion of the San Andreas fault. Meisling and Sieh (1980) found that trees around Fort Tejon showed ring-ratio anomalies directly attributable to the 1857 disturbances. The January 1857 Fort Tejon earthquake rupture continued over a distance of more than 185 miles, with a horizontal slip of nearly 3,120 feet; aftershocks continued for some time, some of which Xántus reports (see September 17, 1857).

Logs of the Garlock Fault (predominantly east-west trending fault terminates against the San Andreas Fault less than 20 miles east of the Tehachapi Range) Well indicate a vertical movement of some 4,000 feet in the fault, with horizontal movement indicating the south side has moved eastward possibly as much as 25 miles. According to Grinnell (1905, pp. 9–10):

> The ruins of the Fort buildings cover considerable ground, and point to the great importance of the place. This importance, however, lasted but a few years, and was followed by complete abandonment. . . . Earthquakes have also helped in this leveling process which will at the present rate before long result in the total obliteration of this, one of California's most interesting land marks.

See also Trask (1864, p. 147); Trask notes severe shocks at Fort Tejon May 23 and August 29 which Xántus does not specifically mention, as well as several in the Los Angeles area. See also Agnew and Sieh (1978).

Baird, November 2, 1857, sent eight 10–gallon and half-gallon cans so that "you will be able to keep your next specimens without fear of loss by earthquakes." See also September 17 and November 10, 1857.

10. *Crotalus cerastes,* Sidewinder, a desert specimen.

N°6.[1]

Fort Tejon, Cala
Aug. 28th 1857

Dear Sir/ Your letter of July 16th is received. I will follow your advise in regard to description of birds, & will transmit to you some every mail.[2] The bird which I mentioned to you in my letter N° 2, & to which you refer in your last, is not the Picus Imp; nor any spec. of Picus. I send you at present the de-

scription of, together with a sketch of his head. Enclosed you find descriptions, & head sketches of 3
more birds; so all I would ask you is, to communi-
cate with me the name of the respective birds. ——
I dont think the Picus Imp. is found as far north, I
secured a number of them several years ago on the
Larapiqui in Costa Rico, & found one or two at
Punta Arenas on the Pacific side.[3]
Since my last I secured several small birds, which
I had not yet; and some very large mice. But there
are very few of the last, the commisary where so
many provisions, & in so great a variety are stored
up, ought to be an excellent place for them, but I
could only secure one family there; and a couple
more around the bakery. —— I am much ashton-
ished that there are no Magpies here, nor any of the
Columbidae,[4] saw the Ectopistes migratoria,[5] which
is found I suppose everywhere.
Dont speak sir, about making money of collections. I am long enough in this job, to know something about. After I suply the Sm. Institute, you
know I intend to give a series to the Philadelphia
Academy, and another to the Hungarian Nat. Museum; and should be something left for me after
such disposal, I will be glad if they bring me back
the cash only, what I expend for books!!! Thats true
I have already of some species over 30 even 40
specimens, and in such condition that they could be
done no better, but such birds are most common,
and of the *very good ones* there is no possibility of
procuring so many, on acct of their scarcity.[6]
I am sorry to inform you, that most of the volu-
minous spirituosae spoiled, I went through them
the other day, and to throw way good many interesting specimens. I am replacing their number now
in my register with other objects; and exchanged a
galloon of our alcohol, with the Hospitals Alcohol,
which is 85°, this will answer well I hope for collection, as the weak will answer for Common Phar-
macy use. Any other time you should send alcohol,

put the key in a box, & fill the space with straw, this manouvre will avert thirsty peoples attention, and always safely arrive at the destination. My kegs were exposed to everybodys test, and I have no doubt they drank it, and filled again with water; besides to invite everybody, they marked it on both sides with conspicuous letters "5 galloons Alcohol", so as not to escape attention.

I am much indepted for your kindness, in promising me Audubons Synopsis, but as you remark well it would be of very little use for me here; please to send me instead of Audubon "Brewers Wilson" (As I asked you already in my last).[7] There are in Synopsis all the Calif & Oregon birds, know until 1854 inclusive. And having the Synopsis of Stansburys Exp. with several other Pamphlets of a late date, I think I can get along very well, with such combined armament. ——

I dont know what to think, about my effects. D[r] Hammond wrote me in May that my guns, & effects will be sent the next day per Harlings, as directed, to you.[8] I wrote several letters to Harling at F[t] Riley on the matter, but he never answered a word as yet.

Now I have to inform you Sir on a new misfortune, which will show you, that I am really persecuted by fate in every respect. —— The Ordnance Sergeant of this Post rode down to Los Angeles, and promised me to bring up my mail. He found there amongst other things a large, round package with Washington stamp (no doubt your Mammalia Report)[9] put altogether in a handkerchief, and placed on the pommel of his Sadle. Taking a farewell dram—as the P. O. is barroom also—the horse got mad, broke the halfter, & run away. When cought (about 10 miles out of the town) was everything on her back, except—my unfortunate mail, and in it the Mammalia Report. I related to you the fact Sir; but dont comment on it —— ——

D[r] TenBroeck is since a month in Los Angeles, I exspect him every day home, but I dont think he

will favor my enterprise in any way, because Capt.
Gardiner wrote to him also on the subject, but he
never took any notice of. ——

At present the Dragoons gone from here to Oregon,[10] and instead of the light carabine to which I
was accustomed already I have a big musket, at
least 10 lb in weight, this circumstance cooles great
deal my passion & devotion to collection that's true!
I am entirely lost in imagination why they dont
send my gun!

I wrote you in my last, that Ft Tejon will be abandoned very probably, and requested you to procure
for me a good post if the above report be true; I recommend again dear Sir the case to your kind attention, and let me know any movement which should
be made in Washington in regard to Ft Tejon. ——
In a late Los Angeles Spanish Paper I see a notice,
that the Depart. of the Pacific suggested to the Secretary of War the establishment of a New Military
Post in the *San Gorgonio Pass,* if this should be the
case, I liked very much the new post on that place, I
think it must be *at least* as good for collecting, as Tejon, even in many respects has advantages over this.
There is a fine running stream, several small lakes, a
great Cactus desert (running parallel with the
cañon) and the valley is very broad. Beside is more
southern Climate, and not at all known. —— What
you think Sir about the plan of going there? (You
will find San Gorgonio Pass on the Map (R.R.R.)
about 70 miles SE of San Bernadino).[11]

My amunition has gone entirely last week; I was
under the necessity of procuring here from the Sutler some at an exorbitant price, (and he had shot
only N⁰ 6 the smallest) but sent word to some
friends in San Francisco, who will supply me by &
by. Meanwhile you may make some arrangement
for a new supply, which shall reach me as soon as
possible, until then I will do my best to procure my
ammunition. I liked very much, if you could send
me a bag smaller shot, as N⁰ 10, it is called—I think

mustard shot, the german name for is „Dunst"—
for small Silvias,[12] Parus, Trochylus[13] etc N⁰ 10 is
altogether to large shot, even half charge is so
large! ——
   The other day made their appearance that red
bellied large Picus,[14] of which I have seen quite a
number in your collection; they are very numerous.
                                        Very truly yours
                                              LXdeVésey

P. S. The other day I had to go down to Los Angeles
for a Power of Attorney, and noticed near San Fernando Mission on a desert *a great number* of a very
small species of Lepus, they not longer than 6
inches I suppose, and are dark brown, with pale
reddish face.[15] —— There I noticed a great Lanius[16]
also, and some other birds, which are not found
around Ft Tejon. I made arrangement with the gar-
dener at the mission, gave him the necessary instructions and he promised to procure me anything
he can.

---

1. Letter No. 5, dated August 3, 1857, was lost on the *George Law;* see
November 10, 1857.

2. Baird, July 16, 1857:
   > You would not do amiss to lay in large stock of skins of birds of all
   > kinds. If in good conditions you can find eggs a good market. . . .
   > You had better commence a sort of systematic list and description
   > for all your birds from time to time numbering the descriptions by
   > the numbers of the specimens. If you could send on such listing . . .
   > we could then tell you the [species] and what to do next in getting
   > more specimens.

3. See Xántus, November 16, 1857. This turned out to be *Phainopepla
nitens,* Phainopepla. Baird, October 17, 1857:
   > I received yesterday your letter of Aug. 28 (No. 6) with its notice of
   > birds. The plan of sending a sketch of head, and an accompanying
   > description is a very good one, facilitating very much the identifi-
   > cation of the specimens, and 53, 194, 198 which is the Ptiliogonys
   > nitens, a species frequently met with in the Southern border of our
   > western region, as far east as El Paso.

Xántus made no collecting expedition to Central America; according to Madden (1949a, pp. 33–36), Xántus applied to Sherzer and Wagner (see November 10 and 16, 1857) to go as a collector with them and was refused.

4. Dove Family.

5. Properly *E. migratorius*, Passenger Pigeon, now extinct. According to Dr. Amadeo M. Rea, San Diego Museum of Natural History, it is more likely that he saw *Zenaidura macroura*, Mourning Dove; Grinnell (1905, p. 12), noted that these "were to be seen by the hundreds."

6. Baird, October 17, 1857:

> Notwithstanding the uncertainty about making money from collections, I still think that it may be well to look a little forward to it. Even after kindly supplying the Smithsonian and Phila. Academy and the Hung. Mus., you will doubtless have duplicates which may be disposed of to your advantage. At least there will be no harm in looking to something of this kind. And of one thing I can assure you that though the birds of which you have most specimens are the most common . . . no species from S. California is as common but that it is wanted by collectors & all western specimens are in demand.

7. Baird, October 17, 1857:

> The Synopsis of Audubon was sent some time ago and will doubtless have reached you ere this. You are mistaken in supposing that there is any edition of Brewer's Wilson which contains any species not in the Synopsis. This edition of Wilsons was published in 1800[?] just after the Synopsis, and was made up mainly from it; the succeeding editions have been merely printed off from the same stereotype, plates adding on the titles, the dates of printing to make it fresh.

8. Charles Harling enlisted in the U. S. Army Medical Department, March 1856, and was assigned to Ft. Riley in June of that year as hospital steward, where he would have certainly known Xántus. According to William McKale, Museum Technician, U. S. Cavalry Museum, Fort Riley, Kansas, there is nothing to indicate why he should have been responsible for Xántus' goods unless it was an extra assigned duty, or a promise made to Xántus. He left the post in October 1858; see November 16, 1857, March 1, and September 1, 1858.

9. Baird (1858d).

10. Problems with the Cayuse Indians in Oregon prompted the sending of reinforcements north to Col. Steptoes' command; see July 15, 1858, note 1.

11. San Gorgonio Pass was an easy grade, discovered during the Railroad Surveys in 1853. As the only large break directly through the mountains, it forms a great draft channel for ocean winds that rush into the vacuum caused by heated updrafts rising off the desert east of the mountains; as a consequence, it is one of the windiest sites in California, witnessed by sand-abraded wooden posts and deeply fluted rock, and today is the site of hundreds of wind generator "farms"; see also Russell (1919?).

Baird, October 17, 1857:

> I have heard nothing of the proposed change of Post from Tejon to Gorgonio, but will make enquiries on the subject & I [would] consider this as a much better locality even than Fort Tejon as farther south and more likely to catch scattering summer visitors from the Gulf of California.

And undated, but probably February 14, 1858:

> As to the new post I will do what I can, but I was informed that there was no intention of abandoning Tejon. Would you wish to leave before June or July?

12. Sylviidae: Old World Warbler Family.

13. Genus of Hummingbirds.

14. *Melanerpes lewis,* Lewis' Woodpecker.

15. Baird, October 17, 1857:

> The little rabbit of Los Angeles is probably my Lepus trowbridgei which I have seen from San Diego.
> *Lepus trowbridgei,* named by Baird in 1855, is now *Sylvilagus bachmani,* Brush Rabbit.

16. *L. ludoviciana excubitoroides.* Loggerhead Shrike. Baird, October 17, 1857:

> The next bird, No. 200, is evidently a Lanius but of a species entirely unknown to me if your figure expresses accurately the length and proportion of the bill.

For Xántus' General Register description, see September 12, 1857, note 7.

No VII.

Dear Sir / I received your letter of July 16th last mail, and was disappointed to learn, that you do not receive my letters regularly. I wrote to you every mail, which left the Fort, since I am here. The respective dates of my letters were as follows: June. 5. — Jun. 29. — July. 20. — Aug. 3. — Aug. 25. — One I wrote from S. Francisco, & this the seventh.

I received last mail the Report on Mammals from page 321. (Spermophylus Spilosoma) to the end, and so the Ordonance Sergeant lost the pages from beginn to the 320th page inclusive.[1] Be so kind now Sir, and send this deficit. Audubon, & the steel scale arrived also, my warmest thanks for your kindness.

———

I was extremely glad to find, that the 3 inch rule corresponds precisely with my surrogate used until now. I manufactured it of a flattened bladder, & divided in ¼ inches.

I find in Audubon, that the Picus Imperius is an Oregon & California bird. Until for the last two or 3 years I paid very litle attention to N. American birds, & was under the impression that P. Imp. is a Central American bird. Taking in consideration that in the Regions mentioned by Aud. the bird is very rare, and more abundant in the high mountains of Costa Rica, & Yucatan, I believe still that P. Imp. is a native of those Countries, and the few found so far north as Oregon, are only "Oisseux errants" —— I found the species invariably in high mountains, where mountain torrents rush in deep gorges, the ground is moist and the sun hardly ever penetrates through the gigantic forest trees. They fly on trees only, when something approaches, else they are on ground like the Woodcocks, & feed on ants.[2] —— As these are some like places in the mountains hereabout, I may come yet across some, and in that case I surely get them, because they are not very shy.

The rat, I noticed in my first letter, is no doubt the Neotoma Mexicana, but I got one since I mentioned the first, which is very different in size. I measured both minutely and submit the result to your examination. N⁰ 52 is an adult female, N⁰ 637 is an adult male. They agree with the gen. characters, color, etc perfectly, as given in your description. But the 1st is a slender, comparatively small animal, while the 2d is a heavy, large, & quite a clumsy looking fellow. — — I dont know whether on act of larger size only is anybody authorized to make a new species? but you may find in something perhaps, which would justify a making one. I could not procure their skulls, both were fractured entirely, but I will get plenty specimens yet no doubt. —— I enclose herewith a rough sketch of their residence, they build it here in narrow valleys, close to water, in the bush, but select the highestmost, and very slender bush trees. They have two houses. One on the tree, the other on the ground, beside to the tree itself, and surrounding bushes, it is about 6 feet in diameter, by 4 high. The entrances (from 6–10) are on the ground, but the dwelling in the centre of the heap, consisting of feathers, moss, dry herbs, etc. arranged very neetly. The upper residence is generally about 15 feet high on the tree, with a fine gallery above, to protect against the inclemency of weather, and is arranged very softly inside. —— If a dog only smells the lower habitation, the inmate runs instantly in his upper house, if you attack this with some missile, he darts down at once like lightning in the ground house. *And then,* there is no possibility to get him out again. When arrivinng at this stage of the manovre, I destroyed carefully their habitation, but never could find the rat, they have several subterraneous passages, for their last refuge.[3]

——— ——— ——— ———

In my last, I sent you description of 4 birds, and I am mighty glad, there is none of them in Audubon. Of the 2^{d} one (with the long decurved bill) there is no genus; not even family in Audubon. —— The 3^{d} one I presume is a Lanius, already described by Aud., although I did not examine him yet.

I identified several birds with them cf Aud. Examined & compared already my Muscicapas,[4] & Trochylide, the result I submit to you in the enclosed pages. —— I have three Muscicapas, & 1 Trochylus, not described in Aud., you will find here the description, & please to inform me whether they are described already, or not, and of their name if known. —— One of the Muscicapus (as you see) is very large, 7½ inches in length, & 13 in extent.

You shall refer only to the number, affixed to each *species* with red ink, and as I keep a copy of my descriptions, I will know accordingly the species you mean. To have some order in the description, please to number my 4 birds, as they described the crested black bird N^{o} I,[5] that one with the curved bill N° II,[6] the Lanius N° III,[7] and N° IV[8] the last, to have it corresponding with my Copy. —— Yesterday I noticed a Trochylus, much larger as any of the described, entire black or dark brown, (I could not make out precisely) with red head. I was just loading my gun and when ready to fire he was out of sight.[9]

I was informed of a bird, inhabiting the high mountains hereabout, with a very long tail, very long legs, and extremely small slender body; with greyish brown general color. He is reported as very shy, as never flying, but running *faster as a horse* (the words of my informant), it is called popularly "Racer, or Race bird."[10] I never noticed any although I been everywhere around, where they reported to exist, but I presume it is the Tetrao uropharicanus,[11] so common in far West.

—— —— ——

At first sight, (before securing any) I thought they were all Max. Jays swarming hereabout. Now I see, the greatest number is *Garrulus ultramarinus Bonap.*,[12] but there is an other species, which I secured in many exemplars, and is not described in Audubon, which may prove still Max. Ja. You will find here a short description, & please let me know who he is. —— At the same time I would ask you to inform me of the relative value of each bird, that I may pay attention *chiefly* to valuable species, and not lose time with very common ones.[13]

⸻ ⸻ ⸻ ⸻

I was under the impression, that you are going to publish the P. RR. Reports with illustrations, if this should be the case, I would be much indebted endeed, if you could let me have the illustrations also. I would be very glad, to have a series of the Smithsonian Reports also, of which I have seen only a few in possession of Dr Coolidge,[14] but never had them, and never read them. You could send them out occasionally, if you send stores for me, or any of my effects. If you did not purchase yet Brewers Wilson, better let it be. I think I can be very well without it now.

Dr TenBroeck is in Los Angeles yet, he is there since nearly 6 weeks, and I don't know when he will back.

Is Dr John L LeConte[15] gone to Honduras? or not —— I never heard a word of him, since left the States.

Mr Forbes has not written yet to me, nor Wells Fargo & Co.

Sincerely yours

JXdeVesey

---

1. Baird, July 16, 1857, asked if Xántus had received some 47 sheets of the Mammal Report and promised him a supply as soon as possible, October 17, 1857:

[I am] very sorry for the loss of the sheets of the Mammal report as I cannot replace it just now. I got half a dozen sets of each sheet as it passed through the press, and have distributed them all and I cannot get any complete copies now unless by some chance, until the plates are all finished and the volume bound. I will try to accomplish this however, as soon as I can.

See also November 10, 1857.

2. See August 28, 1857, note 3.

3. Baird, November 16, 1857:

Your account of the habits of the Neotoma is deeply interesting. I have little doubt that you have [?] new species, but can't decide till I see the specimens—Look sharp for the *Neotoma californianus* and *cinerea*. . . .

Frederick W. True, (1894, p. 354) credited Xántus with a new subspecies, *Neotoma macrotis simplex*, Type #3651 USNM:

Similar to *N. macrotis*, but all the under surfaces and the feet white, the hairs being of this color to the roots. Tail rather sharply bicolored. Ears very thinly clothed with whitish hairs.

4. Xántus uses "Musciapa" for Flycatchers, Kingbirds, and Phoebes.

5. *Phainopepla nitens*, Phainopepla; General Register I:

Male. Total length 8, Extent 11¾, Ext of the wing 5¼, tail 4½ inches. —— The whole bird is of a shining black, which when exposed to light, plays into gold green. The seven outer quills of the wing are white, enclosed in a narrow margin of black. Towards the tip of the quill, the white color is lost in gray, and the gray at the extremity of the tip in black. The 3d quill is the longest, the 2d & 4th equal, then the 5th. The tail consists of 12 feathers, all rounded. At the top of the head the bird is ornamented with a beautiful black crest, 1 inch long. —— Tarsas feet & claws black, the bill also, which is very short, & the upper mandible terminates in a fine hook. —— Iris red.

Female. Total length 8, Extent 11¼, Ext of the wing 5 inches. — — Throat, & whole underpart light brown ringed with cinnamon; and [?]. Back grayish-brown, wings dark brown. The seven quills are of a dirty white color, margined with dark brown. Tail cinnamon. —— Crest a little longer as in the male, & of a dark brown — — nearly black color. Bill, tarsus, & feet as in the male.

The young resembles much in color, the young Sialia Wilsonii, blue gray & black, tinged with white spots, and striks all over.

The birds came here, the 1st part of June, they inhabit a very high altitude, and craggy peaks, which are almost inaccessible. They are extremely shy; if they notice something approaching at more than 500 yards distance, they fly. They are only by sunrise & sunset visible, at this time they dart down in the deep cañon like lightning,

and sound continuously a peculiar but very disharmonious cry. —
— I am informed by hunters that they build their nests of the higher
most clifs, on projecting pine & cedar trees, which are nohow accessible. By opening them I found in stomach invariably the small
seeds of the Chaparell bush. Where do they get water, I am unable
to tell, as I never noticed any of them within two miles of any water.

6. *Toxastoma redivivum*, California Thrasher [?]; General Register, II:

12. —— 13. —— 5½. ——
Length of the tail 5½. —— Bill very long, of a dark horn color, and
curved downwards. The upper mandible is notched at the base on
both sides, having in it, situated the nostrils. Upper and lower mandible is covered at the base with stiff hairs all round. The margin of
the mandibles runs nearly to the eyes, by which arrangement the
bird can open his mouth like the Caprimulgidae, ready to swallow
objects of great size.
—— Iris bright carmine. Above the eyes a pale yellow stripe passes
back about ¼ of an inch in length. Under the eyes a bunch of white
& brown speckled very fine & very short feathers, which cover the
ears. Top of the head, back, & wings gray brown, primaries a litle
darker brown. 3d quill the longest, next second, then 4th ——
Tail consisting of 12 feathers, above very dark shining brown, below pale brown, rounded in the shape of a fan. At the base of the
tail, below & above extremely fine cinnamon colored feathers. Chin
& vent very clean chamois; throat & breast bluish brown. Legs dark
brown. Tarsus feet & claws slaty.
The bird has the habits of the Turdi; frequents very dark brush, &
never have seen him to fly. If you approach him very closely—say
2–3 yards—he runs like lightning to the next bunch of brush, & so
on. It is very difficult to secure a good specimen as you are bound
to fire at him at a distance of some yards only, else he is not visible.
—— The bird is not very abundant nor extremely rare here, and I
think he could be caught in numbers by setting out birdtraps in the
places, which they frequent. ——
In the stomach of both I found Coleoptera, & Caterpillars.

7. *Lanius ludovicianus excurbitioides*, Loggerhead Shrike, General Register, III:

Length 9. Extent 12¼. Ext. of the wing 5¼. Length of the tail 4¼
inches. —— Bill black, slightly curved downwards, the upper mandible terminating in a hook, & is cut in like a tooth of a saw. At each
side of the upper mandible—4 stiff hairs. —— Head, back, & wing
coverts slaty. Throat, breast, belly, upper & lower tail coverts white.
From the upper mandible passes a black band on each side of the
head, which terminates behind the ears in two points, in the centre
of this band is situated the eye. —— Wings redish-black, with a
white band crossing diagonally the centre of the quills. Second quill

the longest, next the 3ᵈ then the 4ᵗʰ. —— Tail rounded, with 11 feathers, the 3 outer ones having a white patch at the end, else black. The other feathers whole black, tarsus dark slaty, so feet & claws.

The bird was secured in sage bush—artemisia—had in his stomach a quantity of small cicadidae.

8. *Toxostoma bendirei*, Bendire's Thrasher; General Register, IV:

the *adult female* is 10 Inches long, 14 in extent, & 6½ the wing. The tail is exactly as long, as the whole bird without the tail—say 5 Inches —— Iris bright yellow, tarsus & feet light blue. —— Head and back brown, with a bluish-hue. The 4 outer quills of the wing black, the others dark brown, all margined with white. —— 3 white bands cross the wings diagonally, the midle one terminated at the outermost quills in a lozenge shaped patch. Throat & whole underpart white, speckled all over with small brown spots. the tail has 9 feathers, almost of equal length, and dark brown. Except the outher most on each side, which is shorter & of a bright white color.

The *juv.* ♀ & ♂ is precisely the same color as the above described adult ♀, only less in size and the tail very short.

The 3 are all, I ever noticed of these birds, I found them at a very high altitude in dense Pine forest, crying very near like the Garruli. By opening them, their stomach contained sundry little seeds, unknown to me.

9. *Calypte anna*, Anna's Hummingbird.

10. *Geococcyx californianus*, Greater Roadrunner.

11. Now *Centrocercus urophasianus*, Sage Grouse.

12. Now *Aphelocoma ultramarina*, Gray-breasted or Mexican Jay.

13. Baird, November 10, 1857:

It is difficult to say what birds you had best collect largely of. The Maximilians Jay will be welcome also the humming birds and of course all the species seldom seen. . . . Fifty specimens each of all the commonest birds, would be not too many. Get many of the genus. You might perhaps perhaps afford to slight *Picus formicivorus* more for other specimens. The rarer hawks should be [?] gathered up.

14. Dr. R. D. Coolidge (d. 1866) assumed duties as Assistant Surgeon, U. S. A., in 1841, and consequently served at Fort Riley, 1856–58; he advanced in grade to major and surgeon in 1860 and was brevetted lieutenant colonel in 1865 "for faithful and meretorious service."

15. Dr. John Le. Conte (1825–83) was a well-known entomologist, having named nearly half of the 6,000 beetle species then known; as a member of the Academy of Natural History of Philadelphia, he was one

of Xántus' sponsors for membership on the strength of his Fort Riley collections. He catalogued Xántus' beetles and commented (Le Conte 1859, p. 69):

> The present paper contains a list of the species of Coleoptera collected at Fort Tejon, during 1857 and 1858, by the indefatigable naturalist, Mr. John Xantus, (de Vesey), which were found to be remarkable in many resepcts. The number of species obtained (147) is very small for the time during which they were collected, and the proportion of new species (52) is very large. These facts are in accordance with the general principles of the geographical distribution of organized beings in Pacific North America, stated by me at the meeting of the American Association of the Advancement of Science. . . .

He wrote the monumental "Classification of *Coleoptera* of North America" (Le Conte 1861–62). He also collected birds, including the type specimen of *Toxostoma lecontei*.

NoVIII.

Fort Tejon, Cala.
Sept. 17, 1857

Dear Sir/

Although I wrote to you only a few days ago, there is an extra mail leaving the Post, so I avail myself the opportunity to write you again.

The Lynxes which I mentioned to you already are very probably the "maniculatus" variety of the Lynx rufus, as they are spotted.

The Foxes here (I think), are the *Vulpes velox*,[1] & *V. argentatus*,[2] of the last I am quite sure.

The wolves are, one very large grey, with greenish-rufous back, & dark tail (I think the *C. nubilus*.[3] Then the *C. latrans* (very plenty). And finally the black wolf (which I not see mentioned in the list of your report), but which is extremely rare, as it is I suppose rare everywhere.[4]

The ground Squirrell I mentioned to you, is very likely the *Spermophylus Beecheyi. Rich.*[5] I have of them already over 30 specimens, and as many skulls.

The Tamias,[6] I dont know which it is, is very small, tail ⅔ of the whole body, ears much pointed, & half an inch long. On the back 3 dark brown stripes, margined with redish brown. The intervalls grey. Legs grey, the hind ones darker. Sides rufous grey. On the cheeks three dark brown stripes, the middle one crosses the eye. The upper ones unite at the point of the nose, in shape.

Thomomys bulbivorus.[7] Very rare.

Thomomys fulvus.[8] Not very abundant.

The Kangaroo Rat, I mentioned to you is very probably the *Dipodomys ordii*, Wood.[9] although I got none yet. There is an another Dipodomys, I suppose the *D. Philipii*. Gray.[10] I did not notice yet the *D. agilis*,[11] but he must be here also, I think.

Of deers, there is only the *Cervus columbianus*[12] here, about 20 miles NW very abundant.

I should not be surprised, if my rusty Squirrell, with the cinnamon patch on the head, should turn out the *S. ferruginiventrus* Aud & Bach.[13] —— But I must get the lost parts of your Report, before I can positively identify my specimens.

Yesterday I secured a young Neotona Mexicana, which perfectly resembles the *larger* specimen I described you in my last. The ear, tail, & whiskers fully developed, & rather clumsy, not slender as the *smaller* (female) specimen. They wont bait meat, nor cheese, corn, barley, or backen, it seems they live exclusively on the different fruits of oaks. ——

——

I have not Cassins birds of California, but if you will kind enough to procure for me I will be under many obligations. You must not think, that I am entirely destitute, such expenses I will be very glad to refound you occasionally. If Mr Cassin, who knows me very well, has a copy to dispose of he will no

doubt give it to you for me, if not please to purchase
one & charge to me, but I liked to have it illustrated.
Since a month we experienced very few Earthquaque shocks, & their intensity decreases from
time to time. They come some time yet, with heavy
rumblings (like a passing of a railroad car over a
bridge), but the vibration is generally very slight, &
almost always vertical; this a great change in their
nature, as formally the rumblings were slight, the
shocks very heavy, & invariably oscillatory. Our
buildings were considerably injured this spring,
some of them perfectly ruined, but since their re-
pairation not even a crack is seen on them.

With sincere regards

Yours truly

XLVésey

---

1. Swift Fox, not in California; probably *Vulpes macrotis*.

2. Now *Urocyon cinereoargenteus*, Gray Fox.

3. *Canis lupus*, Gray Wolf.

4. Undoubtedly a local name.

5. *Citellus beecheyi*, California Ground Squirrel.

6. Probably *Eutamias merriami*, Merriam Chipmunk.

7. Giant Pocket Gopher, found only in northeastern Oregon.

8. Now *T. bottae*, Valley Pocket Gopher, the only one in southern California.

9. Ord Kangaroo Rat, absent in most of California, including Xántus'
area.

10. *Dipodomys* in southern California are *D. deserti*, Desert Kangaroo
Rat; *D. merriami*, Merriam Kangaroo Rat; *D. agilis*, Pacific Kangaroo
Rat; *D. heermanni*, Heermann Kangaroo Rat; *D. stephensi*, Stephens
Kangaroo Rat. See Hall and Kelson (1959), and Burt and Grossenheider
(1976).

11. Pacific Kangaroo Rat.

12. *Odocoileus hemionus* replaces *O. h. columbiana*.

13. Now *Sciurus aureogaster,* Red-bellied Squirrel, found only in Central America.

No IX.

Fort Tejon, Cala.
Sept. 30, 1857

Dear Sir/
    I forward you herewith the continuation of my descriptive catalogue. As you see, I have 9 species Woodpeckers, of which some—no doubt—valuable. The Certhia[1] may turn out as a *Creeping Warbler,* but I think it is a real Creeper. —— You will find the commencement of my Finches, of which I have over 20 species (fringillinae), and are only the four in Audubon, which you receive at present, in the next sheets I will send you description of the others. —— the *Erythrospiza frontalis, Say*[2] is quite common here, I noticed in my first letter as "a red breasted Carduelis," as Audubon did not get many. I will procure plentyful.
    I have at present 87 species of birds, in over 550 specimens, out of those are only about from 30 to 35 described in Audubon. As I already commenced, will try to describe them as far as I can, and then send them in, (probably the end of October or so).
    In a couple weeks the waterbirds will be here. I experienced everywhere, that the collection of ducks never remunerates trouble, as they are market fowls procurable everywhere & by everybody; so I will get only a very limited number of them (to show that they are also here), but will turn my whole attention to snipes, Cranes, Curlews, etc amongst which there are some valuable species yet, (I think so).
    Yesterday I secured a female *black ground Squirrell.* It has a whole History. —— —— Being out in the

mountains, when at Rest, I noticed a great excitement amongst the Spermophylus Beecheyi around
me. In looking after the cause, I soon found it out.
There was a black fellow amongst them, and the
whole crowd was vociferating & persecuting the
stranger. He run a way, I could not get him. The
next day I saw him again, but being in continuous
persecution by the other Squirrells, was no possibility of getting near to him on the exposed ground. Of
course I could not give him up, but resolved at once
to build an ambuscade near his residence (in a hole,
amongst two blocks of granite). I did so, and
watched from morning until late in the evening yesterday; at last I got him. ―― ―― ―― It may be
the *Spermophylus Couchii, Baird,*[3] but I have not that
part of your Reports, in which the description of
this species contained, I infer only from the index,
which is in my possession. So, being not certain of
the identity, I send you herewith a description of
the Species, together with very particular & correct
measurements. ―― The skull (which is a very perfect one) is very similar to that of *S. Beecheyi* of same
size, although is a little narrower in general, the upper molars a little shorter, & the lower ones *decidedly*
longer. ―― But even it if should turn out as the *S.
couchii,* will be a valuable acquisitions, as you give
his habitation in the Nomenclature, as North Mexico ―― Her appearance is extremely curious here,
being so apparently noticed even by her relatives
the *S. Beecheyi,* who where greatly annoyed by her
appearance amongst them. There is nobody here
who ever has seen before the animal, although
there are several citizens & hunters, residing since 4
& 5 years around the Post. How she could come
here is a mistery, & notwithstanding is hardly imaginable, that she is alone, she must have some mate
or family members no doubt. ―― ――

very truly yours
LXdeVésey

P.S. I almost forgot to inform you, that I was under the pressing necessity to aply to Mr Forbes for ammunition. I requested him last mail to send me some, and informed him at the same time, that by returning mail I will send him the whole amount he expends for; I hope he will do this favor, else I should be really very much disappointed, as here is an article of a very inferior quality on exorbitant prices.

---

1. *Certhia americana,* Brown Creeper.

2. Now *Carpodacus mexicanus frontalis,* House Finch.

3. Now *Spermophilus variegatus couchii,* Rock Squirrel; Baird identified Xántus' "new" species as *S. beecheyi,* the only Rock Squirrel in southern California and very common. See also October 20, 1858.

 N^O **X**

Ft Tejon, Cala.
Oct. 15, 1857

Dear Sir/

I forward herewith continuation of my descriptive Catalogue of Birds, from N^O XXXIII to N^O L (inclusive). I intended to make something like a sketch of each bird, but I cannot spare so much time. Dr TenBroeck is never at home, so I am in fact the Surgeon of the Post. In the morning I have to look out for the cleanliness of the Hospital, then comes the Sick call, then the Morning Report, then to dispense the Sick in Hospital, and finally to enter everything in the books. The ordinary routine of my duty keeps me busy every day until about 11 o clock mr. So you will perceive that only the afternoon is left to me, which I regularly use for hunting & skinning both. I have to make my private correspondence etc

all by candle, which keeps me some time awake
until midnight. I cannot possibly do more. ——
——But I think my descriptions are enough detailed, so as to enable you to identify the respective
specimens. Amongst the 18 here described birds,
there are only *four* described in Audubon, viz
Regulus Calendula,[1] *Silvicola aestiva,*[2] *Trichas Marilan-
dica,*[3] & *Ptiologonys Townsendii.*[4] The last one may
prove a good aquisition, as it seems Audubon had
only a ♀ specimen. My, is a ♂ one, & differs considerably from that of Audubons ♀. The base of all the
primaries & secondaries bright ochre, with the exception of the 3 outer primaries, which are light
straw color. In size he is by ¾ of an inch longer, &
the coloring of tail is different also. But quite positively it is the same Bird.

N⁰ˢ XL. XLI. XLII are (so I think) *Icterus,*[5] but
comparing with Audubons species, they differ from
any of them so much, that I cannot consider them
else, as positively distinct species.

N⁰ˢ XXXVII,[6] XXXVIII,[7] & XXXIX,[8] are probably
Anthus, the first may prove the *Anthus Ludovicianus*
but having no other specimens on hand to compare
with; it differs so entirely from A. Ludovicianus
that I consider it a distinct species.

All the other species I suppose are
Tringillinae.[9] There is amongst them a
beautifull species of *Erythrospiza* (N⁰
XXXVI)[10] not described in Audubon. They were extremely rare until now, only occassionally seen. But
since a couple weeks they appear in flocks from 5 to
10, and I hope to get yet a good series of them, although very difficult to aproach them, being very
shy.

*Possibly a Cassin's
Finch; Xántus' de-
scription is ambig-
uous, making a sure
identification prob-
lematical.*

Lately I undertook a trip to the Tejon peak, the
highest mountain we have here around. I scaled
after considerable difficulties, and reached the highest most point, which is about 3 tausend feet above
the Fort.[11] I chiefly undertook the expedition, to ascertain whether there is anything, what we have

not below. I killed there ½ dozen birds, which seem quite abundant there, although very rare below in the valley. Besides I secured again a Lynx maculatus. I observed from the peak large herds of Antelopes, Mountain Sheep,[12] & some grizzlys—walking on the Western slopes, & lower ridges,—and observed several (some very large) flocks of the Ortyx plumifera, Gould,[13] but could not secure any. It was so craggy, & thorny bush filled the whole desolate region, that I could not persecute anything, considering myself fortunate to have a sure foothold at times. ——

I am packing up everything, the greatest part of my collection is already in boxes, & labelled. As soon, as any opportunity shall offered, I send them down to Los Angeles, to be forwarded by Wells & Fargo Agency to M[r] Forbes.

I received the eyes, and am much indebted for your kindness.

I did not receive yet any ammunition from my friends in San Francisco, nor from Mr Forbes; and consequently my operation dont goes so well, as I wish and as it could.

Until now Dr Hammond returned no doubt and I hope he will forward, or cause to be forwarded my effects at once. I wrote him last mail.

sincerely yours
LXdeVésey

---

1. Ruby-crowned Kinglet, local in the mountains of California.

2. Now *Dendroica petechia,* Yellow Warbler.

3. Now *Geothlypis trichas,* Common Yellowthroat.

4. Now *Phainopepla nitens,* Phainopepla.

5. *Icterus cucullatus,* Hooded Oriole. General Register, XL:

    Male. Bill very stout, nearly straight, & rather long. Upper mandible dark brown, lower yellow,—nostrils round, & not covered. Whole underparts & rump gamboge, tinged with light green; rump more so. Head & neck greenish yellow; the tail nearly even, dark brown, the outer webbs margined with greenish yellow. Second & 3[d] quills longest & equal, the first & 4th next & also equal. Wings as the tail, all the primaries margined with yellowish green, the secondaries very broadly. There are two very prominent bands on the wing (the upper bright, the lower light yellow) formed respectively by the tips of small, & long wing coverts. Whole upperparts yellowish green, tinged with brown.

The *female* is similar in size & color, only duller, the bands on the wings being nearly obsolete. . . . Arrived the 1th days of August, & departed again in the 1st days of October. Is gregarious, feeding in immense numbers on blackberries.

General Register, XLII:

Male. Bill as in the foregoing species. Third quill the longest, second & 4th next & equal; 1st much longer than 5th. Whole underparts & rump beautiful bright gamboge, the sides & breast a litle tinged with olive. Ground color of head, cheeks, throat, & neck also gamboge, the forehead much tipped with orange; as is the forepart of throat. —— The neck, sides of the throat, & head, tipped with dark olivaceous wings, & tail shining black, the 4 lateral feathers of the later margined at their tip with pure white. Primaries a little margined with yellow, the secondaries very broadly towards their tips. —— Two very broad bands of yellow on the wings, formed by the coverts. Back black, but every feather is margined (all round) with a faint yellow, which makes appear the bird, as if covered all over with scales. —— Tail slightly rounded.

Female similar, but not so brightly colored; the feathers of the tail all margined, & the back *tipped* with yellow. . . . Noticed several specimens, but departed very soon (almost immediately) after their arrival in August.

General Register, XLII:

Bill as in the foregoing two species, but more compressed towards the end. Tarsus & toes blue, tinged with brown. Second quill the longest, first & 3[d] a litle shorter only & equal. Fourth again a litle as the former. Whole underparts & rump gamboge; the sides of abdomen much tinged with olivaceous. A longitudinal band of orange on the throat, the base of mandibles & forehead tipped with orange. Head & neck greenish yellow, back duller, & tinged with brown. Tail & wings chocolate, the feathers of the former margined with yellow, as are the primaries. An indistinct band of yellow crosses the wing above, & which is formed by the tips of the small coverts. Tail slightly rounded.

6. *Anthus spinoletta,* Water Pipit. Baird, December 3, 1857, identified this as *Passerella* sp. General Register, XXXVII:

*Possibly a House Finch;
Xántus' description is ambiguous,
making a sure identification
problematical.*

Male. Bill robust, edges inflected, the ridge slightly curved, & terminating in a very acute decurred point. Nostrils round, & partly concealed by the feathers. Head, cheeks, & sides of the neck dull grey. Two longitudinal redish brown bands on the head, and two similar ones on the cheeks. Upperparts brown, streaked all over with dark brown, & redish brown. Quills dirty black, margined with redish brown; the secondaries nearly entire dark red. The 4th & 5th, longest, & equal; the 8th equal to the 1st. Sides dull yellow, all other lowerparts white, streaked with dark brown, longitudinally. —— Tail much rounded, & the feathers pointed; the central ones margined with redish brown.

Female. Much lighter colored in general. All the streakes are light red brown—instead of dark, as in the male—. The tail wood brown, margined & tinged with chestnut. . . .Iris blue.

7. Identification uncertain. General Register, XXXVIII:

*Possibly a Song Sparrow;
Xántus' description is ambiguous,
making a sure identification
problematical.*

Male. Bill of a dark horn color, robust, conical, compressed towards the end; the edges inflected, nostrils round, & partly concealed by the feathers. Throat & abdomen pure white; all other lower parts white, spotted with dark brown. Cheeks & back dull grey, tinged with pale brown. Feathers on the head lanceolate, of a deep chesnut color, & spotted with dark brown. Wing & tail chocolate, the primaries margined with yellowish brown. Third quill the longest, 2d 4th & 5th the next & equal. First shorter than sixth, but a litle longer than 7th —— Tibia redish brown, tarsus ochre, toes & claws (which are both remarkably long) nearly black.

Female. Whole underparts yellow, streaked with obsolete brown spots; but which are on the sides of the throat, & upper breast quite distinct. Head, neck, & cheeks likewise yellow, tinged with light brown. Upperparts yellowish brown, with obsolete brown streaks.

Tail & wings dark brown, margined with rufous. A little smaler as the male. . . . Iris brown.

8. Baird identified this species as *Penecea lincolnii,* Lincoln's Sparrow, December 3, 1857; General Register, XXXIX:

Bill moderately stout, conical, edges inflected, the tip very acute. Both bill & feet of a dull yellow color; claws moderately long, very acute, & laterally grooved. Second, third, & 4th quills longest & about equal; 1st & 5th next & also equal. 6th a litle shorter than 1st. —— Head streaked with grey, chesnut, & black lanceolate spots. Hind neck, sides, & a band over the eye yellowishgrey. A similar band below the eyes, than a dark brown, & again a yellow band. Underparts dull white, the breast, & sides of the throat streaked with very narrow (but still distinct) black *lines.* A redish yellow band across the breast. —— Upper parts yellowish red streaked with black. Tail rounded & woodbrown. Wings the same color, primaries margined with yellow, the secondaries very broadly with chestnut red. Rump, & under tail coverts rufous, tinged with brown & yellow. . . . Iris blue.

9. Sandpipers.

10. *Carpodacus mexicanus frontalis,* House Finch.

11. Mount Frazier, at 8,013 feet, is southwest about 8 miles away as the crow flies, but of much farther access on foot; Tecuya Mountain, 7,155 feet, lies westsouthwest; Grapevine Peak, closer to the fort, reaches 4,800 feet. The Fort lies at 3,300 feet, and one suspects Xántus' "3 tausend" is awry. There is no "Tejon peak" on modern quadrangle maps.

12. *Ovis canadensis.*

13. Now *Oreortyx pictus,* Mountain Quail. See postscript, January 20, 1858.

No XI.

Ft Tejon, Cala.
Nov. 1st 1857

Dear Sir/

I hear at this moment, that the mail goes out to night, so I hasten to send you the enclosed sheets, continuation of my descriptive catalogue of birds, with a few remarks ——

All the birds of course, which I described (or at least try to describe) are *positively* not in Audubons Synopsis; although some in my respects similar, but in more yet different.

I tried to make of two birds sketches Nº LI,[1] & LV,[2] they are far from being correct thats true, but more than perfect for the purpose I sketched them.

I call your attention particularly at Nº LVII[3] & Nº LX, the later is a very large & most beautiful wren[4]; the former a bird which genus I never yet encountered in the U. States. As the description will show you it is a composition of Picus, Sitta, Certhia & Troglodytes, but really what it is, I can not find out. Very likely some genus of the Certhianae, which is not represented yet in North America.

Nº LXI,[5] LXII,[6] LXIII,[7] LXIV[8] are Sparrows but I am not sure of the genus.

I secured last week a pair of Lynxes they entirely differ from rufus, & maculatus. They have not a particle of red on their fur. Back grey, tipped & streaked with sooty & dark black. Lower parts white, spotted with black. The ears likewise white, transversely banded with Black. Ear tufts shorter as in the rufus, & maculatus. It may turn out as the same animal in winter toilet, but its general appearance is entirely & altogether different from any, I have seen yet.

Neotoma's I secured again several together with excellent skulls. Grizzly & Elk skulls also, and I hope to get this day, some good skins of both of the lat[t]er animals. I am sorry I have no trap, nor strychnine, the wolves & foxes making every night a concert here round, which beats surely even the evening prayers of my old aquaintances the Jhakals of Lyria.

The Sutler assured me, that his goods will reach this place about the midle of this month; so with the returning train I will forward to you the collection on hand.

Mr Forbes has not sent me ammunition, nor answered my letter. I am altogether in a wretched

condition with my outfit ended. Since nearly 2
weeks —— having no shot whatsoever—I use brass
filings, and taking in consideration that I file it myself out of buttons epaulettes etc; you can imagine
the delightful position I occupy at present as a
Huntsman, amongst plenty game.

I did not receive since a month letter from you,
nor hear anything from F^t Riley. I wonder what
Harling have to say about my guns & effects?

With sincerest regards
your very truly
JXdeVesey

---

1. *Chamaea fasciata,* Wrentit; General Register, LI:

> . . . Measurements: 6½. 6¾. 3 . . . Bill stout, rather long, slightly
> curved, of a dark horn color. Nostrils oblong & exposed. 3^d quill the
> longest, next 4th, second & 5th next & equal, 1st the shortest
> amongst all the primaries. Tarsus & toes slaty, very strong, the for-
> mer covered by six broad scutellae. Claws black, much arched &
> acute, not grooved. Upper colors bluish dark slaty, tinged with
> brown. Tail & wings brown, margined with lighter; undertail tinged
> with bluish. Whole underparts very pale brick color, shaded slightly
> with bluish & brown, the sides more so. —— Tail emarginate &
> round, & as long as the whole body, without it. —— Female per-
> fectly similar, but less in size. Very rare. Habits & cry perfectly re-
> sembling that of the Parinae.

2. *Polioptila melanura,* Black-tailed Gnatcatcher;
General Register, LV:

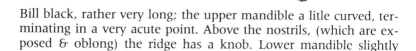

Bill black, rather very long; the upper mandible a litle curved, terminating in a very acute point. Above the nostrils, (which are exposed & oblong) the ridge has a knob. Lower mandible slightly

41.

LI.

♂ – № 557. 540. 606. ⎫ Measurements = 6½ . 6¾ . 3.
♀ – № 607. 608. 704. ⎭ Iris brown.

Bill stout, rather long, slightly curved, of a dark horn color. Nostrils oblong & exposed.
3ᵈ quill the longest, next 4ᵗʰ, second & 5ᵗʰ next & equal; 1ˢᵗ the shortest amongst all the primaries.
tarsus & toes slaty, very strong, the former covered by six broad scutella. Claws black, much arched
& acute, not grooved. Upper colors bluish dark slaty, tinged with brown. Tail & wings brown,
margined with lighter; undertail tinged with bluish. Whole underparts very pale brick color,
shaded slightly with bluish & brown, the sides more so. – Tail emarginate, & as long
as the whole body, without it. – Female perfectly similar, but less in size.
Very rare. Habits & cry perfectly resembling that of the Parinæ.

*Wrentit (*Chamaea fasciata*).*

ascending, & covered by the upper. —— Second & 3rd quill longest & about equal. Fourth only a very litle shorter. First a litle shorter than sixth. —— Upperparts blue, darkest on the head. From the upper mandible to behind the eyes the feathers much tipped with black, forming nearly a black band. Likewise a black band under the eyes. —— A white ring around the eyes. —— Wings brown, the quills margined with whitish grey. Tail black, the lateral feathers pure white. The outer webb of the next ones, & the point & the inner webb white. The third feathers only dirty white at the end. Whole underparts white, the throat tipped, & the sides shaded with light blue. Tarsus, toes, & claws black.

Female similar, but the bill is yellowish brown.

Measurements 4½. 6½. 2¾.

Iris dark brown.

Migratory. Rather rare. Has the habits of Parinae, but a very different, & peculiar cry.

3. *Certhia americana,* Brown Creeper; General Register, LVII:

Bill rather very long, slender, much arched, & very compressed, acute. Lower mandible with the angle very long, & narrow. Upper mandible dark horn color, the lower of a pale flesh color. All lower parts pure white, the lower tail coverts only tipped with pale yellow. Upperparts dark brown, streaked all over with red & white very distinctly. Rump bright chesnut red; a white circle around the eye, & a white band over it, running down the neck. Wings wood brown, with four very distinct bands, two of them of a greyish white color formed by the tips of the small, & long coverts; & two bright ochre, formed by a patch on the outer webb of each primaries & secondaries. The inner webb opposite this ochre patch is white.— —3d quill the longest, 4th & 5th but a lite shorter, the 1st the shortest. —— The tail which consists of 12 feathers, is pale brown, margined with still paler; and is formed exactly like the tail of woodpeckers, the lateral feathers being very small (but placed below the next, not above as in the *Picinae*) & the Rest long, especially so the midle ones. The shafts are very strong, the webbs towards their end very narrow, with their filaments deflected & stiff. The six pointed. —— Tarsus & toes ochre, the former very short, hind toe long, so are the claws, which are compressed, very long, & extremely acute.

Measurements 4¾. 7½. 3.

Iris brown.

Habits, as far as I know, precisely that of Woodpeckers.

See January 20, 1858, note 13.

4. *Campylorhynchus brunneicapillus,* Cactus Wren; General Register, LX:

Whole upperparts chesnut brown, with innumerable very small (but quite distinct) black & white spots. Wings dark brown with the 2, 3, & 4th quills longest & about equal. The outer webb of primaries transversely spotted with light brown, the secondaries undulated with the same. Tail of ordinary length, bright chesnut red, with eight quite distinct transverse bands on every feather, which are broad & rounded. —— Throat & forepart of breast pure white, lower parts of breast shaded with yellowish red, which becomes in the abdomen, undertailcoverts, & sides bright chestnut red, tipped with white & dark brown. —— Bill 1 inch & 4½ long, considerably arched & very acute, the upper mandible being of a dark horn, & the lower of a yellowish flesh color. —— Tarsus toes & claws black, the hind toe with the claw being $\frac{4}{12}$ of an inch longer, as the tarsus. —— The claws are moderately arched, very acute, & laterally grooved.

Female generally paler colored, & wants the white spots on the wing coverts, & midle of the back. —— Although I do not possess a ♀ specimen, I killed one with the above male, but being much spoiled, could not preserve her.

Measurements $5^{10}/_{12}$. $7^{4}/_{13}$. 3
Iris brown.

5. Identification uncertain. General Register, LXI:

Bill brown, rather long, slightly curved; tarsus & toes brown, the former with eight broad scutellae. Upperparts light brown, streaked with darker, & tinged with grey olivaceous & yellow. Rump grey tipped with gamboge. The forehead white. A grey collar round the upper neck, tipped with straw yellow. Breast throat and in fact the whole underpart white, faintly streaked with pale brown & yellow, the undertail coverts more so. Tail emarginate, the feathers much pointed, & with their basal part gamboge, the rest black, margined with white. —— Wings (2^d quill the longest) 7th but litle shorter, the other primaries ⅓ inch shorter) black, margined with gamboge, & two bands across the same color, formed respectively by the outer webbs of primaries & secondaries. —— A single pure white feather on the top of the head.

Measurements 4½. 8¾. 4.
Iris brown.
Secured very high in the Pinewoods.

6. *Carduelis spinus*, Pine Siskin [female?]; General Register, LXII:

Bill as in the preceding species. Whole upperparts brown, streaked with darker. Wings (1, 2, & 3^d quills longest & about equal) dark brown, margined with straw yellow. The basal parts of primaries & secondaries gamboge, but which is partly concealed by the wing coverts. The secondaries broadly margined with white. Tail dark brown, much emarginate, the basal parts of all the feathers pale gamboge. Cheeks, throat, sides, breast, & undertail coverts pale redish brown, streaked with dark brown. Abdomen yellowish white. Tarsus toe & claws sooty black.

Measurements 4$\frac{4}{12}$. 8$\frac{6}{12}$. 3$\frac{10}{12}$.
Iris brown.

7. *Melospiza lincolnii,* Lincoln's Sparrow; General Register, LXIII:

Bill redish brown, rather short, conical, edges inflected, the upper mandible near the point slightly curved, & very acute. Cheeks, upper head, wing coverts, & back light yellowish red, every feather streaked in the centre with dark brown, or rather black. A collar round the hind neck, breast, & upper parts of abdomen light ash grey, with narrow black streaks. Lower parts of abdomen, & undertail coverts pure white. Wings (with 2^{d} quill longest, 3^{d} quill litle shorter, & 5th equal to first) black, the primaries slightly, & the secondaries broadly margined with yellowish red. Tail much emarginate, pointed, black, margined with yellowish red. Tarsus, toes, & claws, transparent pale yellow.
Measurements 5$\frac{1}{2}$. 9$\frac{2}{12}$. 4$\frac{2}{12}$.
Iris brown.
Secured in the woods, out of a small flock. They were feeding on the ground, and making much noise like other gregarious Sparrows.

8. *Aimophila ruficeps,* Rufous-crowned Sparrow; General Register, LXIV:

Male. Bill like the preceding species; Tarsus claws & toes brown. Whole crown bright chesnut red. A collar on hind neck, cheeks, & whole underparts ash-grey; the abdomen inclining to white. —— Back redish brown, streaked with darker. Tail much emarginate, & woodbrown. Wings of the same color, & margined pale brown.

Female. Much fainter colored in general. And the head is only tipped with chesnut, & some black streaks.
Measurements—5$\frac{1}{2}$. 9. 4.
Iris brown.
Observed in the woods in considerable flocks, chipping continuously, & feeding on the ground. Extremely shy. Migratory.

Grinnell (1905, p. 11) refers to "the weird notes of the rufous-crowned sparrow" at Fort Tejon.

No **XII.**

Ft. Tejon, Cala
Nov. 10th 1857

Dear Sir/

I had the pleasure of receiving your letters yesterday, dated Sept. 18th & Oct. 3d, and am extremely delighted to hear that there is at last some prospect of getting my gun[1]; books, & *a new outfit* instead of the one, which fate never allowed me to look even at! —— ——

I am not at all achtonished about the disaster at sea with the only vehicles of our correspondence. If you should happen to travel on the pasteboard barks of that Filibuster Company, you would be of my opinion. I long ago anticipated such affair, as that of the Central America alias George Law, because it was so unreasonable intervall between this and the ½ a dozen, which perished a couple years ago on the Pacific. Such boats as the Golden Age, Golden Gate, etc never would be permitted to leave any European port, they are fit for Lakes or Rivers but nobody would believe (who is accustomed to any reasonable safety) that those boards barraks should attempt the waters of the sea. —— In regard to my letter lost in the George Law, I do not consider worth to copy it, because I send this day my collection on hand, and so the descriptions would be superfluous. My letter in question bore the No V, and was dated Aug. 3. amongst others.[2] I informed you, that there is strong reason to anticipate the entire abandonment of this Post in consequence of the Earthquaque shocks, & therefore I asked you, if that should be the case (which you can easily ascertain there) to procure a suitable transfer for me to some other Post, where I could do something in the way of collecting. —— Even now, everybody is convinced, that Ft Tejon will be shortly abandoned, the Quarter Masters works are already suspended, & the garrison reduced to only 40 men. I would earnestly request therefore you dear Sir, to look out for the movements of the War Departement, and arrange (if the case should require it) my affairs to our mutual satisfaction. There is a rumor prevalent, that at the petition of South Californians (backed by their Representants in Congress) at the *San Gorgonio Pass* will be built a new military Post, if this should be the case, I liked very much to go there in my present capacity, as the geological & topographical position of that Region induces me to believe, that there is large field for work. After all, until June next, (when I am here 12 months) I will exhaust so entirely F^t Tejon, that there will be not a Beetle new to catch it, and my position here afterwards would be not only tiresome & lonesome for me, but absolutely useless for the Smiths. Inst. —— —— I recommend therefore the matter to your earnest consideration, & by time—action.

Dr Hallowell[3] wrote me a letter also, and am much surprised to hear from him likewise, that *he* expects every day a Herpetological collection from me. I am much surprised I say; because although I promised *a series* of my future collection to the Pha. Academy; I told very positively to M^{srs} LeConte, Hallowell & Leidy,[4] that my intention is to store up my whole *future* california collection, & dispose of only after my Return to the States, and only after I wrote some Report or Memoir on the Collection.[5]

I made only exception to this decision in behalf of Dr Leidy & LeConte, whom I promised—respectively—some Paleontological specimens, & Coleoptera, as I never intend to do anything in those two branches, except collect them, and as (especially Dr Leidy) highly deserves support. ——

I am much vexed, that (as you know yourself) I contributed so extensively to the Museum of the Pha. Academy, and they even never noticed it. I sent only to Cassin over 150 species of birds, & you cannot find a line of acknowledgment in the Proceedings. —— This all will not say, that I am abandoning the Academy, on the contrary I intend to

support it as far as my poor & limited abilities allow, but I will notice my contributions myself, before they pass the "fenestras rubiconis." —— —— ——
I noticed an item lately in the New York Tribune, to that effect, that the Smithsonian Institute is going to sell to the U. S. Governement her Museum for a National Gallery, & the Smiths. Instit. does not need anything else as a simple office for the transaction of her Business—, so the item says, now pray is any truth is this statement?[6]

Nov. 11th evening
As I was writing the above, somebody knocked at my door, and made his appearance—(who do you think he was?) Mr Möllhausen.[7] He informed me that he heard much in Los Angeles about my collection, and came up here expressly to see it. —— I confess you sincerely that I felt since some time uneasy on hearing, that Möllhausen is coming & is going to collect (so to say) within gunshot of my kingdom. My old friend the Prince Paul of Würtemberg[8] spoke much to me of his (Möllhausens) abilities; and likewise Dr Sherzer & Moritz Wagner.[9] —— —— —— But since I know him personally, I do not fear him, but on the contrary intend to assist him in procuring specimens at my own ground. —— He was completely beaten by seeing my collection, & he confessed to others this morning, that he passed a sleepless night, and never will attempt to collect here anything, although he came with the intention, to do it.
I tell you *confidentially* that Mr Möllhausen (although he had known it, that I am collecting under the patronage of the Smithsonian) tried to induce me, to sell my collection to the King of Prussia, garanteing that he will confer a great favor on me, especially A. Humboldt.[10] I of course emphatically refused his proposal, and I did that in presence of several Officers, amongst them Dr TenBroeck.
About the 20th this month goes my whole

collection en route to Washington, and I hope you will get it some time in January. —— Concerning my expenses, I dont want that the Smithsonian Institution shall pay the whole; I am willing to pay the half, and the other half may be paid by the Smithsonian, as a support. The next mail I send to you the rest of my descriptive catalogue of birds, (amounting now to about 115 species) and the amount of my expenses also. But you would oblige me greatly if you would have the kindness And purchase on account of the expense money a double barrelled gun for me, not exceeding $15.00, and dispatch it immediately per Wells Fargo & Co to me. Although I hope to get soon my own gun, I want an another, to employ some person to hunt for us on the desert. I hope you can get a very good Belgian or German gun for from 12–15 dollars which will answer perfectly my purpose.

Mr Forbes never answered my letter; but my friends sent me 50 pounds shot of Nos 8, 10, 11 and I am now princely supplied again. I think it would be best to put aside altogether Mr Forbes, he is a merchant prince whom I dont like at all. I can get through my friends from San Francisco anything at least as cheap, as Mr Forbes could send it, and as we have to pay *anyhow*, I should think it is the same. On the *practical* way much better, because my countrymen are my devoted friends, and supply my orders with speed, while Mr Forbes likes to put himself in attitude as a grand Protector, and requires his time for action ad libitum. When Mr Forbes recommended me to Captain Seely[11] of the San Francisco & San Pedro Steamer line, by introducing me spoke as follows: "Captain, this fellow is from the Smith. Inst. and going to catch poisonous insects, and all kinds of wild beast; be so kind and transport his catching apparatus as cheap as you can; you see—we transport ourselves everything gratis for the poor devils. etc etc"

Next mail more   your sincerest   deVésey

1. Baird, October 3, 1857:

> I have this morning received a letter from [Mr. Harding] at Riley dated Sept 15 in which he says that your boxes and guns are boxed up and will be sent to Leavenworth by the first government train. I shall write him again urging all dispatch . .On the whole the articles may be looked for in a few weeks. I will await their receipt that long before making up your new outfit.

2. Baird, October 3, 1857:

> The unfortunate [steamer] George Law has perished and the succeeding steamer leaving San Francisco Sept. 5 is now six days or more overdue. We are thus without any letters from you since that which left San Francisco in the steamer of August 5th.

Named for one of the Atlantic-side backers of the Pacific Mail Steamship Company, she foundered between New York and Havana, September 12, 1857, with a loss of over 400 lives.

3. Dr. Edward Hallowell (d. 1860), a devoted member of the Academy of Natural Sciences of Philadelphia, specialized in herpetology, wrote part of the Pacific Railroad Survey reptile report (1859), and also made important contributions in the pathology of cholera. Baird, October 3, 1857:

> When in Philadelphia Dr. Hallowell was anticipating with great exultation the receipt before long of a large collection of reptiles from you.

4. Dr. Joseph Leidy (1823–91), a professor of anatomy and natural history, a surgeon and pioneer in vertebrate paleontology and parasitology, was president of the Academy of Natural Sciences of Philadelphia, 1881–91, and published frequently in the Smithsonian *Contributions*.

5. Xántus' first mention of writing up his collections in the form of a Memoir; see also November 16, 1857; January 15 and April 15, 1858.

6. See December 28, 1857, note 4.

7. Heinrich Balduin Möllhausen (1825–1905), sent by Baron Alexander von Humboldt to America, served as artist on the Whipple Survey and produced some charming watercolor sketches; Whipple (1856, p. 117) commended his bravery:

> Mr. White and a little Mexican boy were nearly drowned, before the exertions of Mr. Möllhausen succeeded in extricating them from beneath the boat.

Möllhausen's *Tagebuch einer Reise vom Mississippi nach den Kusten der Sudsee* (Leipzig, 1858) was translated as *Diary of a Journey from the Mississippi to the Coasts of the Pacific, with a United States Government Expedition.* When he passed through Fort Tejon he was on his way south to meet

Lieutenant Charles Ives' surveying group which was to proceed up the Colorado River by boat. Besides *Reisen in die Felsengebirge Nord-Amerikas bis zum Hochplateau von Neu-Mexico,* he wrote so many novels he became known as "The German Fenimore Cooper."

Baird, December 3, 1857:

> I am glad you saw Mr. Mollhausen. I was afraid he might miss you. Your immense operations will stimulate him, and all his collections must come to the Smithsonian.

8. Duke (not Prince) Paul of Württemberg (his name appears with both one or two t's) made four trips to the United States between 1822 and 1856, up the Missouri River, through Mexico, Texas, New Mexico, and California, keeping (and publishing) extensive diaries such as *Erste Reise nach dem nordlichen Amerika in den Jahren 1822 bis 1824* (translated as *First Journey to North America in the Years 1822 to 1824* [1828]). Gudde (1933, pp. 301–2) described him in 1850:

> The prince, a scholar and a widely travelled man, tall and corpulent, was very simple, without the slightest conceit and extremely interesting in conversation. Nothing but curiosity had led him, immediately after the discovery of gold, to come to the wild, disorderly California where not the slightest comforts could be obtained— even for money. He had left his escorts in Mexico and knew how to put up with everything. Often I had the pleasure of drinking a toast to Germany with him. I was pleased to note also that he would acknowledge the cordial greeting of a blunt American with a hearty handshake.

His arrival was announced in less formal fashion by Thomas Kerr (see Camp 1929, p. 180):

> Mr Guitaries arrived this evening & a half dozen of German, Ducth [*sic*] Hungarians & French with him: among which is the Prince Paul of Wertimburg

For a complete discussion of this period of Xántus' life, see Madden (1949a, pp. 24–25).

9. Karl Ritter von Sherzer was a Viennese who worked with the German Moritz Wagner; they traveled in North and Central America, 1853–1855, and co-authored *Die Republik Casta Rica in Central-Amerika.*

10. Alexander von Humboldt (1769–1859), German explorer and naturalist, interested in plant distribution, climatology, and geology, made geological trips through Europe, Central and South America; his map of the western United States, which he had never seen, was based on the 1776 Escalante explorations. The map, drawn in Mexico City in 1803, was the most accurate to date. In a letter written August 31, 1859, while he was tide observer for the U. S. Coastal Survey in Baja Califor-

nia, Xántus intimated that he was a special envoy of Humboldt; see Madden, (1949a, p. 238).

11. Captain Seely, who captained on the short merchant runs on the West Coast, was "highly praised" for his conduct when, six years later, his ship ran aground between San Diego and San Francisco. See Kemble (1937).

No**XIII.**

Ft Tejon, Cala.
Nov. 16th 1857

Dear Sir/

I forwarded yesterday per Msrs Starks & Co's train[1] to Los Angeles eight large boxes, containing the collection made by me since June up to No 1000. —— You find herewith enclosed the list of boxes, or better the contents of the boxes specified; and a specification of my expenses on the collection, up to this moment. As I told you in my last weeks, I do not want that the Smithsonian Institution shall pay *all* my expenses here (connected with the collection), I am satisfied if besides the apparatus and other support from there directly, shy[?] pays—as a support from her part—*half* of my expenses. As you see from the specification I had over $90 expenses, and so please to give me credit to $45. in round sum. the fright for this collection I consider cheap enough (5 cents per pound), compared with other expenses. But I made arrangements with my friends in San Francisco to get hereafter everything I may want, at a reasonable price. And I hope never to be subjected again to the piratical treatment of the Sutler of our Post. ——

I requested you in my last, to send me out a Belgian or French double barrelled gun, if possible instantly, but the price shall not exceed 15, at most 20 dollars; the balance of my credit you may remit to me at your convenience.

You will find a copy of my General Register in box N⁰ 7, which with my descriptive Catalogue of birds (to be continued regularly) will give all information in my power.

I had to keep back 3 large fasciculus of Herbarium, several deer & Elk Skulls with immense horn; because I had no boxes large enough to hold them. I have now grizzlys, & a deer also, and will send it with the next transport; I packed up all the smaller object, hoping that they will prove most interesting, & urgent.

_____ _____ _____

Concerning this transport, I trust you will take in consideration the situation I was in. For nearly a month I had absolutely nothing of an apparatus kind; and afterwards to—I had the worst kind of Alcohol, no vessels of any kind; wretched guns, & which I had to change every week, was often short of ammunition, had to perform my ordinary Duty as Steward, Librarian, & Superintendent of the Bakery; had no assistance from anybody, on the contrary had to met with obstacles etc etc

If you take in consideration all this, I confidently hope, you will admit that I did everything possible; and you can conjecture how much more I had done under some protection here, or a better outfit. ——

The collection of Alcoholic specimens, is (so to say) entirely a new collection, the 1th or original one nearly entirely spoiled. When I commenced to re-collect, most of the species I had before, were gone; but never mind I will make a fresh descent on them in the early spring, I am sure I will fill the vacancies. Of the large Crocodilelike lizards, there are I suppose only two juvenile specimens, but as they are not very rare, I will get plenty full grown ones in the Spring.

I took particular care to pack up everything so, as to insure the safe arrival of the specimens, and I trust they will arrive in excellent condition. ——

_____ _____ _____

The Latins said "clara parta, boni amici" and so, I would remind you dear sir, at my agreement with you, that the collection will be stored up with due care, and left untouched until my arrival there. —— But do not think I mean this agreement (suggested by you) liberally. If the Institution wants particularly any specimen (of which I have duplicate of course, & is already known & described), you may take from the collection, & use it. But especially I would request you, to apropriate for my collection a separate room, in order not to mix it up with the Institutions collection. I had not time enough to label properly with my name the specimens, put only the inevitably necessary marks on the labells, and so if you should mix up this collection with that of the Institution, we will be never able to assort them apart again.[2]

I worked hard enough since several years, and never even had the gratification to be acknowledged[3]; now I liked to do something for myself also, viz—to write some memoir at large on my collection in California, & particularly on the birds. —— About fish, reptiles etc I would not care much.

If you find some new species amongst my birds (and I hope you will find some), and you liked to introduce them in your progressing work on birds; I have no objection *provided* you introduce my description. But in order to do this,—I suppose—you ought to publish in my name before, in the procedings of the Academy, or somewhere else. *In this case,* I wanted to name the first bird " —— —— *Hammondii.*" In honor of my excellent friend Dr W. A. Hammond U.S.A. And the Second *"Bairdii"* in your honor sir—provided you have no objection.[4]

—— —— ——

And now, allow me dear Sir to furnish you some items in regard to myself, as our aquaintance will be drawn from time to time closer. —— —— I was educated at the Polytechnical School in Vienna, & after leaving it entered the Royal Artillery. When in

'848 the unfortunate war broke out against Hungary, I resigned my commission, but it was not accepted. I left notwithstanding my Garrison, and offered my services to the *Hungarian* Secretary of War, who accepted it readily and entrusted me with an important mission. The Austrian Governement declared me a deserter, and ordered the sequestration of my property,—but I think I did my duty, and never cared much about material losses! —— You know dear Sir the tragedy, how it terminated, after we fought manly for two whole years against the combined foes of civilisation, at last we succumbed; and I found myself homeless & penniless trown out to Asia.[5]

I came to this country amongst the first of my countrymen, in advance of Kossuth,[6] and by order of President Fillmore I received a grant of land in Iowa, as the other of my fellow Refugees. But actually I never took possession of, but being a good piano player, and a tolerable draughtsmen, I procured a honorable support by teaching for a short time; when I went successively with the Prince of Würtemberg, Dr Wagner & Scherzer, & Dr Krøyer[7] as collector. At last I filled out my hard earnings an expedition into North Minnesota, which failed so entirely that in a moment of utmost despair, & under circumstances completely beyond my control —— I was forced to enter the American army.[8]

With a honest past, very regrettable connections, and a good many enemies at home, I think I was justified in changing my name, and not to carry it on the muster Rolls of the American Military Ranks (?). My name at home was John Xántus de Vésey;[9] but as Véseys are good many, and John Xántus is only one, I took the former.

I told you this circumstances dear Sir with the object, that if you should make perhaps any reference to my collections hereafter, be so kind, and do it either in full *John Xántus de Vésey*, or *John Xántus* alone, as you please. I do not care much about my military aquaintances, but my friends may know it, that I am still living, and doing something.

I requested my family at home to send some printed matter & portraits for me to your care, anticipating no objection on your part. If they should arrive, addressed *John Xantus* be so kind & forward me; I will remit any expenses of course, you may have on them.

As soon, as the Bill of Lading arrives up from Los Angeles, I will forward it to you, which will reach you at the same time I hope with the collection.

Harling wrote me last mail, and says he will forward my effects next mail (Sept. 20), so I hope, they are on route until now.

Dr Hammond I hear returned with a large collection, and is at present very dangerously sick in F^t Riley, he had since several years very violent attacks of Neuralgia.

Very sincerely yours
XVésey

---

1. Probably Starkey, Janion, & Co. which was in operation during and after the goldrush and operated a store and wharf in San Francisco, as well as a mail pickup; see Camp (1928–29) pp. 397–400. John Jackson Starkey, a resident of San Francisco, was involved in some overly ambitious ventures in supplying the gold fields, according to Davis (1973, pp. 250–51.

2. Baird, January 17, 1858:

> You may rest assured that I will rigorously respect yours & ours in regard to your collections. They shall be properly separated from all others, and so kept that they can at once be separated as in the use of the mollusk in my reports. I should regret not being able to include your Fort Tejon species so as to render it complete, but I have already amplified in my letters other remarks to you. My plan will be to draw up a list of Fort Tejon birds, and add to it a description of new species . . . and publish this at once in the Proceedings of the Phila. Academy under your name entirely, and then quote this paper in my book. Nothing will be done with the Manuscript's future at present. . . .

3. Baird frequently recognized Xántus' contributions, as November 16, 1857:

> You certainly have an extraordinary collection and not the least valuable point about it is the large number of specimens furnishing means of extensive comparison.

4. Baird, December 15, 1857:

> Please let me know whether there are any names of persons you would wish particularly to have given to any of your new species. These I shall publish at once in your name.

Baird, January 17, 1858:

> I will bear in mind your wish about a name of species for Dr. Hammond. As to the bairdii I have my doubts. Dr. H. was here a few days ago and we had much pleasant talk about you, your trials and your future. I told him your intentions about a bird of *Hammondii* at which he seemed much gratified.

True to his word, March 31, 1858:

> I have prepared the description of Tyrannula hammondii and shall send in your name to the Academy in a few days.

May 15, 1858:

> I have sent the Academy for publication your *Hammondii* Vesey and *Vireo cassini* Vesey. They will be printed in the May proceedings.

A yellow-eyed junco from Baja California was named *Junco bairdii* (the AOU now considers it a subspecies of Yellow-eyed Juncos, *Junco phaeonotus*). *Epidonax hammondii*, Hammond's Flycatcher, is very close to *E. oberholseri*, Dusky Flycatcher; Peterson (1961, p. 196) remarks that "it is a standing joke among western ornithologists that *no one seems to have an infallible way*" of telling the two apart in the field. See also Xántus, February 2, 1858.

5. Xántus did not have a commission, did not graduate as stated, etc.; for a concise evaluation of the paucity of truth in these statements, see Madden (1949a, pp. 21–49).

6. Laslos Kossuth (1802–94) was one of the leaders of the Hungarian Revolution of 1848; he became finance minister after the fall of Metternich (who had him arrested for treason a decade earlier), then head of the independent Hungarian government in 1849. Ultimately defeated by the Austrians, he resigned that same year, fled Hungary, and went on a triumphal tour of England and America where Henry David Thoreau noted in his journal, May 11, 1852, "Kossuth here."

7. Henrik Nikolai Krøyer (1799–1870), who published in *Naturhistorisk Tidsskrift*, a periodical published in Copenhagen, was a well-known Danish naturalist with a special interest in fish.

8. Xántus joined the Hungarian colony at New Buda, Iowa, where he remained but a year, unable to get along with his compatriots, and joined the Army immediately after, September 24, 1855. Later he tried unsuccessfully to secure his claim. See letters of July 1 and October 8, 1858, and January 14, 1859.

9. According to Madden (1949a), there was no "de Vésey" in Xántus' background. Enlisting under an assumed name was not uncommon in the nineteenth-century Army and usually caused no complications; see Rickey (1981, p. 30). For Xántus it caused problems; he was forced to make some explanation when he knew packages would arrive from Hungary addressed to "John Xántus"; he hoped that his name would appear on publications and perhaps in scientific nomenclature. Nevertheless he continued to sign his name "Vésey" or "de Vésey" or "XVésey" until January 21, 1859, when he was finally out of the Army and used "John Xántus." See also February 2, September 10, October 8, and November 16, 1858.

NO**XIV**

Fᵗ Tejon, Cala
Nov. 24ᵗʰ 1857

Dear Sir/
I just received your letter of Oct. 17, and although I wrote only a few days ago extensively, I hasten to write again, as Mʳ Möllhausen leaves to morrow, & offered to take down to Los Angeles my letter.

I will follow your friendly advise, & will collect as many duplicates of birds, as I can. It was one circumstance which discouraged me much in doing so, and I must tell it to you. When collecting with Dʳ Wagner in C. America for the Bavarian Governement, I entertained the hope also, of which you speak now the second time, and contracted with Mʳ Wagner, that in lieu of pay half of the birds, & ¼ of the other collection (to be made by myself) shall belong to me. After the expedition I retained as my share 1700 birds & mammals, besides a great variety of other things, amongst them about 40 gallons of snakes, fish etc etc As I had to meet that time in Brussels my family, I transported with me my collection, and after paying a heavy import on in London, I offered there for sale. The Brittish Museum picked out some hundred, & offered two shillings sixpence a piece for them, (this was the highest bid!) —— But if I had sold the picked out 300, of course the balance of my collection had become comparatively worthless; so I refused to sell them, and took the whole concern to Amsterdam, from these (after unsuccessfull attempts to sell) to Brussels. In the last place I sold about a dozen new serpents at 5 francs a piece, & about 100 birds at from 3–5 francs. —— After two weeks efforts I gave the collection to an Auctioner, and he sold it in my presence for 1245 francs!!! —— Deducting the commission, import duty, fright, & other expenses connected with transportation of the collection (not counting my personal passage), I realized of this 114 francs, or in plain American something like twenty dollars! —— And I assure you, the collection was in perfect order.[1] Now, how you intend to menage the sale of my california duplicates, remains to be seen; and it will afford me a great pleasure to learn such operation, for times, to come yet.

As it stands the affair with Brewers Wilson, I am very glad, you did not send it.

The steel scale arrived also, although you sent me one before from Philadelphia per Mr Green,[2] this circumstance you probably forgot, and so I can send you back one, if you wish it?

Dr TenBroeck is very kind since some days towards me, and after I gave him your last letter to him; he said (the first time since I am here) he has no objection if I should go out hunting after my hours of Duty; and that he has no objection if I should make an excursion for 3–4 days to the Kern River and Tulare lakes.[3] I will use his offer, as long as it is *fresh*, and start the next week to the headwaters of the Kern River, in the Sierra Nevada, which is only about 40 miles (and so ½ a days ride on horseback) from the Fort. I intend to descend then on some of the larger tributaries, hunting & fishing continuously, and then follow the river on the plains, as far as the shortness of time will allow it. I anticipate a good harvest there, as to my knoledge that part was never worked yet, and I will get no doubt some valuable specimens of fish. —— As I take some Indian boys & a couple pack mules with me, probably I will succeed in procuring some Beavers, Otters, Weasels etc. also.

Flying Squirrell is none here in the vicinity, but I made incessantly enquiries about them, & on *positive* authority can inform you, that in the very place where I am going next week, they are frequently met with, & they are reported as quite numerous around Pitt river. They are of cinnamon color, darker on the back; and according my information of the same size, as that of the Eastern & Middle States. In case I should not succeed to get any specimens, I intend to offer to the Indians there about some premium, to procure it; as my intention is to do with every animal, which positively exists here about, and I will be not able to procure one myself; because I would not like to clear out from this Region, without getting hold of everything procurable —— somehow. —— Of course, I will make such expenses with discretion, and so I hope the Smithsonian Institution is willing to participate in such important expenses. (?)

I am glad, that you ordered some ammunition for me, although I have at present on hand abut pounds of shot yet; but my powder & caps are nearly gone. I hope Mr Forbes will send it as soon as possible, maybe the next steamer.

I did exactly, as you seem to wish it. I sent my collection per Wells Fargo Co to Mr Forbes; requesting both to see, that the boxes are not exposed to water, but kept always as dry as possible. Until this time, the boxes are no doubt in Los Angeles, from there they go the 7th next month to San Francisco, & probably with the outward bound steamer of 20th December leave for New York. I think under this circumstances that you will get them nearly the same time with this letter.

I sent you in my last letter the specification of the collection, together with the list of my expenses; & told you that a Copy of my Register was in box N⁰ 7; thats true it was there, but just the day before I dispatched the boxes, I killed again a Lynx, opened the box N⁰ 7, & packed it it together with his skull, by this occasion I forgot to put in again the Register, & it was left here. I send it now per mail, & you will get I hope before or at the same time with the boxes.

As the lynx is N⁰ 1000, and the Register sent goes only to N⁰ 1000, I note here the measurements of the specimen, in successive order of my Register form, as follows:

♀ 31. $6^{50}/_{100}$ $7^{15}/_{100}$. $1^{25}/_{100}$. 3. $10.^{85}/_{100}$. $14^{10}/_{100}$ Weight 17½ pounds.

I am extremely sorry now, that I did not keep the wrecks of the Parrot, I found in a nest, & mentioned to you. I see it was carelessness, but to late to philosophise about now. I never have seen the bird itself, although I heard that around San Gorgonio, & San Bernadino, even on the timbered lands SE of San Diego, they are sometimes met with. I did't gave up the hope altogether to get one, but the chances are few I see it so well!

You will perceive, that the Departement of my Skeletons is very poor, nearly = 0. But situated as I am, such job is very tiresome for me, and I could it only effect by the neglect of the other branches of collection as only a rough Skeletons preparation takes more time, as the skinning of a dozen birds. But notwithstanding if you *absolutely* wish it, I will do hereafter what I can. Would be not the same, if I would send you whole mammals in alcohol for this purpose. I guess you could effect their skeletonising there much better, as I can here, what's your opinion sir?[4]

If you should mount any of my birds, I call you particular attention to the fact, that *all* my birds are opened from the legs to the anus, in a triangular shape of incision, and none of them is opened on the vent or belly. The long pratis taught me this improvement, that *it is* an improvement, you must admit it, as there are few birds (opened on the abdomen) which look so perfect on their underparts; as my birds which are opened triangularly. —— The taxidermist of the Ph. Academy, was not able to discover my incision, & opened my birds a new on the abdomen, destroying many fine specimens. This blunder made me to call your attention to the fact.[5]

With highest regards

Your very sincere
LVésey

XIV
---
3   Postscript

I nearly forgot to forward the continuation of my descriptive catalogue, which is long ago ready for mail. I send you hereby to species N⁰ CXIV inclusive; as I sent you the specimens itselves, I was this time with description consequently very short; but noted carefully everything by each species, which may usefull for the knowledge of their geogr. distribution & principally migration. —— I call your attention to N⁰ LXVIII,[6] LXIX,[7] & XCI,[8] the last one a very small picus, of which the ♂ is unknown yet to me. ——

Please inform me then, after the arrival of the boxes, of the name of each species, by referring only to the number (red roman mark), I will know it at once then, as I have a copy of this catalogue.

I have again about 100 birds, since my collection left, amongst them several species not contained in

the catalogue yet. Especially an interesting Helinaia,[9] & 2 large Buteos. I secured lately a Sturnella
Ludoviciana[10] also, the first specimen ever seen *here
round*.
  I will successively send you descriptions of everything shall turn out as new to my collection, and as
my specimens are now not so accumulated, I will
try send my descriptions more at length, & accompanied with better sket[ches.]
  Concerning my future transports, I intend hereafter to send smaller parcels, one or two boxes at
the time, in order not to risk so much, as I did at
present.[11] I should be extremely grieved & vexed, if
my collection should sink to bottom or fly in the
heavens on some of those remarkable *staunch crafts*
(as they are ironically called) of the P.M.S.S. Co. —
— Although I hope fortune will favor us this time at
least.

LVésey

---

1. According to Madden (1949a) a complete fabrication.

2. Green's Standard Barometers were made "under direction of Smithsonian Institution"; see Green (1860, pp. 61–62).

3. Baird, October 17, 1857:

> I had a very kind letter from Dr. Ten Broeck by the last mail in
> which he promised all assistance to you in his power. This I have
> no doubt he will do and I will write him again by this mail.

Kern River and Tulare Lakes were enticing collecting grounds. Lt. Derby
(Farquhar 1932, p. 255) found

> the Kern river, a very broad and deep stream with a current of six
> miles an hour, which, rising high up in the Sierra Nevada, dis-
> charges itself by two mouths into Buena Vista lake near its northern
> extremity. Three large sloughs also make out from the river near its
> mouth and form an extensive swamp in the plain upon the north
> bank of the lake.

4. Baird, January 17, 1858:

> It is not necessary for you to take trouble for skeletons. They can (if
> small) be cleaned here in alcohol. Plenty of small skins will be how-

ever desirable. The flesh of animals the size of a hare or even of a fox might be cut roughly off and after disjointing the limbs, the bones allowed to dry. Could not the Indians be got get to do this for the meat?

According to Dr. Rea (personal communication, 1984) skeletonizing takes about half the time or less than skinning.

5. Baird, January 31, 1858:

I have seen many collections of specimens but nothing within my experience comes up to the perfection of finish of your skins in every respect. The skins are all that could be asked. Just right, not too much or too little stuffing. May I say that they are much better than your Kansas collections. The packing of the [?] vials attracted especially my admiration, as well as of the nests. Everything was perfect.

6. Identification uncertain. General Register, LXVIII:

Bill stout, like that of *Parinae*. Upperparts olivaceous, darkest on the head. Wings wood brown, margined with green, the 2^d & 3^d quills longest & about equal, the 4th but litle shorter. Tail the same color, & a little emarginate. Whole underparts chamois. The sides & breast shaded with yellowish brown. Tarsus blue.
Measurements 5^4/$_{12}$. 9. 4.
Iris brown.
Habits of Parus or Sitta. Only two Specimens seen.

7. *Seiurus noveboracensis*, Northern Waterthrush; General Register, LXIX:

Upperparts dull brown, undulated with darker brown. Throat white. All other lower parts very pale rufous yellow, the breast & sides spotted with brown. Tail even, dark brown, the lateral feathers white, with the exception of a long brown shade at the lowerpart of the inner webb. Next feather has a white patch at the end. ——
Wings wood brown, with the 2^d quill the longest, 1st & 3^d next & equal, the 4th only a litle shorter, & all margined with light brown. The wing coverts & secondaries broadly margined with dull pale brown. Claws extremely long, & very slender.
Measurements 6. 10. 4^5/$_{12}$. Iris blue.
Secured in the Swamp, on the ground, picking insects out of the mud. They are occasionally seen in very small flocks (5–6), always in Swamp. Habits of Helinaia.

See also January 20, 1858.

8. Identification uncertain. General Register, XCI:

Bill rather short, very slender, & very pointed. Bristles white. Head black. A white band above the eye, running back & upwards, uniting with that from the other side, & forming a conspicuous ring around the neck. This is succeeded by a black band, enclosing the

eye, and running in similar direction across the neck. This is again succeeded by a white, & this by a narrow black band. Whole underparts yellowish white. Back pure white. Wings & tail black, the former spotted with quadrangular white specks very regularly. The 3 lateral feathers of tail white, transversely banded with black.
Measurements 6⁵/₁₂. 12³/₁₂. 5⁶/₁₂.
Iris blue.
Only the one specimen noticed.

9. Now *Vermivora,* Warbler.

10. Now *S. neglecta,* Western Meadowlark.

11. Baird agreed, January 7, 1858:

Hereafter you had better send your collections by single boxes at a time, not waiting for two or three. If a number come together they have to be kept a while in San Francisco so as not to crowd the steamer. . . . Mr. Forbes had a good stock of boxes in store [?] of these he sent forward some of yours and four others that had been kept over from the previous steamer for the same reason.

And March 2, 1858:

I hope you will continue to send in your collections box by box so as to avoid too great an accumulation.

N°**XV**

Fort Tejon, Cala,
Decemb. 10th 1857

Dear Sir/

Yours of 2d ult. reached me last week and am very happy to hear that some apparatus are coming; although I heard nothing about the box from San Francisco, whence Mr Forbes writes me last mail, that he forwarded for me the ammunition & alcohol.

I had the intention to write you at some length, on my latest collection, but I was just now notified that the mail leaves today, instead of the 14th as usual, so I could not get ready in time with my mail, & write you only a few words this time.

Herewith enclosed you find the Receipt of eight boxes collection, I sent last month to you care of Mr Forbes, I hope they reached you safely, as I took particular care to pack them well for the voyage. I hope, you will tell me at once your opinion *frankly* about it, in order I shall make the future specimens more agreable to your wishes, if I had mine own way with those.

I have about 25 birds again, new to my collection; foxes, deers, rats, etc.

I am sorry you could not raise more of the Explor. books; I hope however you will try to get at least Emorys for me this is what I mostly liked, to translate it. I translated last year Stainsbury and Marcy, they are just now published in Hungarian language, and I will make by it a nice profit in "every way."[1]

Sitgreaves is important for Nat History, therefore I am glad to get it; but not fit for translation, as there is hardly anything in it, as pictures (as far as I can recollect it)

I hope the next mail will bring me tandem aliquando' some news about my effects from F^t Riley; God the almighty help me!

I am Sir

Yours sincerely
LVésey

<hr>

1. In *Levelei Ejskamerikábol* (Xántus, 1858b), the "translation" is more like "plagiarism" in his detailed use of everything from text to illustrations of Stansbury's (1852) *Exploration and Survey of the Valley of the Great Salt Lake of Utah* and Marcy's (1853) *Exploration of the Red River of Louisiana*.

Fort Tejon, Cala
                              Decbr 28th 1857

My Dear Professor/
    Your letters of Nov. 2d & 16th came to hand, to-
gether with the collecting box, & other package
from Mr Forbes, containing ammunition. ——
There are some good articles amongst the outfit, &
will do my best to employ them to the most advantage.[1] I am only sorry you forgot to send me boxes
for nests. I do not like to pack nests in layers mixed
up together, this way of doing business is good in
absence of everything; but I think where a collector
has some time, and besides access to boxes, each
nest ought to be packed separately, to keep it in perfect natural condition. But now is to late to lament,
I will try again to make some boxes myself, at least
for the more delicate nests; as I intend to gather at
least some hundred nests the ensuing spring.[2]
    Also the pins, I have long ago a very good assort-
ment, I wrote to Professor Wagner who—although
my letter reached him in Africa sent long ago several pounds to me of the very best quality. It is a
strange thing indeed that in the U.S. there are not to
be had such things!
    You forgot the Gypsum likewise, I sent for some
to San Francisco. Although I never use it by skinning, I prefer it to stop wounds much to Cotton,
and I employ ably for this purpose, when killing
specimens, I found it always very serviceable, if not
indispensable.
    I am under many obligations, for the book,
pamphlets etc, I received by mail a Patent Off Report (1856)[3] & two last Reports of the Smith. Institution (1855, '56),[4] and I had the mortification to
see, that the secretary of the Sm. Inst. is not particularly in favor of collecting Specimens, explorations,
putting up museums etc etc or of anything pertain-
ing to Natural History; although I believe the
knowledge of Nat. history is more beneficial to

mankind, as any abstract knowledge, like Meterology, Isothermology etc, which would be settled satisfactorily in 6 millions years to come yet![5]

Your wishes, in regard to forwarding you some birds, I anticipated largely since long, in sending over 700 Specimens, which I hope arrived safely ere this. —— My birds at present stands as follows:

147 Species

1278 Specimens

The Postmaster of Los Angeles sent my Register back, informing me that he could forward it only as a letter, & it would cost 4 dollars & 75 cts; under this vexatious circumstance I packed up yesterday (only for the sake of the Register) a box, containing besides the Register over 100 birds, & will forward you with first chance down. There are amongst the birds some, which I had formerly, but forget in box in the storeroom, amongst others the Ptiliogonys Townsendii Aud. —— By the by I see in Woodhouse[6] that he found this bird quite abundant in N. Mexico. It may be, but Mr Woodhouse found every bird quite abundant, *extremely common, very common*, etc there; which indeed must be a rich field. I presume, he brought home several thousand accordingly.

I could not say that, of my field here, I consider *quite abundant* only about 10 or 12 species, and the others, rather rare. When secure even a dozen specimens of one, but never noticed any more of them; I on my part cannot consider the species as quite common. —— The idea on this subject may be very varying according to the relative impression, but I should consider always the proof of assertion, *the quantity of specimens secured actually.*

You are much mistaken Sir, in supposing that my black ground squirrell is only a variety of the Spermophylus hereabout, you will surely convince yourself of the contrary, as soon as the specimen reaches you; or I should believe, that poor myself am also only a variety of some Spermophylus![7]

I thought myself, that the Trochylus named as colubris, was an other one, but Audubon description is so indistinct & short, that I regarded in absence of specimens as the colubris.[8]

I do not know who named *Picus formicivorus*,[9] *that* but the name is a great mistake, as I had plenty opportunity to watch closely & minutely this species, being quite overflow with them. This woodpecker had never an idea to eat ant, it leaves entirely & exclusively on acorns, & oak sprouts. They store up in an admiring manner their great stock of provisions for winter, & spring; by boring dry oaks full with holes all round, so as to fit in each hole an acorn. I procured some fine specimens of this granaries, and one for instance being only 3½ feet high, & 20 inches in diameter, contains 195 acorns, hammered in the holes so accurately, that it requires a very sharp forceps to pull one out.[10] I will occasionally send you one of this pieces some of them are really a „Cabinets Stück" as the Prince of Würtemberg would call them.

I wonder, I cannot find in Audubon an immense Vulture, which leaves here. I think it is fully as large as the South American Condor; with a red naked head & neck & entirely black or dark brown, with light underwings. They are quite numerous, but as yet I have no specimens, being entirely confined to the high mountains; but I am informed some of them measure from tip of wing to tip of wing fully 18 feet. I think this statement cannot be much exaggerated, as I myself often mistook them on hills for mounted men. I liked to know the name of these birds, I will secure some soon no doubt.[11]

Amongst my latest aquisition are several birds, principally large Falconidae, very likely of great interest, however I will notice them in their turn in my descriptive Catalogue to be considered regularly, as usual.

I would only call your attention at a fox, which I secured lately, and I cannot find any description agreeing in the least with him. The specimen is a male, & the measurements are as follows:

Length to base of tail   25.
Tail to the end of vertebrae. . . . . . .17.
" " " tip of hair . . . . .20^{50}
Length of side hairs of the tail   3^{15}
Hight of ears . . . . .3^{35}
Fore arm . . . . .8.
Midle claw . . . . .6^{5}
Hind feet . . . . .11.
From snout to occiput . . . . .6^{40}
Whiskers . . . . .3^{20}
Weight in pounds 12¼

General color above dark grey, streaked with black, and a distinct black line passes from top of the head all along the upperparts, to the extremity of the tail. Ears, feet, whole underparts (with the exception of throat, which is pure white) including underpart of tail red. End of tail black.

This fox is called by the Spaniards Zorra el pardusco, or simply pardu Zorra;[12] and by the Americans "Crop fox," it is considered as a very rare animal, & the skin of course very valuable. I was offered as much as 25 dollars for the skin by the Post Sutler. —— I am sorry I could not prepare the skull, it was much fractured, he took to a tree where I fired 5 revolver balls in his head.[+] But the jaws & tooth are in perfect condition, & so you will be able to find out *who* he is.

I am anxious to know your opinion about the wolf I sent you in last transport. That Lupus is called here the *yellow wolf*,[13] And is considered even rarer as the *black wolf*. I could not find any

[+]You must know, I kill every large game with revolver. Although a hazardous operation; still, having no double barrell gun, is much better as nothing, no doubt. Notwithstanding the uncertainty of such hunting, I killed lately a Lynx at 78 paces when running up the hill; and some days ago a Cayote at great distance, also running. ——

distinction between him & the cayotes, (of which I
have several specimens) but still I believe it a distinct species from any wolves I have seen. —— I
poisoned one again the other day, but was to late. I
found him only after 2 days in the bush, & by that
time his cousins or perhaps grizzlys eat him half up.

Dr Hammond wrote me extensively on his late
collection, and I was delighted to hear that he collected amongst other things as many as 200 mammals; & although My pupil H. Brandt (whom I recommended to you long ago, & renew my
recommendation now again) was at the D^r command, still the collection was no doubt considerable.

I liked very much to go once with such a government expedition, to show the people at large, what
a collector can do, when he has plenty transportation, plenty time, & one company of soldiers to his
command; who hunt & pick up everything for miles
around; and the *soi disant naturalist*, has only to
pack them, and labell them, (if he takes this trouble
at all.)

I do not allude certainly to Dr Hammond, I know
he is devoted to science as fervently as anybody
can, and I know that he collects himself as well as
his assistants. But I speak at large of the Govnt Naturalists, who—with some very few exceptions—
could do certainly a hundred times more as they actually do.

I have now 13 woodpeckers, and almost every
one of Audubons Troglodytes, besides some others,
not described by him.

As a remarkable fact I note to you, that the 6th of
December I caught a serpent in open ground, quite
lively, & pugnaciously defending himself. The thermometer stood at 45°. It is the yellow serpent (I
think coluber), with brown & red spots, I sent you
some in my last collection.[14]

Dr Tenbroeck promised me everything as I told
you; but he never gone further as promise. I asked

him after his kind conversation to let me go to the
Kern river but he thought he is going there himself
to hunt grizzlys. He nothwithstanding stopped in
his house for a couple weeks, then he went to Los
Angeles for a months spree. He returned last week,
and instantly received an order to proceed to Cajon
pass[15] & report for Duty to Major Black.[16] He has
gone accordingly yesterday morning, & the charge
of Medical Dep[t] at this post left by special Department Order to my care. —— I am confined accordingly as much as possible, but still prefer my present
position to the humbugging of D[r] Ten Broeck; and
doubtless I will procure as many specimens hereafter, as until now.[17]

Although nobody know the exact meaning of the
great expedition to Cajon Pass, it is generally be-
lieved that somewhere in the Cajon or Gorgonio
Pass a Post will be built immediately, or at least a
fortified camp against Mormon depredations.[18]
Could you not ascertain this dear Sir, and act according my previously notified intentions?

*Xántus found the Long-billed Marsh Wren (*Telamotodytes palustris) *"in a rotten
cane bunch near the water, uttering a rattling sound, like wrens do in general. Never
noticed any more of the species, although diligently searched similar places; but I am
informed on reliable authority, that this species is quite common and the most numerous wren in the settlements on Kern river, and Tulare lake; near the swamps, &
sloughs. . . . I considered at first sight the species as the* T. hyemalis Vieall, *but after
a minute examination I am satisfied, it is quite a distinct species, one not described in
Audubon." Xántus identified this bird in the General Register as "Troglodytes."*

Finally, I notify you, that having some payment in San Francisco, I asked Mr Forbes to pay 5 dollars for me to a gentleman & charge to the Smithsonian Institution.

Now I am rather so long, must close wishing you a happy new year, I remain Sir

Your sincere
LXdeVésey

---

1. Baird, November 2, 1857:

Despairing of ever getting your guns in a reasonable time, I have sent off to New York today a fine large chest packed full of traps scarcely, by speaking, for your use. From the enclosed list I trust you will see that we have duplicated as far as possible the first lot and in part improved on it. The chest is one that Dr. Hammond had this summer in Borgas pass, and which he brought back full of nice things. (By the way, I have just had a letter from the doctor stating that he was coming in in a few days on sick leave.) I have put in as many of the tin preserving cans as the chest will hold but I am not sure but that I have omitted some of your memoranda as I mislaid one slip on which I had put down what to send, but I tried to recollect everything. If anything more is wanting let me know.

The invoice is attached:

1 wooden chest	4.00
2 copper tanks @ 8.50	17.00
1 wrench[?]	.75
8 tin cans with screw caps	2.75
2 canisters powder 0 size	1.00
1000 percussion caps	1.00
2 shot belts	1.00
1 powder flask	.50
1200 printed labels	5.00
4 packages insect pins	1.25
48 pieces cork	3.00
2 oz. vials	.30
6 bottles strychnine	3.00
1 lb. campher	.65
Wooden - paperboard boxes	1.25
Can insect powder	.50
" arsenic	.40
2 cans saltpeter & alum	.80

1 Sitgreaves report   <u>2.00</u>
miscellaneous books   46.60
[The actual amount is $46.15]

2. Baird, January 31, 1858:

The boxes for nests I do not remember your asking for. It would however have been difficult to have sent enough to have done much good without increasing greatly the bulk of the invoice which I was desirous of reducing as much as possible so as not to wear out our welcome in the way of free freight.

3. "Report of the Commissioner of Patents for the Year 1856. Agriculture" (U.S. Patent Office, 1857) contains articles on raptors and rodents "injurious to Agriculture" with extensive descriptions and illustrations which would have been very helpful to Xántus.

4. *Annual Report to the Board of Regents, January, 1855.*

5. William H. Dall (1915, p. 189), letter from J. D. Dana to Spencer F. Baird, August 27, 1849, while Baird was applicant for the position of Assistant Secretary:

As to your application to Professor Henry. The fact is that Henry has no idea of requiring, yet a while, a curator. He intends to have nothing to do with the Exploring Expedition Collections or any other government property. I regret that he takes this stand,— for collections are better than books to the naturalist; they contain the whole that was ever put in words on the subject, and they illustrate a thousand times more. He is more interested in the library and publications,—both very important purposes,—but the plan is one sided— and not of the wide comprehensive character I had expected from Henry.

In the 1856 *Annual Report,* Henry, p. 41:

It is not the design of the Institution to form a general museum of all objects of natural history, but of such as are of a more immediate interest in advancing definite branches of physical research.

He proposed removing the Museum of the Exploring Expeditions which filled a large room in the Patent Office and reinstalling it in the Smithsonian; without careful reading it might have sounded to Xántus as if he intended to close the Museum altogether.

6. Dr. Samuel Woodhouse (1821–1904) accompanied Lt. Sitgreaves in 1851 to the Zuni and Colorado rivers, and reported on the natural history of the region. From Cabo San Lucas, Xántus refers sarcastically to Woodhouse's identification of *Acanthylis saxatalis,* Rock Swift (now *Aeronautes saxatilis,* White-throated Swift) made while standing on

Inscription Rock, New Mexico, without obtaining a specimen (Sit-greaves 1853, p. 64); Xántus, September 14, 1859:

> I wish I had this time the eyes of one of our American naturalists, who accomplished notoriously such feat, as to name even & describe a *swallow on wing*, and that most minutely, not forgetting even dimensions of tail, tarsus, feet etc. of course the swallow was never before or after seen yet, and we can suppose the creature was expressly made (contrary to all destinations of swallows) for the benfit of the inscription or hyerogliphic Rocks.

Actually Dr. Coues made a special pilgrimmage there on July 3, 1864 (quoted in Cutright and Brodhead 1981, p. 58):

> It is a grand mass of Old Red Sandstone. I clambered to its top, like Woodhouse, without my gun; and there in airy circles round my head dashed the birds he called *Acantylis saxatilis.*

7. See Xántus, September 30, 1857; Baird, November 10, 1857:

> Your black Spermophylus is a curious animal. It may be the *S. couchii* . . . a black variety of the [blot] showed me just such freaks of [blot] are often met with.

He eventually identified it as *Citellus beechyi;* see October 20, 1858.

8. See note 23, June 5, 1857.

9. Now *Melanerpes formicivorus,* Acorn Woodpecker. Xántus incorrectly takes *formi-* as referring to ants.

10. Baird, January 31, 1858:

> Your remarks about the habit of *Picus formicivoros* are most interesting. Just such facts as will give the great part of your professed work and I hope you will succeed in gathering up many such. I had heard of this before but the facts have been contorted in favor of the Jays.

Grinnell (1905, p. 11) also found them prevalent:

> Of all the birds of the neighborhood, the most insistent upon our attention were the California woodpeckers. The oaks furnish these droll birds with a generous livelihood, so they seem to have plenty of time for all sorts of nonsensical performances. Their medley of quavering nasal notes echoed among the oaks from daylight till dark. Sometimes a "carpintero," as the vaqueros call this bird, would repair to the roof which yet remains on one of the large barracks and now used to shelter the hay crop, and selecting a loose shake, would pound on it for a half hour at a time, making as much noise as a lather, and evidently enjoying it. The wood-work under the eaves and around the doors and windows, which we were told had been shipped to California around the Horn, was perforated with holes made by the woodpeckers to fit the white-oak acorns. In some places the boards were quite symmetrically inlaid with acorns, just as the old doors were studded with wrought nails.

11. Xántus' field description of the California Condor that he found "quite numerous" is interesting in the light of the condor's present population of so few birds confined to a narrow mountain habitat in southern California; to the west and southwest condor sanctuaries exist today within 20 miles of Fort Tejon. See also February 18 and April 15, 1858. Baird, January 31, 1858:

> Is not your large vulture the Cathartes Californianus? this is nearly as large as a condor, with black head. By the way the eggs of this will be one of the greatest prizes you could dream.

12. In Spanish, "dusky fox." Baird, January 31, 1858:

> The fox you describe is wonderfully like my *Vulpes littoralis*. Why is it not *Vulpes*[?], not the true cross fox. And the fur really is of little value. The black line along the top of back and tan settles it being a *Urouyas* not a true *vulpes* to which the cross fox belongs.

13. The only wolf is *Canis lupus*, Gray Wolf.

14. *Coluber* are racers, none of which fit Xántus' description; to be expected is *Thamnophis sirtalis infernalis,* California Red-sided Garter Snake, not on USNM printout.

15. Cajon Pass was the main pass between Los Angeles and the Great Basin country eastward; troops had been stationed there 1847–48; its name was occasionally confused with that of Tejon. See Hussey (1950). Brodhead (1973) quotes Elliott Coues who passed through the tollgate there in 1865 and commented that the "pass is a narrow, deep, tortuous canon, the roughest I have ever traversed on wheels."

16. Xántus must have meant Major George Alexander Hamilton Blake (d. 1884) whom he identifies correctly March 1, 1858; Blake became major of the First Dragoons in July 1850 and served with distinction during the Mexican and Civil wars, distinguishing himself at Gettysburg.

17. The surgeon's side of the coin was expressed in a letter to Baird by Dr. Coues while he was stationed at isolated Fort Whipple, and sounds as if it could have been written about Xántus (Brodhead, 1973, p. 24):

I have absolutely *nothing* to do here, officially, and so all my time can go for Natural History, but my Hospital Steward is a wretched stick, and a good deal of a rascal, in a small way, to boot, who wouldn't if he could, and couldn't if he would, help me in the least.

18. Tensions between Mormons and Gentiles erupted in the ugly Mountain Meadows Massacre of September 1857, when California-bound emigrants from Arkansas were murdered in ambush after an ostensible truce given by a small group of Mormons led by John D. Lee. Military posts were put on alert to insure the safety of Gentile travelers. The threat was considered serious enough that James Buchanan delivered "Message of the President of the United States Communicating, in Compliance with a Resolution of the Senate, information in relation to The Massacre at Mountain Meadows, and other Massacres in Utah Territory, May 4, 1860" to the first session of the 36th Congress; Xántus notes on May 1, 1858, that troops were dispatched to Salt Lake City when the "suppression of the Mormon Rebellion" began. See November 16, 1858, note 8.

Fort Tejon, Cala.
January 15th 1858

My dear Sir/

Your letter of Decbr 3d reached me just now, together with Dr Hallowells,[1] LeContes, & Coopers[2] Reports, please to accept my humblest acknowledgments for your attentive kindness. I received of Mr Forbes this mail a bill of lading of the package containing Cassins volume etc, but the package itself has not arrived yet.

As I told you in my former letters, you may publish my birds in my name, if there should be any new species; and you may publish the life of my birds also, in your forthcoming Report; to show Geogr. distribution, habits, migration etc.

But we are going dear Sir very rapidly from the arrangement, we made together at my coming out here; and a new proposition in your letter, threatens not only to go further still, but break to pieces my whole design.[3]

Hoping, that you will accept with as perfect sincere good faith my Remarks on this very matter, as my intention is indeed; I take the opportunity to remind you dear Sir, that at *your own* suggestion we determined to concentrate my whole collection in the Sm. Institution until my Return, when I had to write some Memoir on the Collection, and then dispose of the collection itself. —— Although my intention was a different one before, but I cheerfully agreed in your proposition, hoping that at last, after 15 years disinterested collecting, I will take *some positive* in the literary World; & with this view I refused every offer (coming from different quarters) & every inducement. Still I collected number of species, & not number of specimens.

Subsequently you advised me to collect in large quantities, all the species, because by doing so, I could sell them, and realise some money. I overpowered my bitter reminiscences; & did so, as you advised me. In the hope sir, that I will be able to realize something, I gave up all my literary correspondence for home (which brought me in something at least monthly), turned the nights to days, spent every cent of my miserable monthly pay; & with this sacrifice & this energy I brought up my collection already to a very respectable *quantity*, which (if it goes so for a year) will beat no doubt every Governement collection, not excepting Wilkes Expedition.[5] (always the quantity of specimens understood of course)

Now, dear sir, supposed I *present* my surplus specimens to the principal European Museums; what will I sell?

And, supposed, I am through with presents, & have still some specimens on hand for sale, to whom shall I sell, if I already presented them to the *principal* Museums?

These are questions, which are certainly important to me, situated as I am!

I cannot help, but I must consider dear Sir, that according such proceding, instead of concentration, would be inevitably a *uni*versal distribution & dispersion, which system I cannot comprehend, how could profit me either scientifically or materially.

Besides, the principal Museums of Europe are so rich, that their runner out, or Janitor has generally twice as much salary, as my whole earthen property, so they can send here any amount of collectors, if they want; or buy specimens if they prefer. —— When I proposed once an Expedition to the Eastern Tributaries of the Amazon, and asked the aid of the Principal European Museums by reference to the most eminent European personages; amongst the few Museums, who did not consider worth even to a reply my letter, was the Bremen Museum, although in the civilised 19th century it is a social rule to answer every respectable letter.

I dont want to do anything for these Museums; they *never* did anything for me.

As to publishing my new species, you may do so, with the collection already sent in, as you say "it is important for science," although I am not quite of the same opinion. If my collection were the *last* on the N. American continent, I would aquiesce in it, because I would consider it important, that the work should be complete. But how many species will be discovered after me, and we know very well, that the work even containing my species, in some months after its publication, will be again incomplete, having been discovered *again* species, not contained in it.

Knowing as you do, dear Sir my circumstances; you must admit, that it is with some sacrifices on my part to lead such a life as I do; principally if we consider, that I made myself so a perfect slave of collection, & submitted myself to the impertinences, & continuous chincanes of persons, who can never apreciate my objects, whose intellectual capacity is below 0, and who still are my lords, with absolute power over me!

I wish to publish after my Return some Memoir on my whole collection here, which—no doubt—will give me more credit, than anything else; and will place me in some position in the scientific world. The surplus specimens I want to sell, so as to realize something, or regain at least a part of my expenses.

This is all, I wish; and I hope you will support to your best, my wishes; by considereing *hereafter* that my collection is intended to be *concentrated* in the Smithsonian Institute, as a Deposit, not to be disposed of until my Return.

I wish—as I requested you already—to understand me fully, and not to consider, by no means, my Remarks, as any kind of offence; I expressed myself with frankness, and hope you will regard it no otherwise. To avoid even the slighest shade of any unpleasant feelings between us, which would very painfull to me certainly, I would request you, not to refer to the subject in your answer at all. And we shall continue our procedings undisturbed as ever!

——— ——— ———

I never intended to mention again Möllhausen, but as you do it, I make a concluding Remark. —— As he visited me immediately after his arrival here, he promised me to do so again the next day, and I offered to hunt for him & with him as long as his stay here continues. More yet I made up a nice assortement of my duplicates, numbering exactly 60 specimens, and intended to give him as a present, when he shall visit me again. But he came not the next day, or the following ones, although I was always home, waiting for him, with considerable loss in my usual occupations time. I met him several times on the Parade, Sutlers Store, etc, but he always evaded my addresses, even turned from me his face, & left when I approached him. I never spoke him again, although he was here over 2 weeks. —— Subsequently I heard from a Gentleman, who was present at the transaction, that as soon as Mr Möllhausen left my Room the first day, he requested Dr TenBroeck to give me permission to hunt with him every day, until he is here. Dr T.B. answered as follows: "what you think Mr Möllhausen, having been so long in America, you ought to know, that it is unbecoming to a gentleman to have any intercourse with an enlisted man, I hope you wont disgrace us, your companions etc"

It seems, Möllhausen followed the advice of Dr TenBroeck, literally. You may tell him if you see him again, how *unbe*comingly to a gentleman, he acted. I on my part forgot, that I ever have seen him; and nothing in the world can induce me in this life, to speak him again!

Very sincerely yours
LVésey

1. John Leconte (1856) had several papers on beetles and Hallowell presented several on reptiles, among them "Notice of a collection of reptiles from Kansas and Nebraska, presented to A. N. S. by Dr. Hammond, U. S. A.," pp. 238–53. [In this volume Hallowell's name is out of place in the index and page numbering is inaccurate.]

2. James G. Cooper (1830–1902), after whom the Cooper Ornithological Society was named, was an Army surgeon on the Pacific Railroad Surveys in 1853–55; he was also a zoologist and an expert on the geographic and biologic aspects of the Pacific Coast, one of the first to write about the natural history of Oregon and California. He named *Vermivora luciae,* Lucy's Warbler, for Baird's daughter.

3. Baird, December 3, 1857:

> I am delighted to hear you are about to send in a collection of your specimens and [?] I look forward to their arrival with much impatience. Please let me know your view in regard to our new species. Shall I publish them at once in your name so as to secure priority? I want you to understand distinctly that I insist that you shall have the credit of naming and describing all the new birds you may collect; your efforts, sacrifice . . . making this your right. It will be a very trifling hardship to go over your descriptions and prepare those of new species for immediate publication.

4. Lt. Charles Wilkes (1798–1877), U. S. Navy admiral and explorer, was appointed to the U. S. Exploring Expedition in 1838 which, in the four years of its existence, touched around the world, including mapping the western coast of the United States. He served with the Coast Survey on his return, and from 1844 to 1861 was concerned with preparing the six volumes of *Narrative of the United States Exploring Expedition.* The *Merrimac* was scuttled just as he arrived to take command; he was responsible for removing the Confederate commissioners, Mason and Slidell, on their way to England.

№ 18.

F Tejon, Cala
January 20th 1858

Dear Sir/
    Although I wrote you only a few days ago, I take to pen again to inform you on some items, which may prove of interest for your forthcoming Report

on Birds, as you are incorporating in it *my birds already sent in.*

1) There is no Flycatcher of any kind here since September, & no Humming bird, there are only a very few Falconidae, & no buzzards whatever.

2) *Garrulus ultramarinus* are only a few, but instead of a quantity of *G. stelleri*[1] makes their appearence since a few days, which were extremely rare in summer & fall.

3) *Picus formicivorus* still continues in immense numbers, they and the Spermophylus Beecheyi are the most numerous representatives of our Zoology.

4) *Picus Mexicanus*[2] left late in the fall. *Picus Harrisii*[3] are more numerous since winter. Picus N° XXIII[4] left in the fall, likewise *Picus N° XXIV, Picus ruber*[5] is more numerous in Winter, although they are constant residents. *Picus torquatus*[6] (arrived here in September) is extremely abundant now, a man can see in a days hunt several thausends of them, they are nothwithstanding very hard to get at, being very cautious & shy.

5) Of *Picus N° XXVII,*[7] I procured since my description several males & females; the female are all alike to the described specimens. But the ♂ is a very curiosly marked bird. Here the description:
Measurements 7½. 14½. 6½
Head & cheeks black, very distinctly lineated with white. A broad scarlet occipital band, (or rather short crest) Behind the scarlet band, a broad white band, recurved on both sides to the corner of the eye. Upper parts as in the ♀. Lower parts white, shaded with pale yellow. The sides & under tail coverts spotted with black, & dark brown. Bill a little stouter as in the female. They are found almost exclusively on dry cedar stumps above (but along) water courses; they are very tame, being approached nearly to hand length.

6) *Pipilo arctius*[8] has left late in the fall. *N° XXXIII*[9] is extremely abundant, is seen in thausands. Likewise the bird *N° LXXIII*[10] (I think a Pi-

pilo) is every day more numerous, they congregate in flocks numbering hundreds. Of *N⁰ LXXV*[11] I procured also about fifty, although they are of solitary habits, they are frequently met with.

7) N⁰ LXXVI[12] very numerous now, & gregarious.

8) Of N⁰ LVII[13] I procured a number. It seems they are by no means very rare, but difficult to notice them only; as they inhabit trees of the most gigantic size, are of very small size, & entirely noiseless.

Bluebirds[14] are both species here, as is the Niphaea Oregona[15] in countless numbers.

I secured a great variety of birds, & in considerable numbers, which are not contained in my collection sent in; but it would be useless to notice them, partly because you have not the specimens themselves; partly because I intend to notice them myself, according to our plan.

I Hope however that the above dates, will be not entirely superfluous items in regards to the migrations of the Pacific birds.

———

I forgot in my last account the leaf tobacco, & pins which I had to purchase for the last collections, I paid for $1.75, & lately for fright of the collecting box & ammunition from Mr Forbes (194 pounds per 10 cents) $19.40. Total $21.15.

Please to credit me then half of the amount viz $10.50;—my act will stand now as follows:

Former expenses	——	$45.65
New	——	10.50
Off draft on Mr A. B. Forbes		$5
Balance due to me		#51.15

Hoping, you send me the gun I asked you to buy for me, you can remit me the Rest at your convenience.

I am Sir

very sincerely yours
Vésey

Postscript

I was wrong, when I informed you of the presence here of the *Ortyx plumifera*,[16] this birds does not exist here. Besides, the *Ortyx Californ*[17] which are very many, there is an other one although similar in general appearance to Ortyx plumifera, still different altogether, & not contained in Audubon.

Length of the male is 11½ inches, & the wing 7½. It has a straight crest of several single feathers, (formed like the Ardea nobilis of Hungary) the longest of which is 2^{10} *inches* & deep black. The others are much smaler & partly entirely black, partly blue spotted with coffee.[+] Head neck & whole breast blue, the upper neck with coffee reflexions. Back, tail, wings, & in fact the whole upperparts light [gray?], the primaries darker. Under tail coverts deep black. Throat & abdomen chetnut, the former margined with white, the long feathers on the sides transversely banded with orange, black, white, & chetnut.
Tibia pale yellow, shaded with orange, the secondaries margined on their inner webb with white, which gives an appearance to the bird, as if having two white bands above the tail.

Iris black.

This quail is called in Southern California popularly the "Mountain Quail", they are found in high altitudes, always amongst Pine forests with chaparal undergrowth, in small flock of 12 or 15 individuals. They are considered as rare, & of very delicate flesh. They are extremely shy, the males generally commence a warning when the enemy is ¼ of a mile distant, the warning passes through the flock like a telegraph, & they immediately fly. The bird is really one of the finest amongst all American birds, (if not the finest) considering her elegant crest, & beautiful

[+]but their webbs are not decurved, or deflected.

plumage. I have some ♂ specimens, but could not get any females yet. The reason is, that the males allow to clear of all females, before they take to flight, making much noise, & beating the ground with their wings, as if urging the ladies to save themselves.

---

1. Now *Cyanocitta stelleri*, Steller's Jay.

2. Now *Picoides scalaris*, Ladder-backed Woodpecker.

3. *Picoides villosus harrisii*, Hairy Woodpecker.

4. *Picoides pubescens*, Downy Woodpecker; General Register, XXIII:

Bill as long, as the head. Bristles over the nostrils white. Head black, slightly tipped with white. A white band over the eye, joining the scarlet occiptal band. Then a band of black, (crossing the eye,) to the upper neck. Again a white band, from the lower mandible, re-curved & nearly joining the other (above). —— Upper parts black, spotted with white, & tinged with brown. Large white spots on the upper neck, below the scarlet band, nearly appearing as a white ring. —— 2d 3d 4th quills longest & about equal, all spotted with quadrangular white spots. The outermost having 5 inside & 5 out-side. The succeeding 4 quills six spots on each webb. The four upper tailfeathers brownish black the succeeding two on each side half black & white. The outermost white with 5 brown spots on. (One at the tip) Whole underparts white, scarcely speckled with brown & black; the sides more so.

5. *Picoides scalaris*, Ladder-backed Woodpecker; General Register, XXIV:

*Yellow-bellied Sapsucker (*Sphyrapicus varius*).*

Bill quite straight, the upper mandible much longer as the lower. Bristles white, the lowermost brown. Whole upperhead carmine, much tipped with white. Upperneck black. A white band from the hind corner of eye passes back diagonally, & extends on the neck in a large white spot, which unites with the one from the other side. This band is succeeded by a black, this again by a white, (but which does not unite with the one above), this again by an irregular band, passing from the lower mandible into the black of the scapulars. Upperparts black, spotted with white. Quills the same, having the four longest 9 spots on the outer, & 5 on the inner webb. Third quill the longest; next 2^d & 4th's equal. The sixth nearly equal to the 1st. The two central tailfeathers black, the next one on each side black margined with white. The next white outside, black halfway up inside, with black at the base, & a small black spot at the tip. —— The two central tailfeathers black, the next one on each side black margined with white. The next white outside, black halfway up inside, with black at the base, & a small black spot at the tip. —— The lateral feathers which much spotted irregularly with black. — — Whole underparts pale yellow, spotted a litle with brown longitudinal streaks, the legs & sides more so. Tail feathers below yellow, having 6 black spots on their inner, and four on their outer webb. Measurements. 6. 12. 5¼. Iris yellow.

Secured about 6000 feet high on small srubbs. Are very rare, & extremely shy. Never noticed them on hillsides, or valleys, —— always on very elevated

6. Now *Melanerpes lewis*, Lewis' Woodpecker.

7. *Sphyrapicus varius*, Yellow-bellied Sapsucker; the General Register, XXVII, varies somewhat from the letter:

Bill rather long, slender, & very acute, lower mandible more so. Bristles white. A very narrow band from the upperpart of the eye passes (curved down) backwards. This is succeeded by a black also narrow band in similar direction. Then a broader white; again a black. Whole upperparts black, spotted all over with white (except the head; & four midle tailfeathers, which are deep black.) —— — — Third quill the longest, fourth much shorter than 2^d, but longer than first. There are on the outer quill, 3 spots on the outer and two (large ones) on the inner webb. On the succeeding four longest quills 5 on the outer, & four on their inner webb. —— Underparts greyish-white, the sides much spotted with black. The outer 3 tailfeathers yellowish-white, spotted with black transversely . . . Length 7. Extent 23½. Wing 6. —— Iris hazel.

8. Now *P. erythrophthalmus megalonyx*, Rufous-sided Towhee.

9. *Zonotrichia leucophyrs gambelii*, White-crowned sparrow; General Register, XXXIII:

Male. Bill yellow, rather short, robust, conical, & compressed towards the end, very acute, the edges of the mandibles inflected, the upper covering the lower. Nostrils round & partly concealed by the feathers. No bristles. Head silver grey, forehead black, which color extends in two lateral & longitudinal bands, running ½ an inch behind the eye. Another brownish black band runs from the hind corner of the eye, forming a narrow circle on the neck. Cheeks, wing coverts, throat, & breast light ashgrey. Sides & lower tail coverts pale redish brown. Back, wings, & tail woodbrown, margined with redish yellow. Rump brown, 2, 3, & 4th quills the longest & equal. First by ¾ of an inch longer than 5th & 6th. Tail slightly rounded, & of a bluish grey color beneath. Tibia dusky. Tarsus & toes ochre (the lat[t]er darker), armed with pointed, rather long, slightly arched, & laterally grooved claws. Two white bands on the wing, formed by the half tips of the wing covers.

Female. Lighter in colors, else similar. . . .

This species arrived here in September, & is gregarious.

Measurements of —— 6½. 10. 4¼.

See November 1, 1857, note 5.

10. *Turdus migratorius,* American Robin.

11. The General Register description, LXXV, is meager:

Upperparts redish brown, tail chesnut. Underparts white, spotted all over with dark brown.

Constantly resident. Only occasionally seen.

12. In Register, LXXVI, no description, only "Seiurus (?)" and "arrived in very large flocks in September, and are here yet." *S. noveboracensis,* Northern Waterthrush, identified later in the Register, CXXIV:

Very rare. Killed every specimen seen. It does not agree perfectly with Audubons description, but having nothing else to refer to, agreed to place them under that name.

13. *Certhia americana,* Brown Creeper; see November 1, 1857, note 3.

14. *Sialia mexicana,* Western Bluebird.

15. Now *J. hyemalis,* Oregon Junco.

16. *Oreortyx pictus,* Mountain Quail.

17. *Callipepla californicus,* California Quail, USNM #10592, 10593, 26750, 26771,80070.

No 19.

Dear Sir/

Your letter of Debr 15 came to hand, & am much delighted to hear that you commenced an aquarium; this was much in need for students of that particular branch of Nat. History. I had the pleasure of seeing the grand one at the Regents Park Zoological Gardens, London, & passed several times several pleasant hours in looking the magnificent exhibition. They have both marine & freshwater Aquarium, put up in a prolific elegant style.

Cassins volume arrived also, but I have only a very few of his species contained in the volume. I am satisfied now, that I have never seen yet the Maximilans Jay, & nobody has seen him ever here round. The species I sent you, must be consequently one, not described yet. —— [1]

If it is in time yet, I would request you to name birds—provided there will be new ones:

1st Hammondii, in honor of my friend W. A. Hammond, U.S.A.

2d Bairdii, as a slight acknowledgment of your kindness toward me.

3d Kubinyii, in honor of his Excellency the Director of the Hungarian National Museum, August Kubinyi.[2]

If there should be more, then we may name one Lecontei (Dr Leconte); Halloweli (Edward Hallowell), & Cassinii (John Cassin of Pha) etc.

Although I have a great variety of birds not included in the collection sent in; considering that I described so many already known, with a much labor and without any use whatever; I must stop now this until your Rept on birds comes out. But I will continue with birds, which I can identify already.

I have to inform you again on a great calamity. Lt Beall with his camels passed here several days ago,

& having no escort he enlisted citizens, & armed them from the ordnance store of this Post.[3] Consequently he took every musket, Carabine, pistol, & sabre on hand; and I am now entirely naked (scientifically speaking)!

Considering that the Missouri river is now frozen, & wont be open for navigation before the spring, I cannot *reasonably* expect the arrival of my F[t] Riley guns before an other year or so, if they ever arrive. I hope however that you sent out by this time the gun, I asked you for; and in this case I shall continue again operations, as soon as it arrives. Should this hope fail, of course I have to abandon then everything, although I anticipated a very rich collection in the Spring.

I have a great quantity of skulls now but there being some (Cervus Canadensis) of so enormous size with antlers on, that I am entirely lost as how to send in, having nowhere such boxes, as to receive them. As a last resource, I think to saw of[f] the antlers from the skulls, & pack in so; you could then nail them on again. But I will try yet to get boxes, before I do this expedient.

I secured the other day a gopher, which is probably a new one. We cannot assume it to be a young in *January*, & the species is not larger as a common house mouse, of a dark chesnut color.[4]

I have now 12 blackhair deers of all ages & sexes; & so probably more, than all collections in the whole U. S. together. —— But amongst the number, I have a fine old buck, which I am inclined to believe (you must not laugh) is a new species!

The average weight of the Cerv. Columbiana may be considered as 65 pounds. This is however fully 114 pounds, without intestines & blood. The dimensions are as follows =

from nose to occiput		14 inches
" " " eye		6 "
" " " ears		13 "

" " base of tail   74 "
tail to end of vertebrae—   6½ "
" " tip of hair ———   11 "
Hight of ears ——— ———   10½"

You will perceive by this, the enormous difference between this specimen, & the average measurements of a full grown blacktail deer. But this all is but nothing in comparation to the formation of antlers, which is exactly as follows

Although according your Rep[t] on Mammals, there was secured one Cervus Columbianus at Puget Sound, where on the fore branch was no fork at all. By this specimen seems the hind fork the main one, & the fore branch only a side; and as the fore branch is duly forked, the hind one is nearly straight, resembling a single joint of a lance, moreover it is flatt entirely, & not rounded like all other horns of the Cerv. Columbianus. It may prove as a variety only of the C. Columb, but still it is a very interesting one I should think.[5]

I killed the specimen lately not far from the garrison in a Pine forest, out of a gang numbering 5 specimens. There was a full grow doe amongst the crowd, & 3 fawns. I am sorry I could not secure any more for a fuller investigation, although I wounded 2 fawns, with the revolver, the old had 4 balls in the body, & my charges were exhausted.

I had quite an adventure last month, which I certainly never anticipated. —— At San Domidio,[6] distant from here 30 miles north, a man was shot in the legs, & I was ordered to see him. The man being dangerously wounded, I stopped there a couple days, & went out hunting in the mountains. There was from 2–5 feet snow that time everywhere in the Sierras. After reaching the top of a rocky hill, I descended on a ridge (swept clear from snow by wind) into a deep gulch, & when near the bottom— behold a herd of Bighorn then numbering at least 300. —— I fired at once in the crowd, & although my gun loaded with duck shot, I wounded one of their chieftains, a huge horned fellow. The others got frightened, & run in all directions hill up on the opposite side; but the snow was so deep in the gulch, that they could not go, they sunk at each jump, to their neck. By this time I went up with the wounded one, but scarcely approaching him; to my great astonishment he posted himself in front of me, then made a desparate charge, & struck me in the abdomen with his forehead, that I tumbled several feet of, capsized a couple of times.

As I had in front my filled hunting bag, his blow was not so violent as it had been no doubt, without this preservative; so I recovered soon; & just as he was preparing for a fresh attack, I dispatched him with revolver. I commenced now, in highest excite-ment, a furious descent on the fugitives, & killed four more of them in an area of about an acker. —— Then I skinned the big warrior, but I was not able to carry his skin with head home. I left them there, & with the assistance of a couple mules ar-rived just in time to save them; as there were al-ready several Cayotes on the hill sides.

This is the first instance I heard of, that the mountain sheep attacks a man; but certainly I will look out hereafter, as I had a verry narrow escape. —— —— 7

We had a very severe winter here, the severest on record. The road to Los Angeles was blocked up on some places by 15 feet high snow. When last month the Paymaster came up, a Company of Soldiers had to work 4 days, to cut a passage in the snow. At present the valleys are clear, & almost every tree already green, but the peaks are still covered very much with snow.[8]

Lizards & snakes are out regularly, I captured only last week a Ratlesnake.

Very truly yours
XdeVésey

P.S.[9]

I would prefer, if you would refer to me simply as *Mr Xántus*, & describe or publish *simply so* everything, concerning me.

P.S. I

I nearly forgot to say, that I forwarded last month a box (N⁰ 9.) of birds, numbering 135. specimens. The box contains a Copy of my Register also from N⁰ 1 to N⁰ 1000.

---

1. See June 5 and September 12, 1857.

2. August Kubinyii was commemorated instead in *Heliaster kubinji*, a handsome sun starfish from Cabo San Lucas.

3. Lt. Edward Fitzgerald Beale (1822–93) enlisted in the Navy at 14 and arrived in California in 1846 where he was detached for military and messenger service; he became associated with Stockton and Aspinwall in business and was appointed by President Buchanan as the first Commissioner of Indian Affairs for California and Nevada in 1852 with a generous appropriation to develop the reservation. He led an expedition using camels, leaving San Antonio in June 1857, arriving in California, January 1858. Beale proved that camels worked well in North American deserts and thought them "the salt of the party and the noblest brute alive"; the problems were not with the camels but with the mule-drivers who couldn't make the transition in handling techniques. The camels were kept at Fort Tejon and other places for more than a year and used on short hauls in the area; Beale used a pair for personal transport to Los Angeles; some were turned loose, but eventually none of the original thirty-six survived. Beale was accused of using the camel

train and government funds to build a road for his own benefit, charges which were never proved, but he was removed from the position. When Fort Tejon was finally closed in 1864, it was absorbed into the larger parcel of Rancho Tejon, which Beale bought. He held more than 270,000 acres, the highest price paid per acre being $3.00. Beale's account is contained in the Report of the Secretary of War, "In answer to a resolution of the Senate, a report of E. F. Beale of his exploration for a wagon road from Fort Defiance, in New Mexico, to the western borders of California"; see also Gates (1977), Gray (1940), and the proceedings of the meeting of December 22, 1857 (*Proceedings of the Academy of Natural Sciences of Philadelphia* 9:206–10), at which Dr. William Hammond introduced Major Wayne, in charge of importing and caring for the camels in Texas.

4. *Thomyms bottae*. Baird, March 16, 1858:

A gopher size of house mouse in January might well be new.

5. Baird, March 16, 1858:

The deer you mention is a very interesting one. Why may it not be *Cervus macrotis*? This is much larger than the *columbianus* and much longer. You will know it by the tail entirely white all round, only with a black tuft on the extreme tip. It is cylindrical and close haired to near the tip and is quite naked beneath.

And March 31, 1858:

I was greatly interested [in] the Cervus macrotis, deer. The long-eared species is this as I suspected: there was only one of the *columbianus*. The range of the species is thus extended south beyond what was supposed.

6. Xántus meant San Emigdio, 20 miles west of the Fort; Saint Emigdio, a Roman saint who suffered martyrdom under Diocletian, was patron saint for protection against earthquakes; no one knows whether the mountains received their name for that reason, or simply because it was his calendar day when the Spaniards were there, and so named the range.

7. Baird, March 16, 1858:

You had a most unheard of adventure with the bighorn. It will be admirable [advisable?] for you to include in words on the Western Animals.

Xantus' USNM specimens #38387 and 3532.

8. Dr. William F. Edgar (1893, p. 28), who was stationed at Fort Tejon for several years, remarks that "Tejon was the only post in Southern California where snow fell." He had access to the post's meteorological records for 1856–58 which recorded "the mean number of (annual)

snowy days for same time, 9, which snow, when melted and added to the rain water, made the annual precipitation 22.62 inches." See January 6, 1859, note 3. Grapevine Pass is still closed because of heavy snow at least once a year.

9. This footnote is written upside down across the top of the first page of the letter.

No **XX.**

Fᵗ Tejon, Cala—
Febr 18ᵗʰ 1858

Dear Sir/
As I informed you in my last, I sent you the Register in box Nᵒ 9, with 135 birds. I forward you herewith the Receipt of Wells Fargo & Co. ——
—— Yesterday I again dispatched a box (Nᵒ 10) containing
    52 birds
    4 blacktail deers
    2 Cayotes
    2 Spotted Lynxes
    2 Neotomas
    1 Rabbit &
    1 Grey Squirrell.
I hope they will all arrive safely, with or before this letter. And I will forward now as rapidly the collected material, as I am able to procure boxes; which is a rather difficult matter here.
I had to pay fright on box Nᵒ 9 $1ᵒᵒ and on Nᵒ 10 $5⁶ᵒ in all 6⁶ᵒ, which makes in half 3³ᵒ, please to credit me with.
Your letter of Jan 1ˢᵗ came to hand at the time, together with with the Receipt blank, which I return enclosed, signed for $20ᵒᵒ.
I send also continuation of my bird catalogue up to 131——besides these species I have only two

more which I can identify, viz. *Hirundo bicolor,*[1] &
Querquedula Cyanoptera,[2] they are here quite common both. The others (I have already 151 species) I
cannot find out at all. So I rather look for your Report, before noticing them. Of course you can use
all the materials I furnish you in your forthcoming
Report. I agreed to it already in my former letters.

I informed you in my last on the great calamity in
regard to gun, I have none whatever at present.
Now again an another bad look——Major Blake
came in & assumed the command of the Post, issuing at the same time an order, that no enlisted men
is allowed to fire a gun within the limits of the garrison (that means one square mile)——I went to
him, and told them all Cmdg officers apreciated my
object until now and asked him to do the same, and
give me permission to hunt. He said that I could go
once or perhaps (if I behaved myself good (!!!))
twice a month; but he will not suffer that every day
should be fired guns around the post. I hope the
grand major will soon go away again to join his
Regiment in Oregon, and then is all right again. But
should he stay here, of course I had to give up altogether collection, thats clear; although I would be
really sorry, as in the Spring—no doubt—would be
much harvest.[3] I will try what I can, if I should be
bound to abandon hunting, then—to do something
at last—I will gather nests, plants, & coleoptera.

At any rate I will finish here everything until
May, so if you could secure or rather pick out dear
Sir for me a good post (perhaps in N. Mexico or
Utah) I would be very glad to leave this place, but
not until May or June; I liked to pass here about a
year, so as to notice the Migratory & resident birds
quite correctly.

I wrote some time ago to Dr W. A. Hammond, &
communicated with him a favorite plan of mine,
asking him to forward it as far as he can by his influence. I proposed to go out to the Gulf of California, & explore the peninsula as well, as the Sonora

shore, & the gulf islands. I think there is hardly any spot on the N. American continent, which would reward more a caller for trouble, as the Vermillion Sea & environs.[4] That Region forms something like a connecting link between the U. S. & Central American Zoology, & is almost unknown. —— You have some idea now dear Sir, what I could do under independent & favorable circumstances; and you may imagine what amount I could gather there, when properly supported.[5]

If several Scientific Societies, & gentlemen would associate on shares, & procure me a *respectable* outfit, & monthly pocket money, I liked very much to undertake this trip; should you aprove it dear Sir, & should you so sanguine about the results of such undertaking as I am then you could do certainly very much for the realization, & I would request you very warmly to do, what you can. I am very tired of this sort of a chained & humiliating position, in which I am at present, where nobody apreciates my objects, & everybody pushes obstacles in my way.

If this Plan should succeed, I wanted to get then my discharge from service sometime this summer or fall, to go Washington, overhaul there my collection, & start then next winter for Guaymas or La Paz, to commence operations a new (???)

Should however the Plan fail, then please change my Post, as advantageously as possible, I think Southern USa Territory, or F[t] Tucon[6] Defiance[7] or F[t] Union[8] would be tolerable good, provided they can be obtained.

————

Amongst my late collection is a Bufo, of enormous size. I sent some to the Philadelphia Academy from Kansas, & D[r] Hallowell remarked in his paper on them, that they were the largest (Bufo Americana) he ever saw.[9] Now I tell you, the present specimen is at least twice as large as that from Kansas, although I dont know to what species it belongs.

Yesterday I secured the long looked for Kangaroo Rat, and as it does very much differ in color & size from either Dipodomys Ordii & Philippi, I append herewith the dimensions.

Nº 1761.

From nose to occiput	1.85
" " " eye	90.
" " " ears	1.75
" " " base of tail	5.
Tail to end of vertebrae	7.60.
" " tip of hair	9.40
Length of side hairs of tail (near the end)	60.
Hight of ears	85.
Breadt of ears	80.
Fore arm	1.25
Midle claw	22
Hind feet	1.85
Longest whyskers	2.75
Length of hairs on hind toes	30.
Weight in ounces	2¼

Specimen female. ——

In answer to your question, I state I do not know exactly, whether I have to pay for any parcels from San Francisco to Los Angeles; but they charge me exorbitantly from the last place to the Fort. You may have an idea of, if I tell you that I paid for the package containing Cassins birds $2,ᴼᴼ not weighing more than 6 pounds. —— As the express from Los Angeles to the fort stands about in the same relation as for instance the Atlantic & Pacific Steam Navigation Co's, viz: the same under different names; I think they charge me only for one, but at the same time are paid both. Well—I dont care much about such trifles, if they only forward punctually everything, as I do not receive so very much through their hands.

Hoping, that you ere this already dispatched one or the other gun, I am dear Sir

Yours truly
XdeVésey

P.S.
Please send me by returning mail 1 or two sheets of parchment, if you cut it up in small stripes, you can easily menage it by mail.

The tin cans you sent me, are rusty & worn out pieces, leaking all completely, except one small which contained the arsenic; but I have now the copper cans, and will be able to proceed with.

There is only the California lion, the porcupine, & flying Squirrell of the mammals, positively known as existing hereabout; which I cannot get; I hope however to get them yet.[10] Of the resident birds are missing yet two only, the Roadrunner & the large vulture; although I confidently hope to get about 40–50 species more this Spring, of straglers, & wandering birds.

Vésey

---

1. Now *Tachycineta bicolor,* Tree Swallow.

2. Now *Anas cyanoptera,* Cinnamon Teal USNM #59932, 59933.

3. Baird, March 31, 1858:
> I hope by this time you have received the gun and that any restrictions not absolutely required by the interests of the service may be removed. My father, Gen. Churchill, knows Major Blake very well and will write requesting him to give you all possible [aid]. Of course no mention will be made of his not having done so before.

4. "Vermillion Sea" was a name given to the Gulf of California during a voyage of Francisco de Ulloa in 1539, for its reddish cast in winter when "blooms" of dinoflagellates occurred.

5. Baird, March 31, 1858:
> I like much your idea of the California Gulf Exploration. It would be the grandest thing in [?] natural history results of the day. The pecuniary difficulty is a question to be solved, but I will broach it to Mr. Cassin and others. Have you any idea of the cost. The outfit with what you already have would not amount to much: $100 would cover this. But, what amount of ready money would you need?

6. Fort Tucson was established first as the Presidio of San Agustinde in 1776, and Mexican troops were garrisoned there until 1856 when it was occupied by the First Dragoons, then by Confederate troops in 1862, and by 1870 the name was changed to Fort Lowell.

7. Fort Defiance was established in 1851, the first Army fort in Arizona, on the eastern border near Gallup, New Mexico.

8. Fort Union, also established in 1851 to protect against Apaches and Utes and to be a supply depot, was one of the most important forts in the West, lying as it did on the Santa Fe Trail; it was intended to replace the "sink of vice and extravagance" that was Santa Fe. It was abandoned in 1891.

9. Hallowell (1856, p. 251) notes:

> There are in the collection of Dr. Hammond, two very large toads, larger than any specimens of Bufo americanus that I have seen. They measure 3 inches 11 lines in length, (from snout to vent,) the dimensions of the Bufo americanus . . . being but 2½ inches.

10. Baird, March 31, 1858:

> I hope you will get the flying squirrels as I have never any from California.

N⁰ 21.

Ft Tejon, Cala.
March 1st 1858.

My dear Sir/

I am in possession of your letters dated January 10 & 17th; the gun you kindly forwarded came to hand also last week. I intended to try it at once, & went out. But as soon as I tried the 1st shot, came the Sergeant of the Guard, and ordered me home, intimating at the same time, if I try to fire a shot more, he has to put me in the Guardhouse by order of Major Blake. —— I was not out since then, and it is evident I cannot hunt anymore as long, as the Major rules over us with his arbitrary—Turkish Pasha like—power, & arbitrary will.

I am turning round, & upsetting every Rock & log, & dead tree now—in lieu of hunt[1]; and secured already several thausend insects, & an abundance of Salamanders, the last seem to belong to 3 different species. One (the largest) is 8 inches long, shining black, with 13 small bright yellow spots on the back. I may be mistaken, but I think it is the same species, I secured in great numbers in Kansas for the Pha Academy.[2] —— The second species is smaller, very slender, & of a uniform light brown color. —— The third is very small (about 4 inches) very thin, & of a dark brown, or rather sooty black color.[3] ——

I am extremely sorry to be forced to stop hunting, particularly as I advanced so far, & the Spring is already before our doors. I have however some slight hopes, that the Major will be ordered way to Oregon, then is all right again. But if he should not, you may consider the hunting, as closed; I can not expose myself of course to the ruffianism of his satellites.

As to regard to large animals, I am exactly of your opinion. Although I procure everything myself, still having no animal to my command, the bringing in of large specimens costs me always cash. I have to hire generally a mule to bring it home. The fetching in of the Mountain sheeps for instance cost me 10 dollars, & I know very well that such expense goes entirely & solely of my pocket, therefore I never did even mention *such* expenses to you & never shall. Besides this circumstance there is another difficulty not less, the entire absence of large boxes for packing. I had my whole room now filled from bottom to roof with skins, & other large paraphernalia of sport, and to make some room for the Spring specimens, I caused the construction of a *very large* box, which will hold all the very large skins, & which I dispatch to you next week. The box costs 4 dollars, but as it will contain a large amount of large animals & other objects, the expense is I think still reasonable. —— I stop now entirely the collection of large specimens, still I think I did a good service to science in general, & to the Smithsonian in particular, by collecting such an extensive series of *blacktail deers.*

It is a very curious circumstance I never heard of any Prairie dogs existing west of the Rocky Mts; & still hereby are hundreds of them on the Kern river lake plains. They are considerably smaller, as the eastern Species, but in form & habits, even color perfectly similar & they live exactly with owls in company, as they eastern relatives.[4] Have you any account of this animal?

D[r] TenBroeck has returned again, but he never mentions his promise in regard to Kern river; I think he promised me only, that I shall be more willing to dress otters & grizzlys for him, as I was fool enough to do such "job" for him *in infinitum*; hoping he mayt to something for us.

What D[r] Hammond said about my Fort Riley effects? if they are not in Washington yet; you would oblige me much sir by writing in the matter to D[r] Coolidge the present Med. Off. in F[t] Riley. I think he would push on M[r] Harling, & cause the speedy forwarding of my effects. —— From Iowa I received a letter informing me, that on account of the Missouri river being frozen in (!!!) they cannot send my things before Spring, although they are packed up since October. Now there is a good chance for my specimens to spoil altogether in the damp boxes for a whole winter.

I had in general so many bad looks, that an other temper could be easily made perfectly crazy by; it is my fortune to possess a first rate nonchalance disposition, which brings everything to my consideration in the shade of a Charivari!

I had considerable difficulty in drying skins, as it rained for weeks in torrents, however I save everything, & at present we live in regular summer already, the thermometer averaging 65° last month, & the atmosphere as dry as possible.

Where is that college, D[r] Hammond wants to go?[5] I am since nearly two months without direct news from him, and liked very much to write him, should he go without informing me.

Hoping you received ere now the two boxes (N° 9 & 10) I sent you some time ago; the first containing 135 birds & the Register—but the other Skins of Mammals & birds.

I remain dear Sir

Your very truly
deVésey

---

1. In "upsetting every Rock & log," Xántus found a centipede that turned out to be a new species named *Bothropolys xanti.*

2. Although Xántus overestimates the size, this is probably *Ensatina eschscholtzi croceater,* Yellow-blotched Salamander. See Denburgh (1916).

3. Xántus' description of both is insufficient for identification, but "small" and "slender" suggest *Batrachoseps attenuatus,* California Slender Salamander, a variably colored species common in California.

4. Doubtless *Citellus beecheyi* which burrows in the ground, often lives in colonies, and sits on its haunches like the prairie dog with which Xántus was familiar in Kansas, living with *Athene cunicularia,* Burrowing Owl.

5. University of Maryland. Hammond resigned his commission to teach there in 1860; see June 29, 1857, note 1.

N[o]**XXII.**
F[t] Tejon, Cala
March 18th 1858.

My dear Sir/

I received the other day your letter of Jan. 31th & was much gratified to learn that some of the boxes are at last in New York city. I hope to hear this mail *at some length* of that collection, and indeed I am much in excitement to hear your decision on the quality.

I was much mortified to hear, that you sent me *several* volumes of exploration, as I received only one —— —— Sitgreaves. If you could procure both Reports of Emory, & Simpsons, I would be under many obligations, as I liked to translate them condensed for the Hungarian Geographical Society, which has already published in magnificent editions my condensed translations of Stainsbury & Marcy.

Since my last my procedings were a mere nothing, for the reasons already communicated in my last letters. I do however in a stolenwise whatever I can in the time of insects, trapping etc, & some time even by gunning, although my whole this months harvest does not equall a weeks gathering of former times.

I enclose herewith a sketch of a woodpecker,[1] very similar, but still distinct—no doubt to the *Picus formicivor.* The sketch is very faithful, & is made in a similar position to that of Cassins *Picus formiciv,* to show more distinctly the difference between both Species.

Last week I forwarded per Wells Fargo & Co a box again, numbered N⁰ 11 & containing as follows
____

    1 black tail deer
    2 mountain sheep
    50 bird skins (mostly large ones)
    11 skulls (large)
Paid fright to Los Angeles $5⁰⁰ plase to credit me $2⁵⁰.

_____

It seems there is to be built a Fort at or near San Bernadino,[2] there are already four companies at that place, & a great number of mechanics engaged in putting up buildings etc.

Dᴿ TenBroeck is here again, but as he got all the otter, fox, & grizzly Skins dressed by me, what he wanted; he never speaks now about granting me

some kind of an excursion, or even privilege to
hunt round the garrison. He is one of the most ava-
ricious, most selfish, & most chameleon like
"gentlemen" I ever encountered in the Medical
Dept. of our Army.
 I shant ask him for anything more in my life,
thats true. But he shant ask me again for anything
else!
 I am dear Sir

very truly yours
LVésey

---

1. No drawing of this ilk exists with the letter or in the General Register.

2. San Bernardino was established by Mormons in 1851 and held a strategic position on the trade route between Los Angeles and Salt Lake City, but seems never to have had a fort there. There were various volunteer military organizations there in 1854–58 and at least one—the "San Bernardino Light Dragoons"—disbanded in 1858 because they had "no arms, equipments or military stores"; in 1861 Major Carleton urged the formation of a *posse comitatus* to deal with desperadoes, hardly necessary were there a fort there; see Scammell (1950, pp. 242–43).

N⁰23.

Fᵗ Tejon, Cala
April 2ᵈ 1858.

Dear Sir/
 I dispatched to Los Angeles yesterday again a
box, numbered N⁰ 12, and containing:
 19 large Skulls (grizzlies, deers, elks, etc etc)
 7 deer skins of different kinds, &
 2 Bighorn, 1 old male, & 1 young.
 I cannot tell you the amount of freight, until the
bill sent in.

We are since over a month without eastern mail, although at present are semi weekly boats running between S. Fransc. & San Pedro. We dont know the reason of this double failure of mails, but of course are in much excitement; more so myself, as the last epistle from you is dated Jan. 31 at the time, you were not yet in possession of my instalment.

I hope ere this you received the Register & likewise the boxes following the 8 first ones. I send next week small mammals, & some reptiles, as Salamanders,[1] frogs etc etc

We have since a couple weeks very unfavorable weather, it rains in torrents some time for days, or blows a north western that a fellow cannot stand! Nothwithstanding there is everything green around, & the birds commenced already nesting.

The Buteo Swainsonii[2] nests here also in considerable numbers, I procured already eggs. I do not think Dr Brewer described *this* eggs as mine differ from his entirely. Besides they lay from 2–3 eggs, not more. I even found a nest containing *only one*, which had already a large living bird in (embryo). The color is entirely white, rounded on both ends alike, & larger as any Domestic fowls egg.

Hoping to hear soon of you
I am dear Sir

very truly yours
LVésey

---

1. E. D. Cope (1867, pp. 209–11) lists two new species, both single specimens from California of *Pelthodon intermedius* Baird, USNM #4732, and *P. croceater,* from "J. Xantus" at Fort Tejon.

John Van Denburgh (1916, pp. 219–21) questions the provenance, noting that *Plethodon intermedius* has not been found since in California although it is common to the north; in investigating, he found that there had been a mixup at the National Museum, with two collections given identical numbers, and so judged the locality of Fort Tejon as "exceed-ingly dubious." *P. croceater* was also a single specimen, USNM #4701, also confused and subsequently lost and without confirmation.

2. Properly, *B. swainsoni,* Swainson's Hawk.

No**24.**

Fort Tejon, Cala.
April 15th

Dear Sir!

At last the mail of last week brought your letters of Febr. 14th Febr 28, & March 2d, together with several sundry enclosures.

I am glad that the boxes arrived in good order & properly. As to the wild cats & badger I am entirely lost as to the cause of their spoiling. When I packed up those specimens, they were all in excellent condition, & quite flexible. They were all prepared strictly with the Smithsonian Recipe. viz: ⅔ Alum, ⅓ Saltpeter, and with the article purchased by Mr Forbes at my arrival in San Francisco. I am very much afraid now, that several of deers etc will go also, as they were all prepared with the same material; excepting the few lost ones; which were preserved by a new supply purchased by me in Los Angeles. It is evident now, that one or other of the articles contained some heterogeneous stuff which caused the decomposition. I subjected the preservative to a Chemical analysis, but could find no traces of any corrosive substance, perhaps on act of my imperfect apparatus so such analysis, or taste.—— I am decidedly of the opinion, that arsenic is the best preservative after all, & when Arsenic can be bought cheap, ought to be used always in preference to everything else.[1]

As to the paucity of new Species amongst my birds, I am not much disappointed; I must really

confess that I never expected *many*, although I
hoped there will be at least 3 or four! —— ——
Fort Tejon is in a very high altitude, it is over 5000
feet above the Pacific, and accordingly the climate
very temperate. Besides there are no Springs, of *good*
water, all the few rivulets & springs hereabout are
extremely impregnated with alkaline, which no
doubt drives away many birds.[2] As far as I know at
present the topography of Southern California, I believe the San Fernando Mission, the environs of the
San Gabriel river, and the vicinity of San Bernadino
are the very best places for Ornythological researches. They are almost level with the Ocean, the
climate quite tropical, the streams very excellent &
well wooded; which advantages induce good many
Mexican birds no doubt, to visit those places occasionally. I would advise you therefore, that the earliest moment an opportunity presents itself, you
may recommend particularly those places to collectors hereabout.

As to your views, expressed at length in your of
Febr. 28, in regard to my collections, I fully agree,
and heartily endorse them. It will be always my sincerest desire to deserve your kind & affectionate
feelings towards me. And so, my dear Sir in regard
to introducing in your Reports my Specimens, descriptions of any new Species to secure priority, etc
etc I give you entirely a *chart blanch*, you shall act as
you please, being fully convinced that you will always act, as "if our positions were just reversed" —
this is enough for me.[3]

As I have a very great number of insects *again* on
hand, you will do best if you give the Coleoptera for
inspection to LeConte, and the Diptera or any of the
Rest to Ostensacken, nobody can make more real
use of them as those gentlemen. In regard to the
nests certainly their *only* destination was & is, to be
used in Dr. Brewers work. You particularly requested me to collect nests & eggs for his forthcoming work, and I did so *solely* for this purpose. I will

be much gratified, if I can help him in some way
another with my contributions; & expect only a
credit for my exertions, nothing else.

As to the eggs of the Cathartes Californ. I have
much doubt, whether I will be able to procure some
or not; but I will try anyhow.[4] Preparatory to such
enterprise, I carefully read over Dr Brewers article
on the subject and then subjected all the Indians &
hunters (separately) to a strict examination. I am
very happy to announce, that their information on
the subject was *uniform* in every respect; without
exception whatever; and so the nidification of this
vulture can be described as follows:
They build their nests invariably on large pine trees,
in wild mountain gulches; but entirely regardless of
hight, as they build some time at the very top of the
tree, sometime at the midle branches, & very often
on the first branches, only ten or 12 feet from the
ground. They commence the building in March,
and about midle of May are full grown the youngs.
However if they are not disturbed, they will incu-
bate for several years in the same nests, taking very
little trouble to repair the damages made by
weather. The Nest is always rudely constructed of
dry twigs & branches of trees, with some grass inside, which however is trown in without any artisti-
cal skill, so famous by other birds. The nest is of immense size, sometimes 12 or 15 feet in diameter;
and all the hunters concur, that some of them are so
large that a single one would fill a whole wagon to
carry off. They lay 2, sometimes 3 eggs; but very seldom bring out more then 2, sometimes only one.
The egg is rather larger as a common goose egg;
white, with some pale reddish clouds, or hues. The
young bird even when full grown is entirely grey;
but they do not leave the nest, unless turn out, even
when full grown & able to fly. Their parents feed
them in nest as late as July & August sometimes.
One of the hunters tells me the following story: He
knew a nest with young ones, and when observed

that they are full grown, intended to catch them. The nest was not very high, on a projecting branch, arched by several other branches above. He could not go into the nest, but had to scale the branch above, and from there he jumped—straight down into the nest. The young ones (two in number) alarmed at the appearance of the strange guest, flew out, and soon lighted again on the ground in a sage thicket. He descended, and went after them, but at his aproach they flew up again, & joined by their parents, they sailed the whole day above the place. —— The next day he saw them again in the nest, fed by their mother. He soon scaled the tree, and this time captured them both. —— The parents did not attempt to defend their youngs, although they were constantly in sight, hovering above.

In regard to your proposal to make some Report on my Collection to the Surg. Genl or War Dept, I leave to you entirely to act, as you think proper. I will tell you however that any recommendation from Genl Lawson[5] to Dr TenBroeck, or from the War Dept to the Comdg off here, would be of a very litle consequence, as such *recommendation* is generally stiled: "give him all facilities, and allow him collect, provided it not interfere with his Duty." —— You can imagine yourself how differently can interpretated such *recommendation*; a substancial— something like order however would do much good thats true, principally if the quartermaster would be instructed to transport my boxes on governement wagoons to Los Angeles. Very often go Govmt wagoons to Los Angeles to carry down or up officers baggage, and they are always half or less loaded. I asked once Lt Magruder[6] the Quartermaster to send down in such wagoon a box; but he refused to do it. He is even in bed temper, when Forbes sends packages for me to his care, he told once "g__ d__ I am not your agent, procure somebody else, or I send back your traps."

As to my rivalls hereabout—I am certainly not much afraid of Dr Hammond[7] of San Diego, particularly in birds I am sure he will never attempt to run competition with me. Mr. Cassidy[8] I dont know who he is. Möllhausen may tumble over good specimens, but I cannot prevent it if he does so. The only thing is Mr Bridges,[9] who causes me some fear, as he is fully competent collector & threatens my own ground with his operations. He issued a formal Proclamation in several Southern Papers, & offers high prices for Specimens, some San Francisco Papers even wrote a leading requesting people to gather up *curiosities* for Mr Bridges, and offering to receive them from their subscribers,—and acknowledge if any sent in.

As to my memoranda, I would be sorry indeed if you should retain them for my use only, provided they can be of some interest in your Report. I have here in my possession over 200 folio sheet notices, gathered here, and if I shall write some Memoir some future time on this collection, I can do very well without those few.

If you cannot make up dear Sir the proposed *Gulf of Cala exploration* (by the by Dr Hammond & Le-Conte give me very discouraging prospects) then leave me here as the present Post altogether. It is not worth while to change for a short time my Post again; as—having no hopes whatever in the U. S.—I am fully determined to gather up all my forces, and emigrate to Bolivia or perhaps Ecuador the next year; I intend to setle there permanently, and prosecute my collections as far as my circumstances will allow.

If you can sell some birds, I will be glad if you do it, but you shall dispose only of specimens, which are *decidedly numerous*; as Species only represented by a few individuals, I would prefer rather do give away, as to sell, at my Return.

———

I send you list of my further birds, they are all correctly named after Audubon, with the exception of the 2 Hawks, 1 Sparrow, & 1 Warbler, which I could not identify. N⁰ 153 I named *Ibis farinellus*,[10] although it does not agree in the least with Audubons description. My specimen has light blue bill, the legs & feet purple, & the wing gold green, or grass green with golden reflections. The measurements differ also very materially, viz

my specimen —— 22.39.18.
Audubons description   25.42.11¼   Males

Of Water fowls I collected also a great variety, as you will perceive, & the series of owls also considerably extended. I may mention that the *Fuligula ferina*[11] or redhead is here quite common the whole spring. Audubon says this species was never noticed west of the Mississippi (?). ——

In my next box I will send you specimens of each species, not yet sent in; and you will oblige me by publishing again in the Proceedings an *additional* list of my birds.

Do you know Dr Nentwich?[12] he was some time ago travelling in the U.S., and published this winter (he is a Hungarian)—in Pest his travels in 7 large volumes, I mention this, because he devotes nearly ½ a volume to the description of the Smithsonian Institute, & several pages to your own person.—My Kansas letters are also just now published in Pest and make considerable noise.[13] My next work will be already under press, "the history of the Mormons (!!!)"[14]—you can see now, how many operations engage my attention. The last named work however I trust will be profitable as there is great desire *just now*, to know something of the pass of the Mormons, particularly in Eastern Europe, where they seem to grown out suddenly from the ground, like musheroom. Nobody knows anything there yet about Mormonism, & therefore already is announced a Serbian & Wallachian translation of my work, to appear simultaneously with the original Hungarian.

Very truly yours
LVésey

P. S.

I was much surprised, that I could not identify the Mocking bird, & the Pyranga ludoviciana,[15] although I collected hundreds of both some years ago in Louisiana, & had known both their names! My friend Ulke[16]—whom you know I presume— is one of my most humorous & witty correspondents, & who gives me much pleasure with his epistles. He announced lately the arrival of our friend LeConte as follows " Dr. LeConte arrived safely of his long protracted explorations, and as we all expected, he brought home an immense collection — — Spanish Cigars!" etc etc.

---

1. Baird, November 2, 1857, recommended "the following receipt an excellent substitute:

> 8 ounces salt
> 2 grams corrosive sublimate
> 20 grams arsenic
> 1 quart biling water
>
> I am told that it really preserves specimens in excellent condition, specimen after specimen in it for some weeks should be transferred as fresh.

2. Altitude of Fort Tejon is around 3,300 feet.

3. See November 16, 1857, note 1.

4. Xántus did not get the hoped-for condor eggs.

5. Thomas Lawson (d. 1861) became Surgeon General of the U. S. Army in 1836, and as such made yearly reports to the Congress from 1839 until 1857. In his last report (Lawson 1857, p. 263) he informed Secretary of War Jefferson Davis:

> The duty of taking meteorological observations at the various military posts is rigidly enforced; and the medical officers are required

also to make, as far as practicable, contributions to all the branches of natural science.

6. William Macgruder (1825–63) was a West Point graduate stationed at Ft. Tejon 1856–58; he joined the Confederate Army and was killed at Gettysburg. At Fort Tejon he shared quarters with Major Blake and Lt. Ogle.

7. Dr. George Hammond (1831–63) was Assistant Surgeon, U. S. Army, in 1856, one of the many medical men who collected for Baird.

8. Andrew Cassidy (n.d.) worked for the Coast Survey at San Diego, collected for Baird and was cited by him in *Report to the Regents,* 1857 and 1859.

9. Thomas Bridges (1807–65) was an English botanical collector who lived in San Francisco from 1856 until 1865.

10. *Plegadis farinellus,* Glossy Ibis; in the West, *P. Chihi,* White-faced Ibis.

11. Now *Aythya americana,* Redhead.

12. Karoly Nendtvich was a fellow Hungarian who traveled in the United States and published *Amerikai utazasom* (Pest, 1858).

13. Xántus János levelei Éjszakamerikabol, translated and edited by Schoenman and Schoenman (1975) as *Letters from America,* as well as Schoenman and Schoenman (1976), *Travels in Southern Parts of California,* a translation of Xántus' (1860) *Utazas Kalifornia deli reszeiben.*

14. Xántus' "History of the Mormons," according to Madden (1949a, pp. 232–33), was based on Stansbury's *Explorations* and not an original work; it was serialized in seven issues of *Magyar sajitó* in Pest, 1858, but not translated elsewhere.

15. Now *Piranga,* Western Tanager; does not occur in Louisiana as Xántus implies.

16. Heinrich Ulke (1821–1910), born in Prussia, migrated to the United States in 1845 where he became associated with the Smithsonian and, as an entomologist, specialized in Coleoptera; his sizable beetle collection is at the Carnegie Museum, Pittsburg. As an accomplished portrait painter, he maintained a studio in Washington and was known as "The Painter of Presidents."

No 25.

Dear Sir.

Your letters of March 16 & 18 reached me last mail, together with bills, draft etc etc, and I hasten to return to you Receipt duly signed ($71.16) the other Receipt I sent in my letter of Febr 18th No 20. ($20.20) making in all $91.36.

I cannot make out whether you included in this account the expenses, specified in my letter No 18 of January 20th ? —— —— Since that time, the expenses were as follows:

fright of box No 9 to Los Angeles $1.00 half						=	50.
"	"	"	" 10 "	"	"	$560 "	3.30
"	"	"	" 11 "	"	"	$500 "	2.50
"	"	"	" 12 "	"	"	$1250 "	6.25
making of box No 12, $400,			"		400	"	2.00
fright of box No 13 — — —					200	"	1.00
"	"	"	" 14 — — —		100	"	.50
5# cotton batting					250	"	1.25
Total							
					$3360		half:17.30

I send you last week again two boxes, No 13 & 14, containing as follows:

No 13 1 Elk, 1 fox, & 43 large birds.

No 14 85 small birds, 4 small mammals in alcohol, & 4 small mammals skins, 16 small skulls, 1 Egg of Buteo Swainsonii, & 1 can alcoholic specimens (Salamanders, frogs, bats etc etc)

Those two boxes contain *all my* specimens of *all* my birds not sent until now; I secured since that the *American Avocet*,[1] & the *red shouldered blackbird*,[2] which please to put on the list likewise, if you publish an appendix or second series of my birds.

It will be seen, that I sent you in already 1083 bird skins, & 107 skins of mammals—alone. I have on hand about 700 more birds, & about 25 mammals.

The small blue owl,[3] which you call a *very young* specimen, mayt be such. But I can assure, that this species never grows larger. They were many around the buildings the whole winter, all the same size & same color.

You forgot of your list the *Coccoborus melanocephalus*,[4] although I sent in several fine specimens of all sexes & ages (?) You may have overlooked those, I would ask therefore to insert them in their sistematical place.

A citizen was here lately from San Diego, & Lt Churchill sent very kind words from him to me. I was very glad, as this is the only instance (excepting Drs Coolidge & Hammond, & Colonel Cooke) that an officer of the Army condescended so far, as to remember on me. Mr Churchill made certainly a very good impression on me, not only by this courteous remembrance, but in being always very kind & friendly to me, during the whole Ocean voyage as well, as in San Francisco; he even offered me— without being asked for—his purse! —— I hear he is at present commanding officer of San Diego.

Dr TenBroeck expects to go away to New Mexico this month, I wish him good journey; whoever comes here in his place, will do certainly more to advance my collections, as he did.

The troops from San Bernadino left all, for Salt lake; it seems that some of the Anti Mormon operations will be conducted from this side.[5]

Very truly yours
L Vésey

---

1. *Recurvirostra americana.*

2. *Agelaius phoeniceus,* Red-winged Blackbird USNM #12997.

3. Most likely Xántus refers to *Otus asio,* Screech Owl.

4. *Pheucticus melanocephalus,* Black-headed Grosbeak.

5. Among other incidents, two—the Mormon seizure of Fort Bridger in the winter of 1853–54 and the granting of a mail route to a Mormon rather than the incumbent Gentile—led to Colonel Albert Sidney Johnston marching a *posse comitatus* through the empty streets of Salt Lake City on June 26, 1858. Johnston left the city on the 29th, the inhabitants returned, the incident was closed, an arrangement having been made by a friend of both the Mormons and Buchanan without consulting Johnston.

N°26.

Fᵗ Tejon Cala
May 15ᵗʰ 1858.

My dear Sir/
Your letter of March 31ˢᵗ came duly to hand, & I am glad to hear that the collection continues to arrive there in good order & regularly. I dispatched yesterday again a box, (N° 15) containing 150 birds, several amongst them new to the collection. Likewise I enclosed Register from 1000 to 1500.
—— Next week I send you an assortment of nests & eggs, of which I was successful of collecting good many. Although there are far less species as I anticipate, the collection is those withstanding—I suppose—very interesting, & contains no doubt novelties. Besides the nests I send you last year, I collected amongst others nests & eggs of

Chrysomitris psaltria[1]   Icterus Bullocki[11]
Zonothrichia leucophrys   Cyanocitta Californica[12]
Zonothrichia coronata[2]   Pipilo arcticus
Zonotrichia fallax[3]   Trochylus Alexandri[13]
Passerella shistacea[4]   Ptiliogonys nitens
Tyrannula cinerescens[5]   & several others
Tyrannula flaviventris[6]
Vireo Huttoni[7]
Buteo elegans[8]

Buteo calurus (?)⁹

Buteo ＿＿＿ ⁺⁾¹⁰

The nest of the Philogonys nitens is a truly wonder-
ful one, it is like the finest wire sieve, worked transparent with horse hair & mergual [*sic*] fibres. ——

As to the Lagopus,¹⁴ I am unable to say, whether
any of them are found here, but there are two species of grouse (commonly so called) the one ash
grey, the other brown, very similar to the Prairie
Hen. —— It is easily proposed "to look out sharply
on the Tejon Peak" but—mighty hard to carry it
out. Said peak is nearly 4000 feet above the fort,
and nearly as steep as the roof of a dutch Church. It
requires full ½ days goatlike climbing to get up
there, and the ground being loose gravel & rock, a
fellow sometimes tumbles down with the stuff several yards. The mountain has several gulches, over-
grown with tall pines (here are the birds) but the
sides of these gulches are almost perpendicular
granites. —— As soon as Dʳ TenBroeck goes however, I will try to make these another expedition, if
for nothing else to get the grouse (should they not
be Pharmigans)

In regard to the proposed gulf of Cala expedition;
I think with proper menagement could be carried
out. If for instance the Academy of Philadelphia, the
New York, Boston, Charleston, St. Louis, & N. Orleans Institutions, in company with the Smithsonian would agree, each of them had to expend only a
triffle sum, & at the end of the expedition divide the
collection amongst themselves according their share
of expenses. To the present outfit I would require
only plenty of ammunition, about 25 lb of Cotton,
& barrel alcohol (2   10 Gallon kegs, & 4   5 galls
kegs) & Arsenic. The minor apparatus I would
leave to your arrangement. I wanted however as

⁺⁾The lead blue one, I send you in this box (Nᴼ 15), the
female is dark brown.

something *sine qua non*, a good skiff, which would sail *anywhere* in the Gulf. Such a skiff I had when at the Bahamas, I bought her in N. Orleans for 60 dollars, & at the end of my expedition sold it in Key West for $85. When the collector has to hire his boat, for every trip to islands, it costs in 3 months more the the [*sic*] price of a new skiff. To buy a skiff is beyond question the most economical, because at the end can be sold.

To conduct such an enterprise to good success, it is the *principal thing* to encourage the *boys* everywhere to hunt for reptiles etc. & to induce fishermen & hunters to procure specimens. This expense would be not very much (as I buy any serpent, fish etc in Mexico for 5 cent a piece,) still it would be considerable adding to this the expenses which are almost daily, & never can be foreseen, & adding my board etc can easily made an aproximate estimate of my probable monthly expenses. But it would be unavoidable, to hire a small boy, who would do for me such work, which is undispensable & still retards greatly collecting. Such a boy I suppose I can hire for from 6–8 dollars a month.

The outfit would be not much over $100 (including skiff), as you estimate. And you could sent it out via the Horn, or any other route to Mazatlan or Guaimas care of the U.S. Consul. To the rest, I believe the collection can be carried out with $100 per month.

I would be much pleased if you could carry out this plan dear Sir, and I have very litle doubt that it can be carried; considering that by association of several scientific institutes any of them has to bear only a small expense for the 12 months. I believe even private subscription would cover such expense.

As to the travelling there, this point could be menaged very easily. Mr Forbes could give me in some of their boats passage to Cape St. Lucas or Manzanilla & I could go from any of these places in a schooner to the gulf. I could go even in schooner direct from San Francisco for a very small sum of money.

Yesterday came to me the Major (Blake) and told me, he liked to have some mounted birds, whether I would fix some for him. —— I told him frankly, that whenever is in my power to render any service to him, I am ready to do it with the greatest pleasure; but considering that there was no officer of the Army since I am in the service, who afforded me so litle assistance for the pursuit of my collection as he; I am obliged to decline any such service, unless he gives some privilege for hunting at least. — — In consequence of this bold "pronunciamento" we had together a long dispute, & the final result was that he sent for the Sergeant of the Guard; and told him to turn over his order to every Sergt of Guard, & report to the Officer of the Day likewise *..that the hospital steward has his permission to hunt at any time, and at any place whatsoever even on the Parade."* —— He wanted then at first to *fix* for him a Crow, and a white heron[15] (those are his favorite birds) and I am just now engaged to fill this part of my convention. He wants also a whole family of Spermophylus Beecheyi. —— So I am very glad this obstacle is removed, although very sorry that I could not remove it a couple months before, I missed good many Spring birds no doubt.

Mr Banning the Contractor for the Governement fright from San Pedro to this Post was here last week & visited me.[16] He offered at his leave to transport free of charge all my collections to San Pedro or Los Angeles. I will avail myself of this opportunity as far as I can; but Mr Bannings trains go only every 3 months with the Horses, I cannot depend entirely on this conveyance; because it is against our policy to send many boxes at the time. You would do however well, if you would acknowledge in your annual Report this offer from Mr Phineas Banning, I would show it him then occasionally.

Dr Hammond wrote me a very long & very affectionate letter before he left for Europe. He promised me to see my friends in Hungary, to whom I gave him letters of introduction.

Please send me a package of new labels, of which you sent me lately samples, they are of a much superior paper as the first ones.[17]

Very truly yours
LXántusdeVésey

---

1. Now *Carduelus psaltria*, Lesser Goldfinch.

2. Now *Z. atricapilla coronata*, Golden-crowned Sparrow.

3. Now *Melospiza melodia fallax*, Song Sparrow.

4. Now *Passerella iliaca townsendii*, Fox Sparrow.

5. Now *Myiarchus cinerascens*, Ash-throated Flycatcher.

6. Now *Empidonax difficilis*, Western Flycatcher; Xántus' specimen is one of four type specimens from which the original description was written.

7. Hutton's vireo.

8. Now *B. lineatus*, Red-shouldered Hawk USNM #105729, 10573.

9. Now *B. jamaicensis*, Red-tailed Hawk USNM #10568, 10571.

10. "Lead blue" *Buteo* with dark brown female suggests *Accipeter striatus.*

11. *Icterus bullocki*, Bullock's Oriole, is no longer a valid species but included under *I. galbula*, Northern Oriole.

12. Now *Aphelocoma coerulescens*, Scrub Jay.

13. Now *Archilochus alexandri*, Black-chinned Hummingbird.

14. Ptarmigan.

15. *Casmerodius alba*, Common Egret.

16. Phineas Banning (n.d.) was one of the founders of a stage line between San Pedro and Los Angeles and as such was undoubtedly drumming up business; in December 1857, he was listed as Captain of the muster roll of the Union Guard, one of the several military units organized to keep order in Los Angeles; see Layne (1934). He was an entrepreneur who "enthusiastically" provided services for the Army that invariably turned out to be of considerable benefit to himself; Browne

(1869), a contemporary reporter, described him as "big of heart, big of body, big of enterprise—the life and soul of Los Angeles County."

17. Baird, March 16, 1858:

> I understand you to say that you intend to be referred to as John Xantus de Vesey, and have had the labels so printed for you. Do you prefer to omit the de Vesey?

No**27.**

Fᵗ Tejon, Cala
May 29ᵗʰ 1858.

My dear Sir/

I dispatched yesterday again a box, numbered Nᵒ 16; & containing nests eggs etc according the detailed invoice annexed hereby. You will see, that the box contains 88 nests, with 257 eggs; representing 31 distinct Species. Soon, I send another box, with several others not included in this.

It is in general very hard to form any adequate idea of the troubles connected with oological collection, if somebody is not aquainted with *practically*. I know very well, that accordingly my troubles will be never acknowledged as they should—generally; I hope however that you at least sir will apreciate my efforts in full, particularly if you expose once the said collection *to your view*!

In the small collection of nests, I made last year, there were *two* very important mistakes committed; which I wish you would correct at once as follows ——

1.) There was 1 nest labelled as corresponding with *Icteria auricolis*.[1]

2) And there was another, given as the nest of the *Tyrannula Richardsonii*.[2] Both those nests were given to me by a soldier, and as he could not tell me to what birds they belong, I show him every bird in my collection, and he assured me quite positively

that the 1st belonged to the Icteria Auricolis, and the 2d was labelled. —— I have now several of those nests, and accordingly I discovered at once the blunders, to our great fortune. So the 2d is the nest of the *Vireo Cassinii, formerly Huttonii,*[3] as you will see if you compare with the nests of *this* bird sent in the present box. —— As to the 1st I do not know to what bird it belongs, until I see it personally, it is however not the nest of the *Icteria auricolis,* leave it therefore blank. Every nest in the present collection (box No 16.) is correctly lalabled [*sic*], as every one was taken personally by myself, after identifying the bird most scrupulously. —— There are however some nests, which are labelled only with the No of the corresponding bird, because I did not know the name of the bird. —— Such nests please to compare with the corresponding bird, and fill out accordingly the labell.

I am much inclined to stick firmly to my belief that I sent you in my *first* collection 2 distinct species of *Orioles,* the Bullocki; and an another under the next number. There is of the last, one specimen in the box with these nests, labelled ♂ No 1963,[4] and I wish you would subject it again to careful examination on the following ground ——

She builds her nest *entirely* different from that the the Ict. Bullocki; and has in many respects different habits. I sent you several nests of both birds, and you will convince yourself of the great difference between the architecture of each. Besides, as the I. Bullocki builds her nest invariably *suspen*ded, and whenever practicable on high oak trees, the Icterus No 1983 build her nest invariably on the top of small bushes, firmly secured the bottom into forks, as the following sketch will show it.

You will see by comparing the two nests, that they are constructed of an *entirely* different material, and that the nest of No 1963 is much more elaborately finished, principally inside, as the nest of the I. Bullocki. —— I collected many of both, and in

the fine brown nests of the bushes found *invariably* the pale colored bird (as Nº 1963.), and in the white coarse nest on oak trees, always the I. Bullocki. I say this circumstance, because I thought at first also myself that the nests are only varieties, amongst young & old bird birds, or varieties arising from the different material for construction, the bird has at her command; but I found within an acre 2 or 3 nests of both kind, the I. Bullocki having white nest on oak, and the Icterus Nº 1963 having brown nest on an elder or willow, the first invariably suspended, the last firmly secured between forks. (?)

As to the eggs, it is true I cannot make out any material difference, but if you take 100 eggs of the *Icterus Bullocki* herself, you can not find two amongst such enormous number, which are perfectly alike, even the size of them is entirely different. Some time amongst 5 eggs in one nest, there will be 1 or two flatt ended, 1 or 2 sharp pointed, & 1 or two nearly round, accordingly differing much also in size. The markings of them are no key whatever to go after, they are of 1000 kind in every 1000 eggs! —— —— —— ——

I enclosed likewise in the nest box some of the *Vireos*, to which the nests belong, I suppose they are the same I sent last year (Vireo Cassinii) but may be other species; they seem rather more pale, & smaller (?)

I secured the other day a bird, which I suppose is
the *Nucifraga Columbiana*,[5] although it differs slightly
from Audubons description, particularly in size, my
specimen is a male and measures as follows
13⁴/₁₅.22⁶/₁₂.10.

And just today I shot a *diving duck*,[6] which I never
saw in the U. S. yet, and cannot identify her from
Audubon. The is a male also, with black bill & pale
blue feet. Whole head, neck, & underparts pale buff,
still paler around the legs. The center of the neck
spotted white & black all round, and a black band
on the upper part of the neck about 4 inches long.
Wings & tail entirely black (glossy) the scapulars
deep glossy chestnut and the back mottled with
dirty buff & black, resembling regular scales. A
slight occiptal crest pale chesnut. Iris light blue.

Measurements—20½.36 ½.16.

I met last week in the Creek a Querquedula cyanoptera with seventeen young, not bigger as a
sparrow, which circumstance proves that they nest
here, they are however very rare at present. The *Himantopus nigricolis*[7] & *Ibis farcinellus* nest here likewise.

As a slight acknowledgment on my part for the
volume of his birds, I sent some weeks ago to Mʳ
Cassin an assortment of small birds. Of course I
wanted to send the package paid, and wrote accordingly to Wells Fargo & Co agency at Los Angeles, to send me in the bill. The birds were in a small
candlebox, not measuring over one cubic foot, &
weighing about 4½ lbs, and how much you think
he charged me?—17, say: seventeen dollars! It was
certainly a foolish courtesy on my part, because I
could as well send it to your care in one of my
boxes, for nothing; but now to late to reflect and
suggest as—*factum infectum fieri reguit*! A very plain
proverb!

I am sorry, the gathering of nests cost me the loss
of two species birds, which I can perhaps never get

again. Being loaded with ropes, sticks, & basket—of course—I could not carry with me in addition a— gun, and I met a bird the other day of the size of the *Piplo fusca*,[8] which was entirely blue, the same blue as the underparts of the *Garrulus Stelleri*, having only the scapulars brown, she had a bill like the Carpodaccus, or perhaps stouter yet; I am quite sure of those marks, as the bird was only a couple yards distant from me. I believe she had a crest also, although of this I am not quite sure.[9] The other bird I met the day before yesterday, she was a flycatcher, much larger as the *T. Cooperi*,[10] entirely grey, with a pale yellow or white collar round the neck. She had erectible dark crest.

I never noticed any of those birds before or after, although a Hunter tells me that the former are magnificent songbirds, & quite abundant between San Diego & Fort Yuma (?)

I procured now several Badgers again, although they are all much smaller in size, as the one sent in last year, & which unfortunately spoiled. Some of this days I will descend on the prairie dogs also.

I received duly your letter of April 18th, together with the sheet of parchment, & the Rapacious part of your bird Report. I expect with much excitement the continuation. ——

I am skinning now all the large snakes, & have already a bucketful of them.

One of my large Grizzlys has spoiled entirely I am at a loss to guess even the cause; as the other continues still in an excellent condition.

I cannot imagine, why Harling dont send my effects from Ft Riley, their intrinsic value is more than $250, but they are much more worth for me. I would be much vexed, if they should be lost. I hope however that your letter to Dr Coolidge will have the desired effect, and he will *make him* dispatch at once my effects.

My other things from Iowa are by
    Richard H. Musser Esq[11]
    Editor of the Dem. State gazette
    Brunswick City
       Missouri
if you will undertake the trouble dear Sir, as to
write him to forward to your care at once my effects, you will oblige me much. Mr Musser wrote
me last fall, that the river is frozen, accordingly he
could not send them until spring. I instantly directed him, to forward it in the early spring. He
writes me in his last, he would not risk the forwarding as he *supposes* I am gone also with the rest of the
mankind against the Mormons! and asks me to tell
him, whether I am gone or not (?!) Mr Musser
however is only a simpleton; but else a very good
hearted gentleman, & quite attached to me.
              Very truly & sincerely yours
                      deVésey

      Contents of box N° 16.
1 nest & 4 eggs of Buteo N° 1961.

1	" "	1	" "		Buteo elegans.
1	" "	4	" "		Buteo N° 1253 (B. Calurus?)
1	" "	2	" "		Trochylus Alexandri
1	" "	2	" "	"	Costa[12]
1	" "	2	" "	"	Anna[13]
1	" "	3	" "		Mimus polyglottus[14]
2	" "	6	" "		Icteria auricolis.
2	" "	7	" "		Icterus N° 1963.
12	" "	45	" "		Icterus Bullocki
39	" "	106	" "		Spiza amoena.[15]
1	" "	2	" "		Paserella shistacea.
1	" "	1	" "	"	townsendii.[16]
1	" "	2	" "		Pipilo fusca.
3	" "	13	" "		Tyrannula verticalis[17]
1	" "	1	" "	"	flaviventris.
2	" "	7	" "		Vireo Huttonii, or Cassinii (?)
1	" "	2	" "		Zonothrichia coronata

1   "   "   3   "   "   "   fallax
1   "   "   4   "   "   "   leucophrys.

_____

74. "   217. "

Carried over—
74 nests & 217 eggs
3   "   "   6   "   of Ectopistes Carolinensis[18]
1   "   "   1   "   of Ptiliogonys nitens
2   "   "   8   "   "   Carpodaccus frontalis.[19]
1   "   "   4   "   "   "   lawrencii.[20]
1   "   "   2   "   "   Peucea lincolnii.[21]
2   "   "   4   "   "   Spizella __? __(like N⁰
                           1559.)[22]
1   "   "   4   "   "   Miodioctes Wilsonii[23]
1   "   "   3   "   "   Helinaia colata.[24]
1   "   "   4   "   "   Charadrius vociferus[25]
_____   4 eggs of Corvus corax[26]

_____

88 nests & 257 eggs in all.
14 bird skins
1 skull of a gopher
1 "   "   "   Neotoma Mexicana.
Register up to N⁰ 2000 inclus.

                             JXántus de Vésey

Fort Tejon Cala
May 29th 1858.

_____

1. Now *I. virens*, Yellow-breasted Chat.
2. Now *Contopus sordidulus*, Western Wood-Peewee.
3. Now *V. solitarius cassinii*, Solitary Vireo.
4. No. 1963 does not appear in the General Register.
5. Clark's Nutcracker.

6. *Dendrocygna bicolor,* Fulvous Whistling-Duck. Baird (1858b, p. 771) lists a single specimen, *D. fulva,* USNM #10399, which was from Xántus at Fort Tejon.

7. Now *H. mexicanus,* Black-necked Stilt.

8. Properly *P. fuscus,* Brown Towhee.

9. Probably *Guiraca caerulea,* Blue Grosbeak.

10. Now *Contopus borealis,* Olive-sided Flycatcher.

11. Colonel Richard H. Musser (1829–?), was admitted to the bar in 1854, established and edited the Democrate State Gazette, and Anti-Know Nothing newspaper. See January 14, 1859.

12. Now *Calypte costae,* Costa's Hummingbird.

13. Now *C. anna,* Anna's Hummingbird.

14. Northern Mockingbird.

15. Now *S. americana,* Dickcissel.

16. *Passerella iliaca.*

17. *Tyrannus,* Western Kingbird.

18. Now *Sitta carolinensis aculeata,* White-breasted Nuthatch.

19. Now *C. mexicanus frontalis,* House Finch.

20. *Carduelis lawrencii.*

21. Now *Melospiza lincolnii,* Lincoln's Sparrow.

22. Possibly *Spizella passerina,* Chipping Sparrow.

23. *Wilsonia pusilla,* Wilson's Warbler.

24. Now *Vermivora celata,* Orange-crowned Warbler.

25. Killdeer.

26. Common Raven.

Fᵗ Tejon Cala
June 15ᵗʰ 1858.

My dear Sir/
Your letter of May 2ᵈ came safely to hand, and I heard with pleasure that box N⁰ 11 arrived in good condition.

I informed you in my last, that I forwarded a whole box (N⁰ 16) of nests & eggs; since then I dispatched again a box, numbered N⁰ 17 & containing 14 mammals
   121 birds &
   1 bunch of Herbarium
Amongst the birds there is the red Duck I mentioned in my last letter, & the Nutcracker, also many hummingbirds of all species here around. Amongst the mammals are 2 badgers, I have several more on hand, and soon send you some large ones.

At present I have only 3 birds, not yet sent in, the large white egret, a small black diving duck, & a blackbird (brown & white spotted).

Of nests & eggs, I procured almost every one species nesting here, with the exception of woodpeckers & swallows.

Of snakes I have of course many species not contained in my last years collection as most of them were spoiled — as you know. Lately I captured several specimens of a lizard, which I never noticed yet here. It is about 10–12 inches long, very smooth & splendent of a light yellow color (chamois) with cinober red head & throat.[1] —— Years ago I collected on the West India Islands (Bahamas, a species very much like this, if not the same, but these live on barren sand ground far from any trees, and those I found invariably on old pine trees, generally under the lose bark.

I secured several specimens of a Ratlesnake likewise, which I never have seen before, it is called the black ratlesnake,[2] is found only in high altitudes

around swamps, lined with rocks, it is much inferior in size to any other species, (except the Prairie
Ratlesnake,[3] & in fact is entirely black, with dirty
yellow rings all along the body, very similar disposed to that of the Louisiana Elaps.[4]

I found a nest of Geococcyx Mexicanus[5] with
young birds in, 5 in number. The nest was placed
on an open sand plain, about 20 ackers in extent,
surrounded by chaparral, and was placed in the
hole of an old cotton tree trunk, about 5 feet from
ground, as follows:

The nest was sticking out at large from the hole,
and consisted of several coarse weeds as foundation, lined very carefully with fine roots & cotton
(obtained of some shrub or flower). Next day I went
there again, but their mother left them, the young
birds were dead & perfectly cold.

It seems you named dear Sir my birds as *Vésey*, although I particularly requested you to name as
Xántus; I would be sorry if the former should be the
case, as the birds would be lost for me entirely.

The Wagon road expedition is just here, they established a station with us, & their route will be in
full operation the 16th of next month. They run
from St Louis per Rifle Rock, the Cherokee Country
Southern Comanches to San Antonio. From thence
per El Paso & Fort Yuma[6] to Ft Tejon. From thence

via Fᵗ Miller[7] to Sacramento city. —— We can certainly say as the whole movement *difficile est satyram
non scribere*. When there is already an established
steam mail line, which performs their duty in 20–
22 days from post to post; now this *turtle line is established*, to vex the whole corresponding community, with their stage & mule mail.[8] —— It is only
pity, that they dont take their route a little more
circuitously, if the company had established for
instance a watering station somewhere in upper
canada, and another in Behring Straits. The undertaking of this mail improvements, would be still
greater humbug, as it could be intended for nothing
else!

Very truly yours
LeVésey

---

1. Probably *Xantusia vigilis*, Desert Night Lizard, a new species that lives
in the thatch of Joshua trees; see November 16, 1858, note 5. Grinnell
(1905, p. 12):

Unfortunately Xantus failed to record the dates of capture for most
if not all of his specimens, and also species are included which were
very likely not taken within many miles of the Fort and whose precise locality therefore must always be in doubt. This is true of other
animals than birds; for example, the type of a lizard (*Xantusia vigilis*) is given as "Fort Tejon." This animal is abundant in the tree
yucca belt of the Mojave Desert. It strikes me as extremely probable
that the type specimen really came from there, not nearer than sixteen miles from Fort Tejon, and in an altogether different faunal
area. Furthermore the tree yucca itself has been ascribed to Fort
Tejon, but I am very sure it does not actually occur within sixteen
miles; not so very far on the map, but a long way off, faunally.

John Van Denburgh (1895, pp. 525–27):

The first representatives of *Xantusia vigilis* were found at Fort Tejon,
California, by Mr. John Xantus, who furnished the three specimens
upon which Professor Baird based his original description, pub-
lished in the Proceedings of the Academy of Natural Sciences of
Philadelphia for 1858. Nothing more concerning it appeared until
May, 1893, when Dr. Stejneger recorded two specimens secured by

the Death Valley Expedition in 1891. Nothing has been known about its habits, and this very intersting species has been considered one of the rarest of our reptiles . . . In reality, *X. vigilis* is the most abundant lizard in the territory it has chosen for its home. It seems to be peculiarly dependent upon the presence of tree yuccas. A glance at Dr. Merriams' [*sic*] map shows that these weird plants grow in each of the localities from which the species has been recorded, viz.: Fort Tejon in the Canada de las Uvas, and Herperia, in California, and Pahrump Valley, in Nevada.

Essig (1965, p. 806):

Some animals were also taken here and in the neighboring region, notably the desert tree yucca lizard, *Xantusia vigilis* Baird, which was no doubt collected in the tree yucca belt of the Antelope Valley some fourteen miles from the Fort.

Xántus, November 2, 1858, chagrined about having to collect eggs and nests and not being able to attend to other branches, comments that

there are but few reptiles here and I am amost sure, that my collection contains specimens of every reptile found here within 5 miles round.

Dr. Kenneth S. Norris (personal communication) says that although *Xantusia* is most frequently found under *Yucca brevifolia* logs, it also can be located under *Agave* thatch and other dead logs (even fallen pinyon logs) or other desert habitats that provide crevices where, being extremely thigmotactic, it can find close shelter. There are Joshua trees on south-facing slopes near Fort Tejon, well within a day's walk, as well as other *Xantusia* habitats, and Dr. Norris thinks it not unlikely that it could have been found at Fort Tejon itself.

2. No rattlesnake fits Xántus' description, although *Crotalus scutulatus*, Mojave Rattlesnake, is more likely to be found at high altitude.

3. *Crotalus viridis viridis*, Prairie Rattlesnake, a subspecies of Western Rattlesnake.

4. *Elaphe*, Rat Snakes, none of which match Xántus' description; possibly *Lampropeltis getulus*, Common Kingsnake, NMNH #4285.

5. Now *G. californianus*, Greater Roadrunner, which nests on the open ground; if left unprotected and without shade by the parent, the midday radiation is quickly lethal to the nestlings.

6. Fort Yuma was established in 1850 on the Colorado River, just below the mouth of the Gila River, and in 1851 moved across the river to a site formerly occupied by the Topographical Engineers. Established to protect an immigrant route to California, it later served as a depot for the forts in Arizona because it could be supplied by ships coming up the Colorado River; see Leavitt (1943). It had a longer life than most of the

western forts because of its strategic position but was finally rendered obsolete by the railroad.

7. Fort Miller was established in May 1851 on the south side of the San Joaquin River, about 150 miles above Stockton, in the foothills of the Sierra Nevada, an area now covered by Millerton Lake. It was abandoned in 1858, temporarily reoccupied during the Civil War, and finally closed in 1864. Mansfield (in Frazer 1963, p. 190) reported that Fort Tejon would control the country "south of the Tula River, whilst Fort Miller controls all north of that river."

8. By July 1, 1861, the Overland Mail Route replaced the Pacific Steamship route, in operation since 1848 with an average time in transit of some 30 days. Popular objection to the monopoly of the steamship line and the growing population in the West prodded Congress to establish an overland mail route; for $600,000 John Butterfield contracted to supply twice-a-week service between Fort Defiance in New Mexico and Fort Mohave on the Colorado River, guaranteeing a delivery time of 25 days or less. In 1858 a station for the Butterfield Overland route was established at Fort Tejon, situated across Grapevine Creek from the parade ground (see Cullimore's diagram and U.S. Postmaster General 1860).

No29.

Fort Tejon Cala
July 1st 1858

My dear Sir/
 The day before yesterday I forwarded again a box, numbered 18, and containing

3	nests of	Trochylus	Anna, with	6	eggs	
1	"	"	"	Alexandri		
1	"	"	"	Costa		
2	"	"	Tyrannus	verticalis with	7	eggs
1	"	"	Tyrannula	Richardsonii	" 2	"
1	"	"	Vireo	Cassinii	" 2	"
3	"	"	Mimus	polyglottus	" 6	"
8	"	"	Icterus	Bullocki	" 25	"
3	"	"	Icterus	No 1963	" 9	"
2	"	"	Ectopistes	Carolinensis	" 4	"
1	"	"	Silvicola	aestiva	" 4	"

1	"	"	Helinaia colata	"	3	"
1	"	"	Pipilo fusca	"	4	"
1	"	"	Chrysomitris pinus	"	3	"
1	"	"	Carpodaccus frontalis	"	1	"
1	"	"	Carpodaccus N⁰ 1156.	"	5	′″1

31					81	
Carried over						
31 nests					81	eggs
2 nests of Passerella Shistacea with					3	"
1	"	"	Passerella Townsendii	"	1	"
1	"	"	Tyrannula cineresens	"	2	"
11	"	"	Spiza am	"	18	"

---

46   105

In all 46 nests, with 105 eggs. The box contains besides 15 birds, 14 out of that are Chrysomitris, and a blackbird which I could not make out as to the species. —— ——

Amongst my late ornythological aquisitions is a finch (I believe a Coccoborus) with about as broad a Bill as the head. General color redish-grey; the head & throat ultramarine blue, the abdomen a little tinged with the same blue. There are two bands of a redish yellow color across the wing. Measurements $6^{10}/12.11^{6}/12.5^{2}/12$. The bird is a male one, and very likely adult.[2]

Lately I added to the collection several fine foxes, and a beautiful blackfooted Racoon.[3] I found the other day the remains of a fox, which seems entirely different from any I have seen. It is of a pale yellow color, long & not very bushy tail, & the animal very small. Fortunately there are all the parts belonging to the animal, although the skin dried to the bones.

I tried to get some Prairie dogs, but had this time no success, I fired at several, and killed them undoubtedly, but as they never leave their door, and keep up their barking with their hindquarters on the holes edge, it is extremely difficult to manuver them out. I am quite satisfied, they are not known yet, and will get some anyhow. —— They are precisely similar to those on the West Kansas plains, but much smaller, I think not more than half their size.

Our troops are going all tomorrow, en route for Oregon, where it seems the war whoop commences to reign again. We will have no garrison here at all, except the permanent staff. Some dragoons are ordered here its true from New Mexico, but they cannot be here before the next month or so. Major Blake is here and is the Comdg off until further orders; — Dr TenBroeck has sold already all his effects, and expects every mail his transfer to some other parts of the world. I wish his hopes would be realised the soner the better.

I am much obliged for the Copy of the Congress act, passed on behalf of the *Hungarian* Reserve, & which you kindly forwarded me. I hope my land affairs will be quite settled now at last, as the only impediment of their sale was the uncertain title until now, but this is removed by the act, which grants permission for preemption, or entering. My only anxiety is, that the bill says *„all who continue to inhabit those lands etc"* and this construction mayt be taken literally by my enemies. I hope however that my being in the U. S. Military service, will be enough reason for having been absent from my lands; what you think dear Sir?[4]

Bird Reports I received only the first sheets (Rapacious birds), but nothing since.

> I am very sincerely
> Yrs truly
> LVesey

---

1. *Carpodaccus cassinii,* Cassin's Finch; General Register, CXXVIII:
   The head of the ♂ entirely blood red; each feather of tail margined distinctly with white. — The ♀ has no green tinge at all on the

upperparts, & the secondaries are broadly margined with white. Head streaked with dark brown & white. On the lower parts no tinge of yellow, it is pure white, distinctly streaked with greyish black.

2. Dr. Rea suggests that this is an immature Blue Grosbeak.

3. *Procyon lotor.*

4. See July 15, 1858. This is the beginning of Baird's involvment in Xántus' Iowa land claim; by February 2, 1859, Baird warned that "The Iowa Land situation I fear is in a bad way" and delineated the requirements of the law. Xántus evidently gave up and mentioned it no more after October 8, 1858.

No 30.

F*t* Tejon Cala.
July 15th 1858.

Dear Sir/

By last mail I received punctually your letters of June 2d, also the very fine map of Emory, & bird Report 161 f. f. I am sorry to announce that pages 65–160 are again lost, as I did not receive them; if you could suply me Sir therefore, I would be under many obligations.

I took the bird, which you call *Pipilo oregonus*, always as Pipilo arcticus, as it agreed very well with the description in Audubons Synopsis, are they *all* P. oregonus, the whole lot?

July 17th

I abruptly broke my letter the day before yesterday, and although it was my intention to write at some extent, I must confine myself to few lines as the mail goes out presently.

The 15th inst arrived two Companies of 1st Dragoons from F*t* Buchanan,[1] brought along many sick, & consequently I am very much engaged since on my Duty.

Fᵗ Johns,² Fᵗ Miller, & Fᵗ San Bernadino had been abandoned entirely, & the respective garrisons left on steamers for Oregon to reinforce Col. Steptoes Command.³ From San Bernardino all the Quarter-masters Commissary & Ordnance property has been already transferred to Fᵗ Tejon, & the buildings etc etc sold by auction.——Consequently there is no military now in S. Bernardino, & is not likely that there will be some soon!

Dʳ Herndon,⁴ who had the charge of the Med. Dept in S. Bernardino was here yesterday also, & left this morning for San Pedro en route for Oregon. He is a very nice gentleman, & had known me be-fore [?] Dʳ Hammond, who requested him (Hern-don) to take care of me, if he should meet me in the Dept. Although Dʳ Hammond never mentioned to me such things, I found out that he recommended me to almost everybody in the Pac. Dept, with whom he is only even slightly aquainted. I was shown several of his letters, and he says always „any service rendered to my friend L. Vésey, will be regarded by me as a personal favor" —— —— I am extremely sorry, that I will be never in a position, where I could do some substantial service for Dʳ Hammond, who certainly is one of the noblest hearted gentlemen, whom it was my good fortune to meet, and gain to a friend—in my very darkest days.

Very truly yours
JXántus de Vésey

---

1. Fort Buchanan, along the Santa Cruz River, was one of a cluster of forts developed in 1857 on the Mexican border in southern Arizona. It was poorly situated and unhealthy; it was attacked and burned by Con-federates in 1861.

2. Fort John was one of the names for Fort Laramie, Wyoming, estab-lished as a trading post in 1834 near the junction of the North Platte and Laramie rivers.

3. Major and Bvt. Lt. Col. Edward J. Steptoe (d. 1865) of the 9th Infantry was commended for "gallant and meritorious conduct at Cerro Gordo and Chapultepec" in 1847. By 1858, the Cayuse Indians were well-armed and planning war. Steptoe took to the field "with the intention of chastising them," and instead suffered the disastrous Battle of Tehoto-nim-me on May 17. General Clarke (see December 2, 1858) called in troops from distant posts, including Fort Tejon, re-organized the troops and finally subdued the Indians in September. See Clarke's and Steptoes' correspondence (1959, pp. 343–50).

4. Dr. James C. Herndon (d. 1877) was appointed Assistant Surgeon in the U.S.A., February 1856; a Virginian, he was "dropped" from the roles, November 1861, when he joined the Confederate Army.

N⁰XXXI.

F^t Tejon Cala
Aug 1st 1858.

Dear Sir/
    Yesterday I sent down to Los Angeles per Bannings train one box, numbered 19, & containing:
    "5 galls alcoholic specimens."
there are several specimens amongst those, not yet forwarded before, unless they will prove young ones. There is however 1 land turtle, & 1 fish, the only specimens I noticed hereabout. I could get plenty fish from the Kern river & Tulare lake, but as Williamson¹ & lately Möllhausen sent in abundance from those places, I do not consider worth while to do so. If I could go to the headwaters of the Kern or Mojave rivers, or to the upper Tulare plains, where there are many small rivulets, & waters in pools I have no doubt, that I could get good many new things in the fishing line, but it seems I will be never able to carry out this plan as long as in the service. Should I however get my discharge at the proper time I mayt go there & fish for a fortnight or so.
    My time of service expires the 4th of September 1859; to tell you something about my plans dear

Sir, would be very difficult task on my part; as I must confess you frankly I have no plans whatever, which I could call "settled plans." I am however under the impression, that it would be the best for me to leave our northern Continent for Bolivia, Ecuador or even Chili; where I *think* I could gain some respectable livelihood. —— —— —— As I was educated in a firstclass military Academy, I am a tolerable good topographical draughtsman, speak several languages, & besides play Piano. With such capacities an American could build up his existence if not fortune, but we Hungarians *cannot sell* our capacities. I tried often to turn to my advantage my education—I found many kind friends in the U. S. who assured me always that *„whatever has been unhappy in the events of my past few years, will bring me by their ready aid blessings"* I am sorry to say however, that nobody went yet further as kind promises & assurances, and I succumbed to fate, *as simpathy alone never saved a life yet.*

We Europeans, are not like Americans, what is incident to the life of almost every succesful American, occurs but rarely to Europeans; the American has no idea what exile & expatriation means; he is always & everywhere at home, everybody speaks his language etc, and so the small caprices of fortune develop only his energies, & *he* becomes as a people instead of theoretical dreamer or amateur in sciences, practical *dollarman.* The American gentleman pressed by want adopts *whatever* presents itself at the moment to provide for his necessities & never feels degraded; this principle is very honorable I know but still the European in face of such facts even clings tenaciously to his past, & like the young Spartan who stole the fox, makes no grimmace while famine eats his bowels out!

I had excellent introductions to several high standing Americans when I landed in New York, I had recommendations from Lord Dudley Stuart,[2] from Cobden,[3] Roebuk,[4] Bright[5] etc everybody received me well, but *nobody* lend his hand to build up some future for me. Although nobody refused openly his assistance, everbodys *act* seemed to say „help yourself."

I tell you dear Sir, that speaking six languages, playing piano, & being a good topographical draughtsman, after all efforts I could never bring higher up my existence, as to 25 dollars a month!!!

I asked once a gentleman, (who received me very hospitable, & I passed several days in his family circle) to help me to some standing in the topographical bureau, or Coast survey. He said he would do anything for me *but this*. He never tresspasses on his principle, which is never patronize, or protect to protect, let everybody fight out his own happiness. —— This is a very respectable principle I confess, and ought to be introduced in every branch of the State engine. But in my opinion it had been proper (to say the least) if the General had reversed our position, & had considered my peculiar case. How he had felt, if deprived of all his property, had been obliged to run only with naked life to a strange country, & had received such *answer* from a supposed friend! —— —— The General is at present in Washington, holding one of the highest offices of the Union, & I liked to know, whether amongst the legions of the employs in his Department there are *none*, who receive their bread by favor & protection?! —— —— —— —— Subsequently I tried to get a situation as collector in one of the several Ground exploring expeditions, I asked Englemann[6] Agassiz[7] & several others to interfere in my behalf, but never succeeded; although my capacities were very well known, and I was already a Citizen of this confederation,[8] some naturalists employed were foreigners in *every respect* & to say the least, certainly not equal to me in their capacities.

All such tricks of fortune exasperated my feelings somehow, and after several adventures, reduced to last—I enlisted in the army, considering more honorable to serve a great Republic in any capacity, than beg favor of people who never understood me.

I did not know that time the exact position of the army in this country, and I had not the farthest idea, that in the American Army only the officers are considered *men*; and the others something like a *last class negroes.* This is however a fact, and so my connection with this *Republican* army, and all its degrading and humiliating incidents has shown me human nature in a new aspect, and probably when my enlistment expires, I will be better prepared for riding the tide of life, or—as Burke says—for buffeting its waves.—— —— ——

I beg pardon dear Sir for indulging in such a long strain of moralizing upon my private affairs, which certainly cannot interest you much; but I feel sure that my hard experiences, & gloomy days have led you to appretiate what I have said; and you will consider as quite natural, that under such circumstances is better for me to leave this country for some other one, as soon as possible. —— —— ——

Your letter of June 13th arrived with usual regularity, and am glad to hear that the large box of mammals escaped all dangers.

Making use of your friendly offer, I took the liberty of advising my sister & mother, to send me some small things per Dr Flügel[9] of Leipzig. I informed the Doctor likewise of your permission, and asked him to forward to your care, should he receive something for me. Should be any expenses connected with this forwarding, of course I will reimburse you dear Sir as soon, as the package arrives. It will contain books, & daguerrotypes, & some small souvenirs, (as cigar cases, camp chair, slipper, cap etc) from my lady relatives & other friends; which are all exempt from Duty I suppose.

Ere this Dr Coolidge is undoubtedly in Washington, and perhaps informed you what became of my books, instruments, guns, etc Should they, or the

Iowa box arrive, please send me out as soon as
you can.
Very sincerely yours
LVésey

NB
The labels arrived just now, and they are very welcome, as much superior to the old ones. ——

---

1. Robert S. Williamson (c. 1824–82) graduated from West Point and
led the California segment of the Pacific Railroad Survey (see Williamson 1856). He remained in California and became responsible for meteorological observations and barometric experiments on the West
Coast. Xántus met him as he was preparing to go to Cabo San Lucas,
and Williamson asked him if he would make barometrical observations
there; a typical Xántus encounter ensued, February 11, 1859:

> Lt. Williamson requested me to make barometrical observations for
> him; but he wants them made hourly, and of course there is no
> possibility to do such things, as I am always out in day time, I told
> him however if he gives me a barometer & pays the expenses of an
> assistant, & will procure such individual on the spot, instruct him
> & look out, that the observations properly & consciously made. As
> he however could not pay only $10 a month, I hardly think I can
> get a proper person who is willing for that amount observe barom-
> eter from 6 o clock A. M. to 10 o clock P. M. for a year every day.

Xántus' characteristic prevarication shoved him into confessing to
Baird, March 5, 1859:

> I did not wish refuse his request and on the other hand I would not
> take such a burden on me, which certainly would no benefit what-
> ever by my collecting; therefore I made the stupid excuse, that I was
> very willing to do so, but I am already engaged to make such ob-
> servations for the Smithsonian Institution, therefore I could not
> *properly* duplicate the observations for him. His statement was ex-
> actly by which he caught me telling that his observations were
> made in concert & community with the Smithsonian Institution,
> shown me a letter to this effect from Prof Henry & insisted for the
> observations; I promised him to do so, if I can, & if they no hinder
> my other very multifarious—operations. He is consequently under
> the impression, that I am already suplied with a barometer by the
> Smithsonian Inst., which is certainly not the case, therefore *if you*

think sir, that such observations would be *really* important & useful, I would make them or get somebody to make them under my superintendence, if you would send me out a barometer at once.

2. Stuart has proved impossible to trace.

3. Richard Cobden (1804–65) was an apostle of free trade and wrote "Speeches on Questions of Public Policy," edited by John Bright.

4. John Arthur Roebuck (1801–79) wrote on "The evils of a House of Lords" which got him into difficulty with the Canadian government.

5. Benjamin Heywood Bright (1811–89) accumulated a valuable library and shared with Cobden a commitment to free-trade policies. That Xántus had recommendations from these men is dubious.

6. Dr. George Englemann (1809–84), a German physician who came to the United States in 1832 and settled in St. Louis; a botanist in his spare time, he devoted his attentions to the Cactaceae; he also discovered the immunity of the American grape to phylloxera and *Pronuba* moth pollination of Yucca.

7. The classic glacier studies of Louis Agassiz (1807–1873) in Switzerland influenced succeeding generations of geologists. He came to the United States in 1846 and was appointed to a professorship in zoology at Harvard, where he was a brilliant and enthusiastic lecturer and writer. It is doubtful that Xántus ever met him, although Agassiz was aware of Xántus because Baird wrote him, March 17, 1861:

> We have large collections from Mr. Xantus at Cape St. Lucas. The last boxes received made the number up to 52, and about 6000 lots of specimens. The greater part of these of course were marine.

Agassiz replied, April 2, 1861, that he would be happy to receive specimens from Xántus, and October 29, 1863, that he was sorry he had no money to contribute to Xántus' expenses; see Herber (1963; his biographical information on Xántus, p. 178, is in error.)

8. Xántus did not become a citizen until he had to, when he enlisted in the army.

9. Dr. Felix Flügel (1820–1904) was the son of Johann Gottfried Flügel (1788–1855) who had been in the United States in 1810 to study English and returned to Germany to teach it at the University of Leipzig in the 1830s; his contact with Baird resulted in his becoming "representative and correspondent" of the Smithsonian Institution; his son continued his father's interests and in 1861 Baird acknowledges him in the *Report to the Regents*.

No 32.

F[t] Tejon Cala
Aug 17th 1858.

Dear Sir!

Your letters of June 28th and 30th were duly received, & am much surprised to hear that the woodpecker suspected as distinct, should be a P. formicivorus. However as the specimen was secured in winter, it cannot be a young.

As you are now in possession of the Wilkes collection, I think you will be somewhere bound to make up a *general Museum*, instead of a local American, as the plan of the Institute was until now. Whether it is better or not is a question, to be solved by time, but I presume the Institution will be never able to do so much for science hereafter, as she has done when only engaged with American objects.

As to the plan of joining Capt Stones[1] Surveying expeditions, I would have nothing against if appointed & sent out properly by Governement, with some position; but I would never join him only for free subsistence, free transportation, etc etc perhaps to be suffered graciously to accompany his train. Besides I am positively informed, that Captain Stones expedition is very unpopular in Sonora, & looked on with suspicious eyes.

Mr Bannings direction is

> Phineas Banning
> Commission & forwarding
> San Pedro and Los Angeles

The Bird Report is on hand to include page 520, with the exception of the few sheets, lost somewhere on the voyage out. I am already quite conversant with your terminology adopted, and know everyone of my birds by your christening. Although I must frankly confess, I would like much better if the Ornithology would be simplified, and made more readily accessible to the public at large. I believe there is no science, which has more atraction

to amateurs, as the Ornithology, but in the present
state of the science, there are but very few who will
undertake the immense trouble of learning the science, and I am confident if the science follows up
the course, already commenced, in a very similar
position to the Chinese astronomy, understood only
by a few Mandarins. I really do not see any reason
to make genera *sine fine* on the slightest specific dif-
ferences, why could not all the flycatchers be put in
2 genera for instance; and why constitutes almost
every woodpecker a different genus. If somebody
writes a monography of a certain bird family, or
even genus, he mayt dissect them in as many genera & subgenera, as he fancies for the edification of
the *few*, who are perhaps particularly interested for
the same family; but by issuing a general Natural
History, or even an Ornithology of the American
birds for instance. I liked to see such work accessible to the public at large, consequently as simple &
still comprehensive as possible. —— ——
    As to the Passerellas (shistacea & Townsendii) I
presume I solved satisfactorily their difference as to
species. You must only look over their eggs & nests,
& you will perfectly satisfy yourself also. I was
under the impression at first that the red was the female, & the blue the male, but soon found mixed
the sexes in the colors, & was perfectly baffled, until
I succeeded to secure their respective nests & eggs.
—— Of course the boxes are correctly marked as to
the species, because I always killed with the nest
the bird, in most instances both male & female.
    I have again packed two boxes, but have no op-
portunity yet to forward them.

sincerely yours
L Vésey

---

1. Charles P. Stone (1824–87), resigned his commission to lead a surveying party into Sonora, 1857–59, in conjunction with Jean-Baptiste

Jecker, a Swiss/French banker to whom the Juarez government was deeply in debt. The mission was ill-received (Xántus, November 15, 1860, remarked that he "acted certainly very unjustly towards the poor, unoffending people") and was expelled in 1859 although Stone remained on in Guaymas as consul, rejoining the Army during the Civil War; afterwards he went on to varied projects such as surveying in Egypt and serving as construction engineer for the base of the Statue of Liberty.

Baird, June 23, 1858:

> Please let me know when your term of service expires, so that I may know when you would be able to begin. Captain Stone who is in charge of the Survey of Sonora would, I know, be happy to have you join him and would give you I suspect your subsistence and transportation free.

N°XXXIII

F[t] Tejon Cala
Septh 1st 1858

My dear sir!

The 25th of last month I forwarded again a box, numbered: 20., and containing:

1 Grizzly bear
3 foxes (male, female, & their young. same family)
3 badgers
1 Racoon
1 Grey Squirrell
1 Beechers Ground Squirrell
1 Spotted Lynx
2 Calif. Barn Owls[1]
1 Skull of the grizzly bear
2 Skulls of the foxes
1 Skull of the lynx
1 box, containing some fallen out teeth of the foxes
1 fox skin, (prepared by an Indian)

1 remains of an animal unknown (supposed
some kind of a fox)
100 mineralogical specimens
2 pieces of wood, filled with acorns by the Picus
formicivorus and a pair of antlers, corresponding
with the black-tail deer, as marked. When I shot
that deer, and lifted on a mule, the antlers gave way,
being probably near to casting way. They can be
fixed up very easily again, when the specimens
should be mounted, and the antlers are very pretty,
so is the deer.

The woodpecker granaries will be the first specimens probably sent east from here; and I think
would be the very proper *stand* to mount the fel-
lows on, in your hall. (?)

The mineralogical specimens will contain many
very interesting specimens, particularly some basalt
conglomerates, lazuli formations, vitrified coals, &
gold-bearing quartzes saturated with most magnificent micas etc etc

The Racoon is probably a young one, although
the skull was already perfectly hard, as by old adult
specimens.

The grizzly bear was procured & prepared by me
at the urgent solicitations of the Hungarian National
Museum, expressly for that institute. I started the
magnificent specimens (weighed before skinning
845 lbs) in perfect good condition & beautiful fur,
and would particularly request you dear Sir, to keep
the specimen well secured & cured with anti insect
matters, until I can find means to send it home. I
should be Sire fine disappointed, if I could not save
the specimen so long sought after by my friends.

———

Your letter of July 17th came duly to hand, and
in answer I inform you that an appointment from
the Coast Survey[2] to some part of Lower California
would be very welcome to me. I thought some time
ago to serve out my time of enlistment, because

there were coming to me nearly 500 dollars at the expiration of service, by way of travelling expense, rations, etc via Panama as the nearest mail route. But now since the establishment of the Wagonroad, my whole travelling expense, rations etc would amount all told to about $100 only, and I care not much consequently to stay a whole year longer in service for those $100! provided I can get some kind of employment which will provide for me honorable existence.

Harling wrote to me last mail, informing me that he sent of my effects last winter by a Govmt train to Richardsons Express Leavenworth,[3] to be forwarded to your care. He further informs me that soon after hearing, that I did not receive them yet, he requested D[r] Coolidge to enquire into the matter at Leavenworth, which D[r] Coolidge promised to do.— — Did you hear anything more on the subject sir, or do you know the result of D[r] Coolidges researches?

The wagon mail passed this afternoon up from Angeles to San Francisco (the 1st regular mail) & we expect tomorrow night the one from San Francisco to Angeles. The mail came in from Los Angeles in 10 hours (127 miles), and expected to run up to San Francisco in 50 hours.

very truly yours
LdeVésey

---

1. *Tyto alba pratincola,* USNM #17234.

2. The Superintendent of the U. S. Coast Survey was Alexander Bache (1806–1867), who was a Regent of the Smithsonian and, as such, knew Baird. Bache's interests would have predisposed him to entertain Baird's suggestions about Xántus: in 1852 he corresponded with the Secretary of the Treasury because the Pacific Mail Steamship Company had requested a survey of the Pacific Coast from Cape St. Lucas to San Diego because "at this moment there is not a chart published, that I am aware of, on which we can place dependence." See Bache (1852, p. 5). He was

interested in receiving tide measurements since he had recently calculated the first accurate determinations of ocean depth by using such records.

3. According to Larry Jochims, Research Historian, Kansas Historical Society, the first express company in Leavenworth was Richardson's Missouri River Express; Richardson also ran a line between Kansas City and Lawrence in the 1850s.

№34.

Ft Tejon Cala
Septb 10th 1858.

My dear Sir/
   Your kind letter of Aug. 1st (№ 880) was received yesterday, and although the mail goes out only the 18th inst, I hasten to answer at once, after a mature reflexion, every point of your questions ——

   1) As I already told you in some of my late letters, my services time expires Sept 4th 1859, and although the whole period is scarcely 12 months, is nothwithstanding a space of time, at which I look as on a century! When my time of service expires, there will be due to me on acct of Retained pay, travelling expenses, & clothing money not drawn, about $300 in all; but I do not care to lose these emoluments. (And I lose every cent, when discharged on my own request, before expiration of service) provided: I enter an employment, which secures me *for some time at least*, a honorable existence.

   I do not know, whether I could be sent by some authority (for instance Dept of War) *on a special detached service*, and then employed by the Coast Survey. If this possible, I could save those $300, and besides enter at once on the operations in L. California. But in this case, the question arises; *how I* would be discharged the service, & who would discharge me in Lower California the 4th of Sept. 1849?[1] The case, I suppose would turn out as complicated as possible, therefore in my opinion would be the best to get my discharge at once, if you can send me at once to Cape St. Lucas.——I give you however perfect free hand dear sir, without restriction whenever, and beg you to act in this respect entirely so, as you consider the best for my own, & sciences interest. —— —— —— If you detail me on special & detached service until my time expires, to Lower Cala, & place me in employment of the Coast Survey, all right. If you cannot do this (and I dont care much about, you may believe me) then get my discharge from service at once, and send me by the Coast Survey at once to the field. For all emergencies I send you a blank signed by me, which you may please to fill out as application to the Secretary of War, Commander in Chief, or Adj't Genl, as the circumstances may require. The rules of the service require, that when a soldier (or any enlisted men) send in an application to heads of Departments, he shall do it through the Commanding Officer of the Post, where he is. But as you have many friends in all Departments, it will make no difference if you present the application to some Secretary, who then places to his chef for consideration, & action. —— —— —— —— I have seen myself such cases (I mean cases without formality) a young man enlisted in the 2^d Dragoons, and his brother being a member of Congress from Penn, simply asked from the Secretary of War his discharge, which was granted at once. His discharge was made out in the following words: *he is therefore discharged the service by special reasons*; and when the formality is kept, the discharge runs as follows: *he is therefore discharged the service at his own request etc* —— ——

I enclose two letters, if you think they will be of some use for my discharge, you may freely use them. One of them was given to me by Dr Hammond to Senator Bigler,[2] the other by Mr Musser a member of the Missouri legislature to Senator Green,[3] but I never presented them, as my plans changed.——I am assured however, that if either of those gentlemen ask, the Secretary of war for such trifling favor *as a discharge of a soldier,* he will not hesitate a moment to grant it at once!

2) As to F^t Yuma, I am much indebted to Dr Coolidge for his good will, but I must positively I decline my transfer to that sandhill, by many reasons. The medical officer of that Post is a half crazy quarrellsome litle boy, a certain Dr Hammond[4]; and the Comdg Officer a very bitter enemy of all my operations as well, as my humble person.—— But not considering this circumstances, you are very much mistaken in regarding *Yuma* itself as a good place for collection. Here are now 2 Companies, who garrisoned for over a year that Post, amongst them many intelligent men, and I gathered long ago minute information about Yuma. The fort is situated on a sand hill, and surrounded for many miles by sand hills. There are only about ½ dozen willow trees in sight and about as many cotton trees. The nearest timber, whence the garrison gets the fuel, is 18 miles distant, with one word there is no vegetation whatever in sight, with the exception of some Cactacea, and there is no water for 50 miles, around, except the mudy colorado. The whole fauna consists of tausands of Antelopes, uncountable Quails, & Jackass Rabbits, the Cathartes aura, & corvus corax. Everything else is only accidental straggler! I have no doubt, that north of Yuma, and at the mouth of the Colorado, there is good field yet for collections, but you know well dear Sir, how absurd calculation or speculation would be to think that I should be permitted to go ½ a hundred, or a hundred miles from the Post. Therefore a transfer to Yuma would make my situation more

uncomfortable, & more unsufferable as it is even at present, besides it would yield absolutely nothing for science.[5]

Should the Lower California expedition fail, I am determined not to move from this place until my service expires. _____

Hoping that the L. Cala expedition succeeds, and in this case you send me by returning mail the discharge as well, as orders from the Coast Survey, I write on everything now, which I consider necessary for the final arrangement.

1) I wish that orders or appointment or everything like *from the Coast Survey* should be directed & made out as to John Xántus.

2) You ought to give me perfect liberty to procure personally in San Francisco, the ammunition & the like outfit, as certainly I have the best, what I want, and how much.

3) Therefore please to send me *to this Post* before I start as much ready money as you can raise, you may be assured, that I will account minutely for every cent expended.

4) It should be one of the principal stipulations with the Coast Survey, a *good sailing skiff.* I could carry down such craft from San Francisco, either on board, or in tow. I do not believe, I could get one to fitt at the Cape, nor at La Paz.

5) The whole collection will be conducted & carried on as usual, and I hope to the perfect satisfaction of all parties interested in it; but to fishes & waterfowls I consider highly important to get distinct directions from you.

Fishes

To what amount you wish I shall embark in this collection, how many specimens of each kind? To what size shall I preserve them in Alcohol, and from what size shall I skin them? Having my large seine rigged & completed now, I am able to catch in a single day 1000, and more pounds fish, the answer-

ing of the above questions therefore is highly important for the operations. —— *A catching net, & a good small seine send out however by first chance, I have no such implements, & they will be of very good use on such places, where I cannot use my other implements.*
Water fowls.

In regard to this branch, I want to know distinctly, what kind of *North American Water birds* are to be collected in large numbers. Although I will procure of every species to indicate their presence, I want to know of what species to collect many? You ought to prepare a list therefore (I will know the bird only by name) and append *common, rather rare,* or *very rare* this will be enough for me. As to South & Central American water birds, it would be very desiderable for me to possess a Synopsis with the like remarks, of all such birds. Considering however that the furnishing of such an information would robb you of much time you could get perhaps some of your clerks, to compile after your instructions such a list for my use. (?) —— ——

I liked to know likewise to what extent I have to collect, gulls, & principally gulls eggs?

———

I agree perfectly with you, that it is much better to select *one* place to exhaust the Zoology of a country, then traveling round about. I know Collectors in Central America, who selected a good spot in some wilderness, and collected in 6 months twice as much, as their employers who travelled with large expedition tausands of miles through the whole country. —— Accordingly I am under the impression, that passing one season at Cape St. Lucas; the other at or near Mazatlan, with occasional cruising on the intervening islands, I could secure almost every bird of Lower California, & Western Mexico, & intercept all migratory birds. There are scarcely any birds in Lower California or Western Mexico, which are not found (at least occasionally) at Mazatlan, and Cape St. Lucas–La Paz.

It is generally known to collectors, and it shows a careful perusal of Wilkes exploration also, that islands are very poor in birds, insects, mammals etc, but I never consider the hundreds of islands in the Vermillion Sea in this light. The Gulf of California is something like an immense stream, and I suppose her islands a very favorite resort of all birds, on acct of their luxurious vegetation, & quite solitude. $^{+)}$

I might be disappointed, but still I anticipate a great harvest, and I will start as soon as possible with rose spirits to try to beat Mr Véseys F^t Tejon collection—in every respect. —— —— ——

I think, this is about all, I have to say to the final arrangement of the undertaking. The transportation I can arrange, when once on the spot, to this effect however would be of good service, if Mr Forbes of course of your San Francisco aquaintances could furnish me with introductions to commercial houses in La paz, & Mazatlan; and if the Smithsonian Institution would recommend me to the American Counsul at those places, you could do that even perhaps by the State Department.

Another point still, there is passport required in Mexico, do not forget that. And considering that the entrance of said republic in her present convulsive Revolution, & dissolution like State; with guns, kegs of powder, & bags of shot; could create a great suspicion & my coming from San Francisco, could easily bring in somebodys head the suggestion, that I am a disguised filibuster agent or so;[6]——would be very desiderable on my part, & in our mutual interest, if the Mexican Minister at Washington would furnish me with something like a manifesto, identifying my real character & pursuit; such document would cause a good influence in Mexico I know, much better than an American passsport, countersigned by J Buchanan, & all the rest of the Yankee empire. —— —— The Mexican Minister will do

$^{+)}$like the Grecian archipelago in Europe.

172

this certainly, if requested by the institution, and he may perhaps do some more, for instance the exemption from Duty my ammunition, & other outfit etc.

The resumé of my letter would be then

1.) Discharge from service, and if so, appointment to L. California at once.

2.) Ready money before I leave this post, to suply myself with everything necessary to commence operations with.

3.) A skiff from the Coast Survey, or somewhere else.

4.) Special directions on Fishes & Water birds, to be collected.

5.) letters of introduction to commercial houses in Lapaz & Mazatlan, and to the U. S. Consuls there.

6.) Manifesto from the Mexican Minister, identifying my character & occupation.

With this outfit then I am ready to start and to make the other arrangements will be a comparatively small affair for me.

sincerely yours
JXántus

---

1. Xántus meant 1859.

2. Senator William Bigler (1814–80), Democratic Senator from Pennsylvania, 1856–61. Madden (1949a, p. 53) quotes a letter from Dr. William Hammond to Senator Bigler, March 1, 1857, on Xántus' behalf:

> Since he has been in our army he has uniformly conducted himself in a manner to win the respect of any officer with whom he has served. . . . Any service which you may be kind enough to render him will be regarded by me as a personal favor.

3. Senator James S. Green (1817–79), Representative from Missouri, 1847–51, and Senator, 1857–61.

4. Dr. George Hammond.

5. Baird, November 1, 1858:

> I am glad to know your views about Ft. Yuma. The personalities of the fort would of course render it altogether inexpedient to go there:

your informants are however under an error as to its barrenness of zoological results. The birds may not be conspicuous to the mere sportsman, but there are many species to be found. This much I can say: that every collection I have ever seen from there, if of only half a dozen specimens, contained something rare.

Both Baird and Xántus were correct; even Dr. Elliot Coues repeats some of the usual Army stories about the soldier who died and went to hell but came back for blankets because it was cold after Yuma; the temperature often hung at 120° combined with heavy humidity. But Baird was right in praising the bird life there, for Coues (1877, pp. 214–15) gives a delightful account of all he saw in one day.

6. Xántus' apprehension was reasonable; Walker's expedition (see October 18, 1858, note 4) had occurred only five years earlier, and Capt. Stone's expedition had been expelled from Sonora. Baird, also aware of the potential for trouble, wrote the Archbishop of New York in mid-December 1858 in Xántus' behalf:

> Mr. John Xantus, a Hungarian by birth, is about to proceed from San Francisco to Lower California for the purpose of making Scientific observations on the tides of the Gulf for the United States Coast Survey, and at the same time of increasing collections of the Natural History of that little known country for the Smithsonian Institution. To accomplish these results a residence of about a year or more will be required and it will be necessary for him to take a sufficient supply of powder, shot, and alcohol for this length of time. As his mission, though purely scientific and peaceful, may have enough of the warlike in appearance to render him suspicious to the authorities, I take the liberty of asking whether it is in your power to furnish to the Smithsonian Institution then for Mr. Xantus any papers or letters or recommendation to take authorities of the Church or village which would serve to . . . diminish in any way his danger of being seized or interfered with as a filibuster.

My dear Sir ——

I forwarded yesterday again a box numbered 21, and containing 3 bundles of Herbarium, a quantity of Reptiles, bats, mice, insects, & humming birds all in Alcohol, with several other alcoholic specimens. —— The 3 bundles of Plants conclude now my Herbarium, which is no doubt as complete as possible, as it comprises the Fᵗ Tejon Flora from February to October, without intervall whatever. I liked very much, if you would submitt occasionally the plants to the Inspection of either Prof Gray,[1] or Prof Torrey,[2] as I am very anxious to know, what I collected?

I enclose the specification of my expenses since the last settlement. The ½ amount to be borne by the Sm. Institution makes \$38⁵⁵ which you may remit to me in some way or other after the usual appropriation made by the Regents.

In regard to the contemplated Gulf of Cala expedition I wrote to you the other day (10ᵗʰ inst) very extensively; the summary of which was—that by reasons specified I must decline a transfer to either Yuma or other place;—that I am very willing to accept appointment under the coast survey, and am ready to go to any place in the Peninsula etc. I proposed to you to effect my discharge at once, and furnished you with blanks signed by me, and to be used as circumstances will require for application to the proper Departments. I requested you to send me some cash to this place, before I shall leave, in order to place me in position to purchase the outfit for the expedition; and asked you to furnish me letters of Introduction to the U. S. Consuls at La paz & Mazatlan, also to some commercial houses there in order to regulate future transportation of boxes. I asked you further to stipulate the skiff, and cause the Mexican Minister at your city to furnish me with a manifesto identifying my character in order not to be mistaken in those parts for a filibuster. —— At last I requested you to give me special directions about the amount of fish to be collected; and *furnish me with a good small seine* for bayou & ditch fishing, etc.

In addition to those suggestions I have now very little to say, I wish however

1.) that you supply me with a *good* quantity of tin cans (a la Philadelphia academy) of all sizes, to preserve in small and first specimens; those cans are invaluable for collectors, you can fill those cans with

2.) large quantity of assorted, & ready made lino bags, as the making of such things on the field is hardly practicable.

3.) If my guns have not arrived in Washington at the time of the receipt of this letter; be so kind and purchase at once a double barrell gun, with *large calibers & light* for waterfowl shoting. The gun you sent me out last winter, is very good make, & well adapted for small birds, but is not fit for long distance hunting, principally on water, as she cannot bear more than half a charge. A good double gun therefore, *with large calibers & long barrells* is the very principal thing. I shall want for a successful collection; do not delay a moment, but send on at once. I think you can get a very good such piece for from $20 to 25 dollars, and I liked if you would take in consideration my pocket, although I do not limit you as to the price.[3]

Hoping to hear final arrangements by returning mail, I am dear Sir

sincerely yours
J X deVésey

---

1. Dr. Asa Gray (1810–88), appointed to a Chair in Botany at Harvard in 1842, wrote up the new plant specimens flooding the Smithsonian, among them Xántus'; see June 5, 1857, note 6.

2. Dr. John Torrey (1796–1873), an army surgeon who was also a botanist, chemist, and physicist, became New York State botanist and collaborated with Asa Gray.

3. Baird wrote, December 22, 1857, that he had purchased the gun; Xántus did not receive it until January 6, 1859.

N⁰36.

Fᵗ Tejon, Cala
October 8ᵗ 1858

Dear Sir—

In my letters of the 10ᵗʰ & 18ᵗʰ of September I fully informed you on all main points in regard to the Gulf Expedition; accepting the offer to Cape St. Lucas in employment of the Coast Survey Dept, & asking of you to procure *in this case* at once my discharge.

Since that, I am informed that the arrears pay & other allowances due to me from the U. S. mayt be saved; as with *strict* interpretations of the Army Regulations only the minors, forfeit pay & other allowances. The Regulation runs thus:

1797. (Pay department) . . . "Every enlisted man discharged as minor, or for other cause involving fraud on his part, in the enlistment; or discharged by the civil authority—shall forfeit all pay and allowances due at the time of the discharge." —— — — And so, I think, I am entitled to every cent due to me, should I get my discharge; and as the affair stands so, you shall not hesitate a moment to procure it, provided I can go to Cape St. Lucas.

I do not know, whether the Coast Survey means *literally* St. Lucas. But I had a long conversation with a gentleman just in from Lower California, who knows there every spot and he informs me that the Cape itself is a barren tongue, projecting for miles into the sea, without water or vegetation for many miles. The nearest settlement is about 20 miles from the Cape, in a small Roadstead, where several houses stand, & amongst others a Mr Ritchie[1] keeps a large Home for the accomodations of Whalers, who report there often for supplies.— —If the Coast Survey means the last place, (or perhaps a town called San Jose, & only 30 miles distant) is all right; but I do not know how to menage affairs if I am sent literally to the Cape, unless the Coast Survey supplies me with provisions & water.[2]

According all I heard from Mr Richard Forbes[3] (this is the name of the gentleman) Mr Ritchies settlement would be an excellent place for collection & tide observations both, as the country around is much wooded, & his house stands only a few yards from high water.

San Jose would be still more better, as the settlement is located just at the outlet of the Todos Santos valley; which is the most fertile & richest spot on the whole north Pacific Coast, & abounds in Lakes, streams, woods, coffee sugar & other plantations.[4] San Jose is however 3 miles off the beach.

I wish you to take all these important points in consideration, and act as your think proper & most advantageous for the sake of the success of the exploration.

———————

Since my last—I procured a *Roadrunner* the 1st specimen I secure. It is however much smaller as the one described in Cassin, & in many points different; unless this be accounted for young birds plumage (?) I have also a nest & 1 egg of the same bird, Major Gordon[5] of the Kern river ferry procured me at my solicitations; he found it on the top of an old deserted Indian Wigwam, and contained 3 eggs. He however did not blow out the eggs, & successively were broken two of them. The remaining one is in good condition, although likewise not emptied.

I espied the other day a flock of *Gymnokitta cyanocephala,*[6] numbering about 30 individuals. They were feeding on the top of the mountain on acorns, amongst deafening noise. I persecuted them very near the whole day, creeping sometimes for more than a mile distance on my belly, but did not succeed to fire even a shot at them, they were without any parallel shy. ——

I inform you dear sir, that hoping the successful issue of the Cape St Lucas affair, I took the liberty to request my friends in Hungary, to direct all their letters to me *your care* Washington. Hoping you will excuse me for this liberty, what ever expense you may incur in this request by paying postage, I will reimburse you thankfully from time to time. —— All the letters will be directed of course *John Xántus.*

As to my land affairs in Iowa, I have to state, that the following lands were reserved for me & in my name by the General Government (Pierce) to wit:

NE quarter &   of Section 36, Township 70.

NW quarter   of Range twentyseven.

I settled on said lands *prior* to January 22^d 1855, & improved the same for two years, in company with a Mr Ladislaus Madarass,[7] whose lands joined the same.

The improvements consisted of a house, stables, & other buildings, besides 30 ackers land fenced in substancially, & under *actual* cultivation. After nearly two years habitation on said lands, I left and gave the charge of the said lands to my friend Madarass, who continued every since to cultivate & improve them, residing constantly in our common house.

Shortly after I left said lands, I enlisted in the U. S. Army, and am ever since in the service of the U. S. ——

The last session of Congress under pub. 23 enacted a law, by which all Hungarians for whom President Pierce reserved lands in Iowa are permitted to preempt or enter their lands, provided: they can prove, that they were constantly living on their reserved lands.

Now—having had some personal difficulties with aforementioned Mr Madariss—he refuses to give up my lands, pleading that I left them, did not continue the improvements, and did not live on them since years. —— My attorney, who is authorized to act for me, informs me, that he has under such circumstances very little hope to save my lands.

This is the case, as it stands. I must add yet, that Madarass has no document whatever in his hands to prove, that I abandoned my lands; he only takes the proviso of the law to his lucrative advantage. Resume =

1) I settled prior to Jan. 22 1855 on the lands, continued to inhabit & improve them for nearly 2 years.

2) The lands were reserved on my name, & only on my name until the last act of Congress passed.

The question is now, whether my enlisting in the army, & consequent *personal* absence from my lands, deprived me of my right of possession; although the lands were cultivated in my name, still reserved in my name?

I would inform you, that in case I lose those lands, I lose 10,000 dollars, as the lands at present are at *least* so much worth!

very truly yours

LVésey

If the lands are reserved of course John Xántus, and you have to inquire in this name.[8]

---

1. Thomas Ritchie, the only European at the Cape, jumped ship as a young man and took up a semi-native existence, supplying food and livestock to travelers, smuggling, etc. He was to be of considerable help to Xántus, although Xántus never acknowledged it; among other things, he had the only well in the area, from which Xántus drew the brackish water that he walked seven miles to get, loaned him money, took him in during storms, and received Xántus' mail for him.

2. Ritchie's house was on the sand berm bounding the bay of San Lucas, the southernmost point of the Cape, where ships could make port. The next port was San José del Cabo, 20 miles to the northeast, where there was a settlement. No way could the countryside be described as "wooded." As late as February 11, 1859, Xántus was still getting confusing information.

3. Richard Forbes possibly was related to Alexander Forbes; he has proved impossible to trace.

4. The idea that San José was the extension of the Todos Santos valley was held by others, among them a young Englishman, William Redmond Ryan (1973), who wrote in 1848–49 that the San Jose valley "stretches right across the peninsula, from the Pacifc Ocean to the Gulf of California, a distance of not less than from a hundred and fifty to nearly two hundred miles."

5. Major William H. Gordon (d. 1865) attended the U. S. Military Academy and was brevetted major in 1847 for gallant conduct at Churubusco; in 1861 he led the 8th Infantry.

6. Now *Gymnorhinus cyanocephala*, Pinyon Jay.

7. Laszlo Madaraz (1811–1909) was one of the first settlers of New Buda and host during Xántus' sojourn there.

8. The last paragraph, signature, and last lines are struck through but not obliterated.

No 37.

F^t Tejon Cala
October 18th 1858

Ft Tejon Cala
October 18th 1858

Dear Sir/
The last mail brought no letter from you, as it was very likely forwarded by the wagon mail. You ought to direct all your letters *via Panama*, else the mischief the Wagon road will do, amounts to something certainly. The Company mayt kill at first several dozens of their horses, break down half their wagons, and effect some few quick passages, but nobody believes that they should be able to make a winter trip in less than 35–40 days! —— Their first

mail they brought in to Los Angeles (from Memphis) in 21 days, & to San Francisco in 24½, but crippled half their horses, & capsized over a dozen times their ominbuses. —— The Panama route is at any rate the most reliable, & most safe, I think so.

I hope you received all the boxes sent in to include Nº 21, forwarded lately. I have one again packed, waiting for opportunity for Los Angeles; it contains several birds not yet sent in.

The bird Report came to hand to page 704 to include Himantopus nigricollis. Pages 61–161 still missing! I received likewise fragments, (about 4 sheets & entirely without connection) of some fish Report under your cover, but I could not find out who wrote them, to what expedition the fish belong? —— I should be very glad, if you could send me a complete copy (with illustrations) of the Mammals as well as birds by a safe convenience for instance per Mr Forbes; and I am anxious to get a Copy of the Smithsonian Report for 1857, which is probably out by this time. (?)

I am very tired of the Ft Tejon collection now, as I cannot find anything, which is not plentifully represented in my collection already; and as I cannot leave the *immediate* vicinity of the Post. I am suffered to hunt now unmolested around the garrison, but never would Dr TenBroeck consent of my going off a couple days to the lakes, plains, or the Kern River. Consequently I am only occasionally collecting now, and probably I am going to close collections entirely here. —— I think I have now every land bird from these Regions with the exception of the Californian vulture. And of the mammals, I have only 5 species not yet, that the large wolf, the Skunk, the Prairie dog, Beaver & Otter. There are no Opossums[1] here, and I am told, there are none West of the Colorado; and I do not believe there are Porcupines & flying Squirrells; as I offered several months ago *$10 for a piece* amongst all the hunters & Indians, and they had certainly brought me speci-

mens, if there had been any around. (?) ——
Should you get soon my discharge, I intend to accept the kind invitation of General Don Andres
Pico,[2] to spend a week or so in his house at San
Fernando; and get there about 100 bears, and a
quantity of Quails; both of which together with the
Chaparral Cock[3] are these found in 1000 & 1000
everywhere round, even near the houses. —— San
Fernando is just on the road as you know, from this
place to Los Angeles, therefore I would lose nothing
by stopping there some days; considering the
amount of specimens, I could get.

You recollect, what I told you several weeks ago
about Capt. Stones surveying expedition to Sonora;
how right I was you can see now of the adnexed
slip from the *Los Angeles Star, of Oct 9th 1858*. And
the editor of the El Clamer del Publico, who is a
good friend of mine, told me months ago that this
will be case. The People of Sonora will try to remove peacefully Mr Stone; and if he does not
move, they will drive him out by force; but are resolved not to suffer amongst them so large a party
of Americans. —— This all we can thank to Walker[4]
and his vagabond associates, who were constantly
permitted to trample on the lives, fortunes, &
homes of those defenceless unhappy people; and
nobody can form an idea of the suspicion & ill will
they created amongst all the Mexican & Central
American people toward everybody, not born on
their soil.

Anxiously expecting your movements in regard
to the Gulf expedition, I remain
> dear Sir
>> With sincerest regards
>> Yours LVésey

---

1. *Diadelphis marsupialis.*
2. Don Andrés Pico (n. d.) was Commander of the California forces in

the Mexican War, and managed to hold out for eight months until he finally was forced to surrender his forces to General John C. Frémont at Cahuenga, January 13, 1847. On January 3, 1847, W. H. Emory (Calvin 1951, p. 172), marching to relieve the situation in California, recorded:

> After marching a few miles the wide Pacific opened to our view. We passed the St. Marguerita rancheria, once a dependency of San Luis Rey, now in the possession of the Pico family.

Don Andrés and his brother, Pío Pica (the last Mexican governor of Alta California) originally owned the Rancho Santo Margarita y Las Flores north of present-day La Jolla. After the war it was taken over by U. S. troops under General Kearny and over time became the U. S. Marine Corps's Camp Pendleton. See Nostrand (1943); and November 16, 1858.

General Pico continued to be active in political affairs; the lack of order in Los Angeles in the late 1850s engendered the formation of many private military units; on August 15, 1858, General Pico received the petition of one captain:

> General: I have the honor to inform you that my company the Union Guards is entirely destitute of arms, and if not provided soon, it will be impossible for me to keep them together.
> Your attention to this will greatly oblige.
> Your obt servant
> PHINEAS BANNING   Capt U G   Cal S Mil

Pico strongly endorsed Banning's plea; see Scammell (1950, p. 237); also November 16, 1858, notes 8, 9, and 10.

3. Roadrunner.

4. The treaty of Guadalupe Hildago insured that Baja California would remain part of Mexico, and set the border between the United States and that country. Expansionist interests in the United States still felt that the peninsula should become part of Alta California, and a series of filibustering attempts were made to take at least part of the territory. Captain William Walker (1824–60) in 1853 fitted out an expedition, got to La Paz, and declared himself "Colonel and President of Lower California." When he was tried for abrogating neutrality laws, such was the sentiment in California that his quick acquittal brought cheers from the press. He was killed in similar attempts in Honduras.

Despite Xántus' protestations, he echoed similar sentiments, November 16, 1858.

No **38.**

My dear Sir/
Your letter of Sept. 2d came to hand today per
private occasion, it was missent to San Bernardino;
we have at Los Angeles at present a very poor individual of a Postmaster, the complaint against him is
general; he sent the other day for instance all the
official letters for this Post, to Fort Yuma, and the
Commanding officer had to send after an express of
six men!!!

The Southern overland mail continues to make
rather quick trips, the shortest however was 23 days
& 23 hours; considering now that from St Louis or
Memphis takes again about 4 days, to go to Washington; a letter will go by this route under the most
favorable circumstances in from 28 to 30 days. The
Steamer letters average 23 days from Port to Port, so
it is still better & more reliable the last mail route.

I forwarded again this morning per Mr Bannings
train a box, numbered 22, and containng as follows:

     10 Mammals, skins
     75 birds
     10 Skulls of Mammals
     20 nests & 51 eggs
     4 bottles of Coleoptera
     10 Mineralogical Specimens
     26 boxes of exotic seeds.

Amongst the mammals there is a large white
Wolf, 2 fine skunks, & 1 otter; the lat[t]er two animals, I secured just but yesterday, & I hastened to
send in at once. The large Wolf is a present from Mr
George Alexander[1] of the Alamos Rancho, although
he killed her with our Strichnine, and I had to go
there to skin the specimen, & to fetch home. She
weighed 68 pounds—when in flesh.

Just this morning I discovered again a whole family of black Spermophilus, exactly the same kind I

sent you one last year, and you considered as a variety only of the S. Beecheyi. —— This family took up her residence in the Quartermaster Store room, amongst thousands of barrells; I have seen 6 of them all jet black; but the clerk told me there are at least a dozen. I set instantly all my traps, baited with every kind of delicacy, and am watching with intense excitement the result. I was told since I sent you the above specimen, that there are seen some occasionally on the slopes of the Sierra Nevada South East from Tejon, and they are found without exception amongst huge rocks. I never have noticed any, but the one specimen, and now this whole family. —— One thing is sure, all of them are black, no mistake about that, and their barking is altogether different of that of the S. Beecheyi.(?)

I have now nearly the whole bird report here, with the exception of the lost sheets, which however comprise the whole family of Hummingbirds, woodpeckers, & most of the Finches, therefore the loss is extremly important, as particularly shore birds would be interesting for me. I hope when the Volume finished & bound, you will suply me with a complete copy.

The Mammal report is likewise incomplete, all the wolves & lynxes, & foxes to the Spermophils missing!

sincerely yours
LVésey

---

1. George Alexander (n.d.) was a resident of Los Angeles and a member of one of the volunteer units maintaining order in the city in 1853; see Scammell (1950).

N⁰39.

My dear Sir/
  Your letter of Sept. 18th Carlisle[1] reached me a
couple days ago, and read with wonder that you did
not receive any letters from me that time; although
I never missed a mail yet, since I am in Ft Tejon. It
is not unlikely that our Los Angeles Postmaster
made again some blunder, by sending it to the
Sandwich Islands or some other neighbourhood.

  I hope you will find something interesting
amongst my Reptiles of this year, although the collection is by far not such as I had devised. But I was
very much engaged in the whole spring, with those
confounded nests & eggs, and naturally enough I
had to neglect somehow the more important
branches, as birds reptiles etc. —— —— But after
all, there are but few reptiles here and I am almost
sure, that my collection contains specimens of every
reptile found here within 5 miles round.

  Dr Thos Brewer wrote me a letter last mail, asking the permission to describe & photograph the
nests & eggs. In answer I told him, that I already informed you long ago, that the particular purpose of
my collecting nests & eggs was to furnish some additional material for his work. Of course then he
shall use my collection *for illustrations descriptions.*
Dr Brewer seems to be a very polite & nice gentleman, and I am quite glad to have formed with him
in this way an Aquaintance.

  I dont know whether Mr Cassin received the
birds I sent him, he never wrote me a single line,
therefore I am under aprehension that the box was
somehow lost?

  Yesterday I sent of[f] again a box, paying fright
$2⁰⁰. The box is numbered 23, and contains:
  3 mammals, skins
  115 birds
  8 nests, with 30 eggs.

Amongst the birds there are some not yet forwarded. And yesterday I secured another hawk, a
very large one which is new to any collection. It is
somewhat similar to *Buteo insignatus*[2] of Cassin, but
I should think—not the same. I will send in now
rapidly everything on hand yet; so as not to be en-
cumbered with specimens, if I shall go next month
to a new field.

I could not secure any yet of the black ground
Squirrells, I hope however to get some by & by.

It is very strange, when I came here last year,
there was not a single mouse at the Post, & there
are now thousands of them. They are apparently a
native woodmouse, but never moved into the
houses, until recently. We had no cats whatever that
time, and nobody can live now without cats. I sent
you already a quantity of those mice, apparently 2
different species, small short eared, the other large
with broad ears. I have at present again nearly ½ a
gallon! —— If the mice moved in, on the other
hand The Neotomas moved away, but not a single
one is to be seen for miles around. I tried to catch
them in a trap, & it happened sometimes that a
Specimen was for 2–3 days alive in the trap *in loco
suo*; and it is not unlikely that the others got
alarmed by such exhibitions, & put out of sight. I
cannot suggest to my mind other reason for their
entire disappearance. I had also to smoke out several of their strange residences, & this was one of
the causes also—very probably—which frightened
them.

The ducks & geese are here again.

You never told me, what snipe it was, I sent you
some few specimens; nearly like the Wilsons snipe,
but lighter & spotted red. I called them Scolopax
Drummondii?[3]

very truly yours
LVésey

1. Baird grew up in Carlisle, Pennsylvania, and before going to the Smithsonian in 1850, he taught chemistry and natural history at Dickinson College for $1,000.00 a year. He had close ties to Carlisle and often went back, finding it a good place to work; he wrote Agassiz that "I take the remaining material [Report on Reptilia] with me to Carlisle next week and hope to finish before the first of October" (Herber, 1963, p. 143).

2. Now *B. swainsonii,* Swainson's Hawk.

3. Now *Capella gallinago,* Common Snipe.

No **XL.**   Fort Tejon Cala
                                          Novb 16th 1858.

My dear Sir/
   As it was offered me a good opportunity yesterday, I packed up in great hurry a box, and forwarded to you via: as usual. The box is numbered 24, and contains as follows:
   1 nest & egg of Geococcyx mexicanus.
   8 pieces of very remarkable mineralogical
     Specimens
   10 birds
   3 mammals
   5 boxes of insects
   1 package for my mother
   The petrified (very likely clay) pieces were taken by me in a warm spring (185° fahrenheit) only 8½ miles distant from this place, and called Sulphur Springs, or "ojo caliente."[1]
   The lava pieces were found near Elisabeth lake on the hill side, only 15 miles distant from the Post.[2]
   The auriferous quartz pieces I obtained near the fort, on the edge of a precipice above the Tejon creek.[3]
   The remarkable pure lead ore was found when bathing under a small waterfall, within the limits of the garrison.

The insects I collected according to your desire—
dry, and pinned. I am however very much against
such collecting, as I have never seen yet a collection
safely transported to its destination. You may pin
them half an inch deep in the cork bottom, some of
them will jump out, and ruin all the others. I took
particular care to secure them as well as possible,
but I am almost sure you will report them by returning mail as ruined. —— I had considerable
quarrel in this respect with Dr Wagner & Leconte,
but particularly with Count Motchulskii,[4] although
any of them was forced to acknowledge that the alcoholic, or etheric collection is *always* safe, when
properly packed & preserved.

I collected in all 181 species Coleoptera, & am
very anxious to hear our friend LeConte about the
amount of new species, I expect at least *one fourth*
of the sum total; as I inspected minutely LeContes
cabinet in regards to California Coleoptera, before
leaving Philadelphia. —— ——

The package addressed to My mother contains
some curious trinkets from this part of the world, as
South american coins, small birds, nests, native
goldpieces, rattlesnake skins, horned frog etc etc;
and I would request you dear sir to forward it to D^r
Flügel as soon as possible. It seems that my mother
and sister are already in correspondence with M^r
Flügel, and are much pleased with his many kind-
nesses, therefore I might hope Mr Flügel will forward the package as soon, as he receives.

According to my mothers letter Dr Flügel has forwarded me already a couple packages to your care,
and should they arrive I would ask you to forward
them to me as soon as practicable. And should be
there any necessity of opening them, you may do it
of course. They contain however only books, newspapers and the like, including some needleworks
from my lady relatives & friends, as arm chair, cigar
case, purse, cap, slippers etc etc, which are not subjected I should think to customhouse Duty; nor

Portraits which they likewise contain. —— By re-
packing those things I would particularly entreat
you, to look out, as (according invoice) there are
some velvet & gold coucers [?], and to this regard
Mr Flügel has received likewise very *grave* injunctions for caution. —— ——
    I am now half packed up, and ready to start as
soon as my discharge arrives, which I expect about
the mail of the 5th next. I hope you menaged
everything in accordance with my desire, but if you
failed to carry out perchance the plans, I would request you again to get my discharge from served *at
once & in every case*, as I am willing to do everything
in the world, even go as a fireman on the first
steamboat rather, than to have any connection
whatever with the army. I have more than enough
now of this kind of life!
    Your letter of Oct 2^d reached me some days ago,
and I heard with great pleasure that there is such an
interesting specimen amongst my saurians. I cannot
however recollect the species, not even after your
short description, and have not even an idea, which
of the collected saurians should be the Xantusia (by
the by much obliged for the honor!).[5]
    The turtle I found about 400 feet high on a
mountain side, destitute of almost every vegetation,
and at least 2 miles off from any water whatever.
This circumstance I mention because since I found
another of the same species (although a litle
smaller), and — in the water, sunning himself on
the mud.(?) Those two were however all the specimens I ever noticed since here, and there is nobody
at the fort even amongst the oldest residents, who
ever saw a turtle at this place, or even heard of such
thing.[6]
    It would be entirely surprising, if you had no fish
from Kern river & Tulare lake; as Mr Möllhausen
went there *expressly* for that purpose (when here),
and passed there about 10 or 12 days with all the
officers. Dr TenBroeck told me subsequently that

Möllhausen was very much satisfied with the fishing, & collected immense number of specimens.——

As to F^t Yuma, I told you already frankly my opinion, and have no reason yet to change that opinion. I am well aware that under certain circumstances I could do there much, as the geographical & topographical position of the *environs* of Yuma, is particularly inviting; but under such restrictions as I am, there is nothing in the world to induce me again to commence collection. If you only could guess half of the troubles I had to struggle against, you would certainly say I am right; I can only assure you that nothing else as my zeal for Science could keep me so long passive under so many humiliating circumstances.

Of all we see & hear, it appears that much sooner we anticipated, Sonora & L. California will belong to the confederation. If this soon happens, (and it will happen very soon) my operations in the Gulf would be of a double importance for American Nat. History, and I would have a fair start before any other competition on the field.

Through the aid of General Pico I put myself in connection with several gentlemen of Los Angeles, who are quite at home in every part of Lower California; and I gathered already a great deal of information as to the topography of the Southern part of the peninsula, islands, animals etc; and the General promised me recommendations to some of his friends in La paz, San Jose & Gyaimas, which will undoubtedly be of very great service; as the general is considered as one of the greatest Mexican Patriots, & is favorably known all over Mexico. —— He is the very same, who commanded once the California forces against Fremont,[7] Stockton,[8] & Thurbrick,[9] and fought the San Gabriel & Los Angeles batles; although at present he is a good American citizen, and being a member of the California Senate, a very useful & a go a head Statesman. He possesses the celebrated San Fernando Mission by a Mexican grant, and is probably a million of dollars worth (speaking in American phrase) ——

Some days ago arrived at the Post Major Carleton[10] of the 1st Dragoons with family, he visited me and told, that being in Benicia,[11] Lt Churchill recommended me to him very warmly; and offered to do everything in his power to advance my collections. I am sorry, it is rather to late, but I acknowledge nothwithstanding gratefully Mr. Churchills kindness, & sincerely good hearth toward me. It is very pleasant to find such gentleman in such places as I am in; & comes something like a white crow in the Ornythology!

very sincerely yours

LVésey

P. S.

With correspondence will be an annoying thing in Cape St. Lucas, as we shall consider ourselves fortunate enough if we can menage to send epistles every 3 months once so I am informed. But we will square up with plentifull at once.

---

1. In Spanish, "spring" is ojo de agua. Los Alamos y Agua Caliente is a large area south of El Tejon and east of Tejon Pass, covering the foothills and crest of the Tehachapi Mountains; Blake (1857, p. 83) mentions several hot springs in the area, and there are several marked on the USGS Quadrangles, although none are designated as "Sulphur Springs."

2. Elizabeth Lake is more like 30 miles from the Fort; Blake (1857, p. 57), early in October of 1853, described the lake:

> Turning up the valley to the right, we soon reached the borders of a very beautiful sheet of water—Lake Elizabeth. This valley extends towards the Cañada de las Uvas, and we found the trail made by the wagons in their passage from there to the lake. . . . The valley is

comparatively narrow and long, and is about 3,300 feet above the sea. It is well watered, and produces an enormous growth of grass, where herds of deer delight to congregate, not only for food, but for the shelter from view which the tall grass affords.

We encamped on the borders of the lake, and during the night the temperature fell to 29°, and 32° at daylight. Thick ice was formed. It is probable that considerable snow accumulates in this valley during the winter.

Edmond Leuba painted quite a different picture twenty years later (see Chickering 1938, p. 103). Leuba writes of finding "Elizabeth Lake, which they dignified by the appellation of a lake, and beyond, the desert as far as the eye could reach."

3. Tejon Creek does not run through Tejon Pass but some 20 miles to the northeast on the northern flank of the Tehachapi Mountains.

4. Victor Ivanovich Mochulskii (1810–71), born in Russia and a colonel in Russian army, was a noted entomologist specializing in Coleoptera; he traveled in the United States in 1853, and his specimens are listed in various Smithsonian reports.

5. Baird (1858a, p. 255) wrote a cursory and superficial description, considering that he was proposing a new genus:

> XANTUSIA, Baird.—Body slender; cylindrical. Femoral pores. Three folds on the throat, the anterior connecting the ears inferiorly and encircling the head. Pupil vertical. No eyelids.
>
> *Xantusia vigilis,* Baird.—Hind leg extended forwards, reaches the first gular fold, and is contained about 2¾ times in head and body. Claws small. Color above dark brownish yellow, varied with blackish spots on single tubercles. Young vermiculated with yellowish on a brown ground. A yellowish line on each side of the neck, with two others on the nape, making four parallel ones. Under parts whitish. Head and body about two inches long.
>
> *Hab.*—Fort Tejon, Cal. John Xantus. Type No. 3063.

6. The only turtles present in the southwest are *Clemmys marmorata,* Southwestern Pond Turtle, dependent upon water (which Xántus collected), and *Gopherus agassizi,* the desert tortoise, which is terrestrial (and which he did not).

7. John Charles Frémont (1813–90), after his well-publicized exploring trips to the Rocky Mountains, the Great Basin, Oregon and California, returned to California in 1845, where he supported Commodore Stockton (see below) and his Pacific Squadron in the revolt against Mexico. Frémont took General Andrés Pico's surrender without authorization. At the end of the War, Stockton installed Frémont as governor. General

Stephen Watts Kearny was appointed in Washington before word of Frémont's governorship reached the capital; when Kearny arrived, Frémont refused to recognize Kearny, and for this he was tried for mutiny, convicted, and resigned from government service. On 1848 he became a wealthy man when gold was found on his land in California.

8. Commodore Robert Field Stockton (1795–1866). Although he expressed some concern at Frémont's presumption in negotiating a treaty with Pico, he himself assumed unauthorized power in appointing Frémont as Military Governor without clearing it with Washington.

9. Commodore William Branford Shurbrick (1790–1874), as captain of the *Saratoga* and the ranking naval officer of the Pacific Squadron, supported Kearny, and replaced Frémont as governor in 1847.

10. Major James H. Carleton (1814–73), decorated for bravery in the Mexican War, also wrote a standard history of it; he collected and compiled a "Table of Distances," a practical guide to immigrants, and *Special Report of the Massacre of the Mountain Meadows, Utah territory, in September, 1857, of One Hundred and Twenty Men, Women, and Children, who were on the way from Arkansas to California, etc.;* see December 28, 1857, note 16. In the 1860s he was stationed in New Mexico and collected natural history specimens for the Smithsonian.

11. Williamson (1856, pp. 9–10) described this important military establishment:

> Benicia, formerly the capital of the State of California, is situated on the Straits of Carquines, which connect Suisun and San Pablo bays. It is on the north side of these straits, and is twenty-five miles above San Francisco. Adjoining the town is a military post and arsenal, and the principal depot of quartermaster and commissary stores for the department of the Pacific.
> The depot and machine-shops of the Pacific Mail Steamship Company are also at this place.

N⁰ 41.

Fort Tejon California
December 2ᵈ 1858.

My dear Sir

Your overland letter of Oct 18ᵗʰ reached me the day before yesterday; and a steamer letter of the same date some time before. I am extremely sorry

to hear, that you give me but a slight hope for securing my immediate discharge from service; although I cannot see any reason why it should be
denied, if requested by influential persons—like
yourself for instance; Morever it would be not the
first case, I have seen many the like during my short
connection with the army.

I hope however that my letter of Sept 10th (No
34) in which I set forth all my views to a considerable length, made some influence on you, and you
acted accordingly. I expect every moment now your
answer on this letter, and I need not say how much
I should disappointed, if my expectations fail!

If you cannot effect any favorable arrangements
with the Coast Survey at present, this circumstance
shall not change my desire in regard to the discharge. Please to hurry up as quick as possible, I
hope to provide for myself in some way or other in
San Francisco, or Los Angeles.

Under no circumstances whatever I am inclined
to make more collections, as an enlisted men. My
patience is long ago exhausted, and I wonder
only—when reflecting at the post—how I could en-
dure so much humiliation, and so manifold insults.

Even officers, who possessed always my protection—with 2 or 3 exceptions—had only one object
to reduce me to the *honorable* position of a private
servant. Major Carleton for instance, who promised
me everything as regards facilities for collection,
wanted me to stuff & mount birds for him, I did
so—even when the number—in 1 month—reached
the grand total of 56. He then wanted me to stuff
for *him* two specimens of each kind. I had, because
he wants to send some to Generals Clarke[1] & Harney.[2] —— At the same time he sent me two Grizzly,
& five otter skins with positive order to dress for
him the next day. —— —— I of course positively
refused to do such thing, and here his protection
ended, he don't know me any more! His protection
brought him nearly 60 mounted birds, & several

dressed furs. The same protection cost us several pounds of preparations, & many days of hard work; during which of course I had to stop altogether collections!

As to your anxiety of going to late in season to Cape St Lucas; I would state that our object of going there was not the only one, to get Water fowls, but everything else. The Waterbirds on the pacific migrate very differently from those on the Eastern shore. They never arrive in these parts before late in December (at present there is not a single duck yet here) and leave very late in the spring. So should I arrive even in February to the Cape, I could hunt waterfowls for more than two months. —— Besides, our intention was—if I recollect well—to collect for a least a couple years in the Gulf, and to whether the season is late or not for ducks, it cannot be late for general collection. For birds, fish, & reptiles the spring is the very best season imaginable. —— —— —— ——

In regard to the Antelope question, although I think I killed at least one hundred, since I am in the U. S. Still I cannot positively state whether they cast annually their horns or not. I had however a very extensive inquiry made on the subject, amongst professional hunters, & they consider the statement as entirely absurd and say—that the Antelopes cast most positively their horns only with long intervalls, say 3 years![3]

If you refer anywhere to me in print please to say simply *John Xantus*. The first mistake was made by my friends, when—without my knowledge—they elected me a member of the Pha. Academy of Nat. Sc., but I had never any ambition for appendages; and am very sorry that it happened.[4]

Could you forward to the *Hungarian National Museum at Pesth* a whole series of my *vertebrate* collection, I should be under great obligation to you indeed dear sir. The museum has a forwarding house at Bremen Msrs C. A. Heinecken & Co, to whose

care out to be sent the boxes, with injunctions to forward at once to the Museum. If you however know a more convenient mode of forwarding, so may use it at your pleasure, as the only object is to send the collection to its destination safely. ——
——Should you be so kind, as to comply with my wish, I would further ask you, to select out only *good* specimens, perfectly fit for mounting; and affix to every specimen a label, printed as the one appended here.[+]

As all these particulars, (including careful packing, & a list of the specimens sent, to be forwarded to me) will occupy good deal of labor & time; you may engage a competent young man for this purpose, and I will pay any amount of compensation for his services you pay him; as soon as you will pleased to notify me of the sum.

I had a letter from home the other day informing me, that Dr Flügel has dispatched a package to your care for me, which started in the packetship *Helvetia* the 15th of September last, for Baltimore. I may expect therefore to hear soon of it.

I send this letter via Tehuatepec, and hope it will reach you before any other mail route from California(?)

very sincerely yours
Vésey

[+][printed label attached][5]

---

1. General Newman S. Clarke (d. 1860) enlisted in 1812 and was made brigadier general, March 1847, for gallant service at Vera Cruz.

2. General William Selby Harney (d. 1889) was a second lieutenant in 1818, fought Indians in Florida, and served with the Second Dragoons in the Mexican War; he had his stars by 1859.

3. *Antilocapra americana,* Pronghorn, bears true horns, bone with a sheathlike covering, but they are shed every year like antlers.

4. Patently untrue; Xántus assumed 'de Vésey' when he entered the U. S. Army and was elected to the Philadelphia Academy under that name as that was the only one he was using at that time.

5. Baird, March 16, 1858:

> I understood you to say that you intend to be referred to as John Xantus de Vesey, and have had labels so printed for you. Do you prefer to omit the de Vesey?

Baird's confusion extended into his report on birds in the *Pacific Railroad Report* (1858b), where he lists Xántus as John Xantus de Vesey, John X. de Vesey, J. X. de Vesey, J. Xantus, and J. Xantus de Vesey.

No42.

Ft Tejon Cala
Decbr 10th 1858.

My dear Sir

Although I wrote only last week I hasten to send you a few lines again in the hope, that my letter will overtake the former in San Francisco by stage, which we expect from St Louis this evening.

Your letter of Nov 1st reached me yesterday, the long anxiously expected one; but I need not tell you how it disappointed me. You wrote me several times, that you have not the slightest doubt about the success of the Cape expedition, and that it only depended on my affirmative answer to commence operations at once. Accordingly I packed up everything, more yet—I sent down several portions of my baggage already to Los Angeles! Should the expedition entirely fail now, of course I make rather a fool of myself, and the case will be one again, to learn of it in future!

As it seems, that there is but slight prospect for the realisation of the Cape expedition, I would earnestly request you dear Sir to effect my discharge as soon as possible; it is indeed a hard trial for me to vast my life & time in such a situation, in some way or other.[1] I hope to create for myself an existence in California, when once out of the service, therefore my only wish is to be liberated from the army. You promised me personally in Washington, and afterwards to Dr Hammond also that any time I desire my discharge, you will effect it at once; I have now the strongest confidence, that you will do so.

I am much surprised that the grizzly lost the hair of the ears, as the specimen was prepared over 15 months since, and when I packed in the box was in complete order. It must have happened in the box the accident there is no other possibility. I wish however to send it to its destination, as I paid $12 for the beast.

I received likewise the end of the bird Report, and I am glad—I have now complete the whole.

Considering that you are just working the Serpent Report,[2] I gathered up a few yet here amongst my collections, and send this evening in a small can per stage to Mr Forbes, to be forwarded to you with 1st Steamer. I filled up the can with Kangaroon rats & mice, which I had captured some time ago.

I wonder much that Möllhausen collected only so little.

sincerely yours
L Vésey

---

1. Baird, November 1, 1858:

> Your letters 34 & 38 both came last mail. I have now the necessary data about [?] to your California exploration, and if Mr. Bache agrees to the proposition I will then go at once to work about the discharge. I would have strong hopes of saving your back pay also. Mr. Bache will be in town in a week or two, and I will lose no time in finding out what he is willing to do.
>
> In case nothing can be done this winter or spring in Lower California with the Coast Survey, I suppose you will remain quietly at Fort Tejon and make an occasional gleaning over your old field.

2. "General Report upon the Zoology of the Several Pacific Railroad Routes. Part III. Reptiles" (Baird 1858c).

NO**43.**

Fᵗ Tejon, Cala
Decbr 22ᵈ 1858.

My dear Sir

I have just received your letter of Nov the 16th, and as the steamer sails only the 5th of next, I will try this time the wagon mail.

I am glad to hear that you purchased the ducking gun, although I did not receive it by this steamer. The long looked for arrival of the box in Baltimore, makes me very happy, and I hope you will forward it as soon as possible. I will not fail to remit you somehow the expenses connected with the fright etc

I am much indebted to you, in putting yourself to so much trouble in regard to my land affairs, but if you shall succeed in arranging it satisfactorily, you will do much more for me as anybody else has done until now.

In reference to my oological collections, I hardly think there is any specimens, which could not [be] identified, as every box is labelled, & besides the corresponding Nᴼ of the Register tells more about it. Whenever I did not know the name of the bird, I referred on the box cover to the Nᴼ of the corresponding birds, for instance, Nᴼ NN. nest & 4 eggs of Buteo Nᴼ XX. Now in such cases you must look at the bird XX among the hawks in my collection, & you will find to what bird belongs the box Nᴼ NN.—There were some mistakes made last year, but I already rectified those in my letter Nᴼ XXVII, & if you look it over again you can correct the labels at once. —— —— —— It is very true, that there are missing the most common nests & eggs; & I expected to hear long ago such remark from you. The cause is very simple. It is generally my rule, to collect *everything* I come across, & in some instances most common species at first. But *in this case* I had very well known, that it is of highest importance to collect at any rate the rare nests, and as the breading season is but short, you may well imagine yourself how busy I was considering that but a few hours belonged to me everyday. If you please now to consider, that some of the nests were on projecting limbs, often 50–60 feet from the ground; and the taking of some of the nests coast me several hours climbing, and some time the nest was only in building process or containing only 1 egg, I had to leave it there & scale up again a few days afterwards; you may from some idea how I must been at work to collect in a few weeks 197 nests & 579 eggs! —— —— —— The woodpeckers, Jays, swallows, bluebirds had hundreds of nests at the very door of my habitation, & every where around, but I considered more important *in this case* to get nests & eggs of *not common* birds at first, & provided be time enough left yet: get afterwards the more common ones. I run however short, when my mountain birds flow out from nest & the collection of good nests closed; the woodpeckers etc nests were also empty. —— This is however not much of a misfortune, we have now the most desirable nests almost without exception; and if I should not here next spring you must only write to Major Carleton or some of the officers to get for you blue bird, swallow, woodpecker & Jays eggs; they will turn out the prisoners, & will get for you bushels of them. To their extent may serve the only fact, that on a single tree before my doors, there were 37 nests (well counted) of the *Melanerpes formicivorus* alone, not counting the blue bird & Martin[1] nests on the same tree. —— —— ——

To illustrate the difficulty of taking some nests, I
will tell you that the first *vireo* nest I discovered,
took fully four days meditating & devising plans, as
how to obtain it. The nest was situated on a limb of
water oak, which was scarcely an inch tick, nearly
twenty feet long, & projecting over a water, fully 4
feet deep, not including mud. The nest was at the
furthest extremity of the limb, about twenty feet
above water. —— —— Finally, after every device
failed—I chopped logs, undressed, carried the logs
neck deep in water under the nest, & built a regular
lower work (in the log house architecture style),
until I reached to about 12 feet of the nest; I
mounted then, pulled down the limb with a hook,
& got the nest. What you say to such feats?

With the Muscicapa verticales[2] & several humming birds I had adventures of very similar character, the description of all together would make a
very amusing volume, & might be entitled *"The
Ramblings & climbings of a fool."*[3]

If you refer to my descriptive catalogue, you will
notice that the *Robins* arrive here in the latter part of
November, & depart early in March. They do not
nest here. —— —— —— —— ——

————

Your very kind and friendly offer to forward dupplicates to Hungarian Museums is very welcome,
and I take the opportunity to ask you at once, to do
so. The first is of course the Hungarian National
Museum at Pest, and I wish to send her as complete
& as *perfect* a series as possible, of all my vertebrated
specimens. I would of course entirely compromise
in you, & leave to your discretion the picking out of
specimens, labelling, & packing, remarking only
that my reputation at home will depend good deal
of this patriotic present. I would particularly request
you to forward the grizzly, a male & female bighorn, ♂ & ♀ deer, & even such specimens which are
few in my collection, but the Smithsonian Institution having many from other parts, does not need

them *particularly.* Of the later I mention the Geococcyx Mexicanus as one. If you could effect an exchange of my *large* dupplicates (say from 60 to 100
specimens in all) for instance a few of each Robins,
woodpeckers, Jays, Pipilos etc for eastern (American) birds, those could go likewise with the others
to the same Museum & would be very acceptable. I
have a large collection of Missouri & Mississippi
birds in Iowa, but I am despairing of their arrival,
therefore this way would be the only one under
present circumstances to carry out my object. As I
requested you in my last, I liked every specimen
properly labelled, with my name (John Xántus) appended, well packed & forwarded, and than a list of
the Specimens forwarded sent to me. To this purpose you must of course engage somebody, I can
not seasonably tresspass in this manner on your
precious time; but I am very willing to pay for the
services of such individual any amount you may
consider just. Anything may be forwarded to said
Museum.

Hungarian National Museum
Pesth—Hungary
care of C. A. Heinecken & Co
Bremen, Germany
but if you know any other way more convenient to
you, you may use it at your pleasure.

———

The 2d shall be the Philadelphia Academy of Natural Sciences, and I would authorize you entirely to
give her dupplicates in my name as soon as possible, of the vertebrated specimens.

———

The 3d the Royal Hungarian Natural History Society at Pesth, of which I am since 16 years, in fact I
am one of her founders; I wish to send a full series
likewise. Their direction is

Magyar királyi terméspettudományi Társulat
Pesth (Hungary)

———

I wish however distinctly understood, that the Smithsonian Institution shall have the preference of every one of the three; and you may pick out a series for the Institution before dispatching the series to the other Institutes.

The rest of the—still formidable—collection shall be subjected to my disposition, respectively deposited with you until my return when I will supply again the Smith. Institution abundantly with dupplicates—personally.

With the nests & Herbarium shall be done nothing at present, unless used for descriptions. I liked to assort them myself, and dispose then of the dupplicates. Every single specimen shall belong of course to the Smithsonian.

I think I expressed myself very fully, & hope you understood my views perfectly.

very sincerely yours
Vésey

---

1. *Progne subis,* Purple Martin.

2. Now *Tyrannus verticalis,* Western Kingbird.

3. Baird, February 9, 1859, urged Xántus to write his adventures as a "traveling naturalist" because they would be "full of interest" and

> You astonish me more and more with your statement of work, by what you say of the difficulty [?] of egg collecting! I had no conception of them. I certainly now know your worth[?] as an explorer and collector. . . .

No44   Ft Tejon Cala
                                  Jan 3d 1859.

Dear Sir
    Your letters of Nov 1st & 16th I answered the 10th & 24th of last month. Since the above dates I heard nothing from you.

The Eastern mail arrived (steamer) the 28th last in S. Francisco, & yesterday here, but I did not receive the gun, nor the box from Baltimore, or any intimation even of their arrival (?) They may turn up however with the next steamer from San Francisco to St. Pedro in a few days. ——

Racoons are but very few here round, but at the Indian Reserve (22 miles distant) I am informed they are very abundant, & easily captured. D[r] Hays[1] the medical gentleman of the Reservation[2] very often comes to see me, and invites me always to see him, offering his hospitality & assistance; but as I tryed to obtain permission to do so from D[r] Ten-Broeck several times, & he always refused it, of course I cannot consistently beg again as long as I am his slave.

As I gave up altogether now collecting, of course I cannot write you on novelties much. The other day however I made an addition to the species of my birds, by killing on my chicken house a very beautiful *Archibuteo ferrugineus*,[3] she is the first of the species I ever noticed, & in a remarkable fine plumage, greatly varying from Cassins description & illustration, although she cannot be mistaken for other birds, as the characteristics are very marked, & differing from every other buzzard I know.

I am very sorry I had not known before the intention of the Patent office in regard to forest tree seeds, as I had been able to gather plentiful of them. I send a small parcel to the Hungarian botanical Gardens at Pesth last autumn, containing 57 pieces, this was all I collected here. In future however I will keep in mind this branch also, it is with but very little trouble connected.[4]

The weather is quite boisterous here since weeks, at present we have 3 feet snow in average, although on some places 10 & 12 feet, so that the stages cannot pass at all. The thermometer is every morning 6–10° below freezing point.

Hoping to hear soon of you I am
Dear Sir

very truly yours
LVésey

---

1. Dr. R. T. Hayes is listed in the Department of the Interior's *Register of Officers and Agents, Civil, Military, and Naval, in the Service of the United States,* p. 88; the report of September 30, 1861, shows him as one of six employees and the only physician at the Tejon Agency; he received a salary of $1,500.00 per annum at his post.

2. The Tejon Indian Reservation was established in the fall of 1853 in response to the troubles caused by Indians in the area; Hussey (1950, p. 29):

> . . . Indians in vicinity of the Tejón were troublesome, so trouble-some indeed that they appear long before the last months of 1847 to have driven most, if not all, of the few ranchers in the region back into settlements.

The reservation closed in 1863 when the Indians were moved else-where; it consisted of 30,000 acres and was laid out by Beale who be-came Commissioner of Indian Affairs in 1851, to be dismissed in 1854 (see February 2, 1858, note 3). In June 1854, there were some 2,500 Indians on the Reservation, largely engaged in agriculture, but fewer than 300 the following year, according to Mansfield (in Frazer 1963, p. 98). The setting of Helen Hunt Jackson's *Ramona* is in the general area of the reservation.

3. Now *Buteo regalis,* Ferruginous Hawk.

4. The Department of Agriculture, then under the Patent Office, solicited seeds to develop new strains for cultivation.

Fort Tejon Cala
January 6th 1859.

My dear Sir/

The Steamer arrived several days ago, but I am without letters from you, the last being of the date *Nov. 16th*. The gun arrived however safely this morning, I will try in target to morrow.

I hope you secured ere this my discharge from service, should be this not the case, then you might leave it as it is, for the few months is hardly worth while to make so much trouble; and to employ it as well as possible, I am willing to go for there few months to Ft Yuma, *provided*: you can send a transfer to that place at once, and *provided* my expenses of travelling to that Post will be paid, or transportation furnished. By overland mail they charge from Los Angeles to Yuma $50, and of course I hardly could expend about 100 dollars (it costs more or less $100 from this Post to Yuma) and of my pocket for this pleasure; even if I had money to spend.

The cause of my willingness to accept this transfer is, that Dr George Hammond has been ordered to Oregon, and is already replaced in Yuma by Dr Herndon; with whom I am personally well aquainted, & who is very well disposed towards me. Under such circumstances I might expect some facilities in regard to making collections at Yuma.

There is a new Post to be established at Beales crossing Colorado river, 275 miles North of Yuma.[1] Colonel Hoffman[2] is already there locating the Post, and has 2 Companies of Drag's & 4 Companies of the 6th Infantry with him. The Post is intended as permanent, & it seems in connection with the overland wagon protection. Dr Edgar[3] is ordered there as Medical officer. There is however great trouble about new Post, the Hospital-Surgery etc are in tents, and much duty to be done therefore I consistently could not go to such place with the view of making collections. You may however look out in time to secure from there specimens by some of your friends. The location of the Post seems very favorable, as the topography is particularly inviting as far as I know.

Of course I should prefer the Cape expedition to everything else at present, and should this plan not succeed *next* my discharge from service. Only in case of a total failure of both, I am willing to go to Yuma, but even in this case: if you procure the transfer at once & transportation.

Should I start to Yuma about the end of March, I will have 5 months for collection, & likely I will get many specimens. For less time however would be not worth to cross twice the desert, thats evident.

I had always some hope, that I might have a good hunt this winter on the Tulare lake, which is literally covered now with waterfowls, but Dr Ten-Broeck is since nearly 3 months vagabondizing in Los Angeles, I have to do all his Duty, and consequently is out of question such project; he comes home the last day of the month, and goes again the 1st of the next, this goes always so; he comes only not to be reported absent on the Post Return, and as soon as the Post Return goes, he follows in track at once.

I never had any idea of such transaction at all! Is the Smithsonian Report for 1857 not yet out?

Very sincerely yours
LVésey

P. S.
Mr Chas Greenman[4] of Broklyn, a near relative of Prof Henry, desires to be remembered by him. Mr Greenman is a very nice young gentleman, a Clerk at present in the Sutler Store at this place.

1.Xántus refers to Fort Mojave, established April 19, 1858, on the left bank of the Colorado River at "Beale's crossing"; its mission was to control the Mojave and Paiute Indians and provide protection for emigrants. It was abandoned in 1861 and its garrison moved to Los Angeles because of Confederate sympathies in southern California; reoccupied in 1863, it closed finally in 1890 and the buildings were demolished in 1942.

Beale (1858, p. 2) crossed at the present-day Mojave, "the entire distance from that place to Fort Yuma, some 200 miles below."

2. William Hoffman (d. 1884), a Military Academy graduate from New York, served gallantly during the Mexican War, went with the 6th Infantry as a Major in 1852, but did not become a Colonel until 1862 during the Civil War.

3. Dr. William Francis Edgar (d. 1897), became an Assistant Surgeon in 1849, was posted to Fort Miller in 1851, and thence to Fort Tejon in 1854. After an accident he was sent back to the East but returned to Fort Tejon in 1857 after the January earthquake. Edgar (1893, p. 26) describes the Fort as lying

> up in the mountains at what has been called "the head of the San Joaquin Valley." Here the Sierra Nevada and the Coast Range mountains meet and form a pass out of the valley known as the "Canada de las Uvas" (canon of currents). Up this canada some three or four miles in the mountains, where a glen containing a few acres opens into it from the west, and about fifteen miles south and a little east of the Indian reservation of the valley and nearly that same distance south of the noted "Tehachipe pass." . . . The location of the post was among large, umbrageous oak trees that bore large crops of acorns, and therefore had been a great rendezvous for grizzly bears which infested the surrounding mountains. When the acorns were ripe, and for the first few days after the command was encamped there, it was visited nightly by a very large grizzly, which generally stampeded all the horses and mules in camp, until he found out that the carbines of the soldiers were dangerous.

4. Greenman has been impossible to trace to date; he is not listed in any Army Register and was probably a civilian employee. Cullimore (1949, p. 33) does not mention him in his description of the store at the post, although he notes owners, profits, sales, and clerks.

Fort Tejon, Cala
January 12th
1859.

My dear Sir/

It affords me a great pleasure to introduce to you herewith Mr John Feilner a late pupil of mine. Mr. Feilner is a Sergeant in Company "F" U. S. 1st Dragoons, at present stationed at Fort Crook, Pitt river, Cala, with almost positive prospect of a protracted stay there.

He was formerly at Ft Tejon, and having got aquainted with him, & found extremely enthusiastic for collections, I imparted most of my limited abilities to him as regards taxidermical operations; and I can safely say he is well conversant *practically* now with everything in the line.

Mr Feilner has already a considerable collection on hand as he informs me, and very desirous to deposit at the Smithsonian Institution, until his time of service expires; of course he is willing to furnish the Smithsonian Institution with any duplicate specimens of his collection, the Institution might desire to possess.[1]

Lieutenant J. T. Mercer[2] his Company Commander at present does everything for him, to facilitate his pursuits, it would however do much good if you should write him at some time a letter also, recommending Mr Feilner; the Lieutenant—I know him well—is a great friend of the Smithsonian Institution.

Anything you can do for Mr Feilner as regards Taxidermical materials, transportation of specimens etc please do it, and be assured you will highly oblige

your very truly
JXántus deVésey

Spencer F. Baird Esq
    Asst Secretary Smithsonian Institution
        Washington city   D. C.

1. From Cabo San Lucas, April 7, 1860:

> I am happy to hear that Mr Feilner of fort Crook has contributed so nicely in birds, I was sure you would be pleased with him. He writes me at present that he is not suffered how to continue much his collections, as his lieutenant left for the recruiting service, and the Captain has the command, who is not much inclined to Natural History. Mr Feilner now, to do something at least, procured a photographic apparatus & is taking the likenesses of animals, principally lepidoptera, with great success as he reports.

Feilner later became Quartermaster at Ft. Crook, served with distinction in the Civil War and was promoted to captain. He was assigned to duty in the Dakotas where there were Sioux problems; riding ahead of the advance guard, he blundered into a thicket looking for birds and was killed by Indians. See Feilner (1872); a comment by his commander, General Alfred Sully, is appended to Feilner's report, p. 430:

> It was all owing to his enthusiastic desire to collect as many specimens as possible for the Smithsonian Institution. I had cautioned him several times about the risk he ran in going so far from the command, and on the night previous to the day of his death I sent for him to my tent to talk to him on the subject, and I offered him a party of my scouts to protect him, as I was desirous that he should do all he could to forward the scientific researches that he was sent here to attend to; he promised me to accept them, but did not do so.

2. Lt. John Thomas Mercer, 2nd Lieutenant in the First Dragoons in March 1855, fought for the South and was killed in 1864.

N°46. [1]

F[t] Tejon Cala
January 14th 1859.

My dear Sir/

Your letter of Decbr. 2[d] arrived at last—this morning from F[t] Yuma, where our Los Angeles Postmaster pleased to send it, with all the letters and papers received by last steamer for F[t] Tejon!

I am much indebted to you for the trouble you take in my land affairs; I send the intelligence today to my Attorney Judge Musser of Brunswick Missouri for his information; and I would earnestly beg you dear Sir to do for him anything you can, if he should request you for something in regard to the lands.

The box from Europe, which you announce as received at last, of course I wish forwarded to me as soon as possible, the contents are of the highest possible interest to me. The box contains amongst other things my recently published books, and the criticism of every Newspaper at home about them. I wish you had opened the box, and looked on one large volume, which contains a selected & condensed translation of Marcy, Simpson, Fremont & Stansbury, with many illustrations, some of them I hear very well executed on steel.[2] ——

The gun is a very good one as regards shooting although badly finished. I fired in targot the other day (a sheet wrapping Paper) with the following results

Charge 180 grains powder, 2 ounces shot N^O 5.

50	yards	71	grains
75	"	43	"
100	"	27	"
2125	"	13	"
150	"	2	"

Satisfactory enough! —— —— I wish only I could come now soon among ducks, & other fowls on water!

I return herewith the specification of expenses, receipted.

Mr Cassin wrote me a very long & interesting letter, I returned his compliments with a still longer one, which I confidently hope—he will publish as soon, as he gets it.

If you print the sheet, which contains the Xantusia, I liked much if you could get me some 3 or 4 extra copies (only of the sheet which contains the article), for sending them to some of my friends.

And likewise I would like to get some extra copies of the *list of Tejon birds* you are going to Publish

in the Pha. Academys Proceedings,[3] of course I am
to pay the expenses, if there are any.

very truly yours
JXántus deVésey

Prof Baird
Washington

---

1. Note at top of page, not in Baird's handwriting: "44 not received."

2. According to Madden (1949a, p. 223ff.), who gives a thorough discussion of Xántus' plagiarism, it was one book, not "books" and there
were no steel engravings.

3. "Descriptions of two new species of Birds from the vicinity of Fort
Tejon, California" (Xantus 1858, p. 117) is a sparse half-page report on
Tyrannula hammondii De Vesey and *Vireo cassinii* De Vesey. "Catalogue of
Birds collected in the vicinity of Fort Tejon, California, with a descrip-
tion of a new species of *Syrnium*" (Xantus 1859) contains a list of 144
birds with a description of *Syrnium occidentale* (now *Strix occidentalis*),
Spotted Owl, USNM #17200:

> The following list presents the results of ornithological collections
> made in the vicinity of Fort Tejon, in California, during a period
> embraced between the end of May, 1857, and the beginning of No-
> vember, 1858, about 17 months, and including but one season of
> northward migration of the species. The 144 species enumerated
> are not to be considered as all that belong to the region above men-
> tioned, as many birds are so rare, retiring, or difficult of approach,
> that they can only be secured in a series of years. Many additional
> species of rapacious and water birds were seen but could not be
> obtained, and though many of these were readily recognized, I have
> not felt at liberty to mention them in the list, which consists entirely
> of species actually collected within a few miles of the Post, and now
> in the Museum of the Smithsonian Institution. Of all the species
> collected, or observed, copious notes were taken relating to the
> numbers, dimensions, habits, reproduction, &c. These will all be
> made the subject of a special memoir hereafter, and I limit myself
> here to a simple enumeration of species.
> It will be seen from the catalogue that the Fauna of Fort Tejon is
> essentially that of the coast of California, as shown by the abun-
> dance of the California Jay, Brown Pipilo, &c., *Psaltriparus minimus*,

etc., and has only slight relations to that of the interior or Colorado Region.

Some of the most interesting results of the collections made at Fort Tejon, consist in the addition to science of several new species, as *Syrnium occidentale, Empidonax Hammondii, Vireo Cassinii*, etc., and in the increase of the Fauna of the United States by some Mexican species, as *Selasphorus calliope, Dendrocygna fulva*, &c. *Helminthophaga ruficapilla* had not previously been found west of the Rocky Mountains, while *Carpodacus Cassinii* was for the first time obtained west of the Colorado river. (See Appendix for complete list.)

No 47.

Ft Tejon January 21st
evening 1859.

My dear Sir/

About noon today arrived here the overland mail dropping your letter of 16th ult; and an order for the Secr of War for my immediate discharge. —— Dr TenBroek is in Los Angeles yet, & Major Carleton Cmdg the Post requested me to wait until the Dr return, (who is ordered home by messenger) so as turn over to him the Medical stores.

I am packing now, and hope to be in San Francisco about the 29th inst, when I will write you again circumstancially.

Our mails were for the last couple months much behind time, as you see your letter came by Overland wagon 36 days; but still in advance of the Panama mail, as the Steamers letters Decbr. 20th are not *here* yet. —— Naturally enough I do not know anything about particulars you write me by steamer.

Some Falconidae I have on hand will be sent of at once from here & all other things I might find among my things.

My traps & extensive apparatus I take along of course, they will fill about 5 boxes. We expect

Bannings train in in a day or two, and if so they will transport gratis. Should the train however not arrive in due time, I will send of to Mr Forbes anyhow you know how much safety is in baggage—left behind, e.g. Brunswick & F^t Riley.

I hope you have done *everything* I particularly requested you in regard my going to St Lucas?

Now dear Sir, please to accept my warmest thanks, for your kind services. And please be assured, that I will always gratefully acknowledge it, and anything I can do for you to gratify your wishes, just command my services which will be always ready!

very sincerely yours
John Xántus[1]

Please send the European box to me, as soon as possible.

---

1. The first instance of Xántus' use of his real name, which he would use from this letter forward.

N^o48

F^t Tejon Cala 1859.
January 23^d morning

My dear Sir

Your letters of Decbr 16 & 18th sent by Panama, came to hand just this moment. I am glad you agree in main points as to the plan of my future collections, & operations.

In regard to several combinations & propositions—of course—I cannot answer until I had interviews with Lt Elliot.[1] I will try everything to ar-

range with him matters to my best calculations as to
a successful result.

To morrow evening I start for San Francisco via
Los Angeles, and as soon as I settled there matters I
am to write you extensively of course.

I sent off all my traps today to Mr Forbes.

I would like if you would subscribe for me for a
weekly paper for instance New York Herald or
Tribune, and send regularly care of Mr Forbes, who
will find some means I suppose to forward it to me.
I would not like to start out of the world without
knowing that I will get some information occasionally, as how the matters are going on on the Rest of
the World!

I will follow your advice, and dont stop at General Picos at all, I am going through as fast as the
conveyances will carry me.[2]

very sincerely yours
JXántus

I hope you sent your letters for me to S. Francisco,
& not to Tejon?

---

1. Lt. George H. Elliott (1831–1900), U. S. Coast Survey, was assistant
engineer in charge of construction of the San Francisco harbor defenses
from 1857 to 1861. Upon his arrival, Xántus' double identity reached
the crisis stage and he wrote Baird, February 4:

> I called, the next day after my arrival on Lt. Elliot likewise, and
> introduced me as John Xántus. He said that he has no instructions
> whatever yet, only a short notice from the Washington office: *that
> if the Hospital Steward from F^t Tejon a Louis Vésey should present him-
> self, to give him instructions in the menagement of the tide gauge, as he
> is very probably to go to Cape St Lucas as tidal observer"* —— —— You
> will recollect very well dear Sir, that I *particularly* requested you in
> my letter of Sept 10th to be called at the Coast Survey John Xántus?
> You forget this point likely, but I had very unpleasant explanations
> with Lt. Elliot in consequence of this.
>
> I believe it was altogether superfluous to tell Lt Elliot that I am,
> or that I was a Hospital Steward, because he (being an officer)

received me as a Hospital Steward, in a very haughty manner exactly as an Officer speaks to an enlisted man! He told me to go at once to the presidio, where I could eat and sleep with the Sergeants, and one of them will learn me gauge keeping. I told him not to imagine, that I will require months to learn how to menage a gauge, I will learn it in a few hours, or a couple of days, but I have not the slightest intention to live & eat with the Sergeants in the barrack. After many words passing between us, I convinced him apparently, that he has to treat me in a very different manner, because he became gradually a gentleman, yielded to my desire, & read your letters to me.

Baird apologized but tended to pass the blame, March 1, 1859:

Lt. Trowbridge inadvertently used the old one as he had become familiar with it from seeing and hearing so much of Mr. de Vesey until very recently.

2. The trip was nearly a disastrous one, February 4, 1859:

I left F^t Tejon by the overland mail coach the 25th ult and arrived in town the 29th morning. The trap was rather unpleasant as the stage upset twice, all the skin came off my knees & elbow, my face was considerably bruised also, nothing serious happened however and I am at present as well as ever!

《 》

Baird's evaluation and appreciation of Xántus' work at Fort Tejon, which he would not receive until he was stationed at Cabo San Lucas, was expressed in the 1859 *Smithsonian Annual Report:*

Exploration of the vicinity of Fort Tejon and of Cape St. Lucas, by Mr. John Xantus.—Among the very important researches in the natural history of America, the explorations of Mr. John Xantus deserve particular mention. In previous reports, the collections made by Mr. Xantus at Fort Tejon have been referred to. During a residence there of about sixteen months, from the summer of 1857 to the autumn of 1858, although constantly occupied with official duties, he has exhausted the natural history of the vicinity of the fort in the most thorough manner. All departments are fully represented in his collections, which filled thirty-five boxes; the birds alone embracing nearly 2,000 specimens and 144 species.

Professor Bache, the Superintendent of the United States Coast Survey, having determined to establish a tidal station at Cape St. Lucas, Lower California, Mr. Xantus was placed in charge, and reached the Cape in April last. He has since that time made, in the intervals of his official duties, and forwarded to Washington, collections which vie in thoroughness with those of Fort Tejon, and exceed them in number of species, embracing as they do the marine as well as the fresh water and land forms. Of 42 species of birds first received from him, 8 are new; of crustaceans, there are over 100 species, many of them new; while in all other departments the collections have been proportionately great.

The results obtained at Cape St. Lucas by Mr. Xantus add another to the many benefits to natural history as well as to physical science rendered incidentally by the operations of the United States Coast Survey. . . .

Acknowledgments

The Smithsonian Archives permission to publish the letters of John Xántus (Record Unit 7212), and selections from both the out-going correspondence of Spencer Fullerton Baird (Record Unit 7002) and the incoming (Record Unit 52), made this book possible. My thanks especially to Susan Westgate Glenn and William Deiss at the Archives. Also at the Smithsonian Institution, J. Philip Angle, Department of Birds, United States National Museum of Natural History.

I am indebted for help to Elizabeth Bailey, Reference Specialist, The State Historical Society of Missouri; Richard Beidleman and James Enderson, Department of Zoology, The Colorado College; Christopher Brewer, for loan of a plate from *Old Adobes of Forgotten Fort Tejon* by Clarence Cullimore; Marilyn Chang, Government Documents Librarian, Denver Public Library; Mrs. Clarence Cullimore and Clarence Cullimore, Jr., for permission to reprint illustrations from Clarence Cullimore's book on Fort Tejon; Curtis Darling, Kern County Historical Society; Bernard Fontana, Field Historian, University Library, The University of Arizona; Larry Jochims, Research Historian, Kansas State Historical Society, Topeka; Steve Lines, State Park Ranger, Fort Tejon State Park; Kenneth S. Norris, Environmental Field Program, University of California, Santa Cruz; W. Michael Mathes, Department of History, University of San Francisco; William McKale, Museum Technician, U. S. Cavalry Museum, Fort Riley, Kansas; Annegret Ogden, Reference Librarian, Bancroft Library, University of California; John H. Slonaker, U. S. Army Military History Institute, Carlisle Barracks, Pennsylvania; A. R. Rea, San Diego Museum of Natural History (who commented extensively on the manuscript in preparation and generously advised on taxonomy); W. Ann Reynolds, Chancellor, California State University; Ira Wiggins, Professor Emeritus of Botany, Stanford University; Virginia Steele Wood, Naval and Maritime Historian at the Library of Congress; William P. Wreden, for permission to reproduce portraits of John Xántus from *Xántus, Hungarian Naturalist in the Pioneer West;* and the marvelous reference librarians at The Colorado College, especially Julie Jones-Eddy, Lee Hall, Yem Michali, Susan Myers, Robin Satterwite, and Jean Casey Welch. My personal thanks to Katherine Belden, Ava Heinrichsdorff, Cathryn Redman, E. J. Sprague, M. D. Tally, and, for precise reading, Timilou Rixton. If any errors remain, they are, I regret to say, mine alone.

Appendix:
Annotated List of Xántus' Fort Tejon Birds

Xántus, John. 1859. "Catalogue of Birds Collected in the Vicinity of Fort Tejon, California, with a description of a new Species of SYRNIUM. *Proceedings of the Academy of Natural Sciences of Philadelphia* 11:189–93.

When Xántus published Baird's list, he noted, "The names and numbers (on the left-hand side) given, are those of the species in the Report on birds of the Pacific R. R. Survey, Vol. ix." Since this produced non-sequential numbering, actual sequence is indicated by numbers in brackets. Bird names are as published, followed by the common name. Within parentheses are given any name changes from the 5th and 6th AOU Checklist; Roman numerals corresponding to Xántus' General Register entries; and text page numbers when applicable.

[1]   1. *Cathartes aura*, Illig.—Turkey Buzzard. (Turkey Vulture; XCIX; pp. 86, 116, 182)

[2]   13. *Tinnunculus sparverius*, Vieill.—Sparrow Hawk. (*Falco sparverius*, American Kestrel; CVII)

[3]   16. *Accipiter mexicanus*, Swains.—Blue-backed Hawk. (*A. cooperii*, Cooper's Hawk)

[4]   17. *Accipiter fuscus*, Bonap.—Sharp-shinned Hawk. (*A. striatus*; CLI)

[5]   24. *Buteo montanus*, Nuttall.—Western Red-tail. (*B. jamaicensis*)

[6]   26. *Buteo elegans*, Cassin.—Red-bellied Hawk. (*B. lineatus elegans*, Red-shouldered Hawk; pp. 134, 138 n.8, 144)

[7]   32. *Archibuteo ferrugineus*, Gray.—Squirrel Hawk. (*Buteo regalis*, Ferruginous Hawk; pp. 206, 207 n.3)

[8]   38. *Circus hudsonius*, Vieillot.—Marsh Hawk. (*C. cyaneus hudsonius*)

[9]   47. *Strix pratincola,* Bonap.—Barn Owl. (*Tyto alba pratincola;* pp. 164, 166)

[10]   48. *Bubo virginianus,* Bonap.—Great Horned Owl. (CXXV)

[11]   54a. *Syrnium occidentalis,* Xantus.—California Barred Owl. (*Strix occidentalis;* CXXXVI)

[12]   57. *Nyctale acadica,* Bon.—Saw-whet Owl. (*Aegolius acadicus;* CX)

[13]   59. *Athene cunicularia,* Bon.—Burrowing Owl. (pp. 119, 120 n.4; CXXVII)

[14]   51. Owl (too young to identify).

[15]   68. *Geococcyx californianus,* Baird.—Paisano; Chaparral Cock. (Greater Roadrunner; pp. 45 n.10, 116, 148, 178, 189, 204)

[16]   75. *Picus harrisii,* Aud.—Harris' Woodpecker. (*Picoides villosus harrisii,* Hairy Woodpecker; XXV; pp. 100, 103 n.3)

[17]   77. *Picus gairdneri,* Aud.—Gairdner's Woodpecker. (*Picoides pubescens gairdnerii,* Downy Woodpecker)

[18]   78. *Picus nuttalli,* Gambel.—Nuttall's Woodpecker. (*Picoides nuttallii*)

[19]   87. *Syphropicus ruber,* Baird.—Red-breasted Woodpecker. (More likely *Syphrapicus varius,* Yellow-bellied Sapsucker; XXIV, XXVII; pp. 100, 103, 104 n.7).

[20]   95. *Melanerpes formicivorus,* Bonap.—California Woodpecker. (Acorn Woodpecker; 22 n.53, 45 n.13, 86, 92 n.9, 93, 100, 121, 165)

[21]   96. *Melanerpes torquatus,* Bonap.—Lewis's Woodpecker. (*M. lewis,* Lewis' Woodpecker; XC; pp. 36, 38 n.14, 100, 104 n.6)

[22]   98. *Copates [colaptes] mexicanus,* Swains.—Red-shafted Flicker. (*Colaptes auratus,* Northern Flicker; XXI; pp. 11, 22 n.52)

[23]   102. *Trochilus alexandri,* Bourc. and Muls.—Black-chinned Humming Bird. (*Archilochus alexandri;* pp. 22 n.55, 134, 138 n.13, 144, 151)

[24]   103. *Selasphorus rufus,* Sw.—Rufous Humming Bird. (XVI)

[25]   104. *Selasphorus calliope,* Gould. (*Stellula calliope,* Calliope Hummingbird)

[26]   105. *Atthis anna,* Reichenb.—Anna Humming Bird. (*Calypte anna,* Anna's Hummingbird; XIII; pp. 45 n.9, 144, 146 n.13, 151)

[27]   106. *Atthis costae,* Reichenb.—Ruffed Humming Bird. (*Calypte costa,* Costa's Hummingbird; XV; pp. 144, 146 n.12, 151)

[28]   126. *Tyrannus verticalis,* Say.—Arkansas Flycatcher. (Western Kingbird; V, LXVII; pp. 144, 146 n, 151, 203, 205 n.2)

[29]   131 *Myiarchus mexicanus,* Baird.—Ash-throated Flycatcher. (*Myiarchus cinerascens;* pp. 134, 138 n.5, 152)

[30]   134. *Sayornis nigricans,* Bonap.—Black Flycatcher. (Black Phoebe; VI)

[31]   137. *Contopus borealis,* Baird.—Olive-sided Flycatcher. (pp. 139, 145 n.10, 151)

[32]   138. *Contopus richardsonii,* Baird.—Short-legged Pewee. (*C. sordidulus,* Western Wood-pewee; pp. 139–40, 145 n.2, 151)

[33]   141. *Empidonax pusillus,* Cab.—Little Flycatcher. (*E. minimus,* Least Fly-catcher; more likely *E. overholseri,* Dusky Flycatcher; LXVI; p. 74 n.4)

[34]   144a. *Empidonax difficilis,* Baird.—Western Flycatcher. (XII, XL; pp. 134, 138 n.6, 144)

[35]   145. *Empidonax hammondii,* Baird.—Hammond's Flycatcher. (IX?)

[36]   150. *Turdus nanus,* Aud.—Dwarf Thrush. (*Catharus guttatus,* Hermit Thrush)

[37]   155. *Turdus migratorius,* Linn.—Robin. (LXXI, LXXV; pp. 44 n.6, 105 n.10, 203, 204)

[38]   156. *Turdus naevius,* Gmelin.—Varied Thrush. (*Ixoreus naevius;* LXXII)

[39]   159. *Sialia mexicana,* Swains.—Western Blue Bird. (XCII; pp. 101, 105 n.14, 102)

[40]   161. *Regulus calendula,* Licht.—Ruby-crowned Wren. (Ruby-crowned Kinglet; pp. 52, 53 n.1)

[41]   164. *Hydrobata mexicana,* Baird.—Water Ouzel. (*Cinclus mexicanus,* American Dipper)

[42]   165. *Anthus ludovicianus,* Licht.—Tit-lark. (*A. spinoletta,* Water Pipit; pp. 52, 54–55 n.6)

[43]   170. *Geothylpis trichas,* Cab.—Maryland Yellow Thróat. (Common Yel-lowthroat; pp. 52, 53 n.3)

[44]   173. *Geothylpis macgillivrayi,* Baird.—Macgillivray's Warbler. (*Oporornis tolmiei,* MacGillivray's Warbler; CL)

[45]   177. *Icteria longicauda,* Lawr.—Long-tailed Chat. (*I. virens longicauda,* Yellow-breasted Chat; LXX; pp. 139–40, 144, 145 n.1)

[46]   183. *Helminthophaga ruficapilla,* Bd.—Nashville Warbler. (*Vermivora ruf-icapilla;* LXV; p. 215 n.3)

[47]   184. *Helminthophaga celata,* Baird.—Orange-crowned Warbler. (*Vermi-vora celata;* pp. 145, 146 n.24, 152)

[48]   192. *Dendroica nigrescens,* Baird.—Black-throated Gray Warbler. (CXLIX)

[49]   195. *Dendroica audubonii,* Baird.—Audubon's Warbler. (*D. coronata au-duboni,* Yellow-rumped/Audubon's Warbler; CXIV)

[50]   203. *Dendroica aestiva,* Baird.—Yellow Warbler. (*D. petechia;* XL; pp. 52, 53 n.2, 151)

[51]   213. *Myiodictes pusillus,* Bonap.—Green Black-cap Flycatcher. (*Wilsonia pusilla,* Wilson's Warbler; VIII)

[52]   223. *Pyranga ludoviciana,* Bonap.—Louisiana Tanager. (*Piranga,* West-ern Tanager; XLI)

[53]   226. *Hirundo lunifrons,* Say.—Cliff Swallow. (*Hirundo pyrrhonota*)

[54]   227. *Hirundo bicolor,* Vieill.—White-bellied Swallow. (*Tachycineta bicolor,* Tree Swallow; CXXXIII; pp. 113, 116 n.1)

[55]   228. *Hirundo thalassina,* Sw.—Violet Green Swallow. (*Tachycineta, Violet-green* Swallow; LXXXII)

[56]   231. *Progne purpurea,* Boie.—Purple Martin. (*P. subis;* LXXXI; p. 202, 205 n.1)

[57]   234. *Phainopepla nitens,* Sclater.—Black-crested Flycatcher. (*Phainopepla;* I, L; pp. 9, 19 n.33, 36 n.3, 41, 43–44 n.5, 52, 53 n.4, 134–35, 145)

[58]   235. *Myiasdestes townsendii,* Cab.—Townsend's Flycatcher. (*Myadestes townsendi,* Townsend's Solitaire; VIII)

[59]   238. *Collyrio excubitoroides,* Baird.—White-rumped Shrike. (*Lanius ludovicianus excubitorides,* Loggerhead Shrike; III; pp. 38 n.16, 41, 44 n.7)

[60]   245. *Vireo gilvus,* Bonap.—Warbling Flycatcher. (Warbling Vireo)

[61]   250. *Vireo solitarius,* Vieill.—Blue-headed Flycatcher. (Solitary Vireo)

[62]   251. *Vireo cassinii,* Xantus.—Cassin's Vireo. (*V. solitarius cassinii,* Solitary Vireo; pp. 140, 141, 144, 151, 214–15 n.3)

[63]   253a. Var. *Mimus caudatus,* Baird.—Long-tailed Mocker. (*Mimus polyglottos,* Northern Mockingbird; LXVI; pp. 144, 146 n.14, 151)

[64]   256. *Harporhynchus redivivus,* Cab.—California Thrush. (*Toxostoma redivivum,* California Thrasher; II)

[65]   263. *Catherpes mexicanus,* Baird.—White-throated Wren. (Canyon Wren; LX)

[66]   264. *Salpinctes obsoletus,* Cab.—Rock Wren. (CXVI)

[67]   276. *Thryothorus bewickii,* Bonap.—Bewick's Wren. (*Thryomanes bewickii;* CXVII)

[68]   268. *Cistothorus palustris,* Cab.—Long-billed Marsh Wren. (Marsh Wren; LIX; pp. 57, 89)

[69]   271. *Troglodytes parkmanni,* Aud.—Parkman's Wren. (*Troglodytes aedon parkmanni,* House Wren; LVI, LVIII)

[70]   273. *Troglodytes hyemalis,* Vieill.—Winter Wren. (*T. troglodytes;* CXV)

[71]   274. *Chamaea fasciata,* Gambel.—Ground Tit. (Wrentit; LI; pp. 58 n.1, 59)

[72]   276. *Certhia mexicana,* Gloger.—Mexican Creeper. (*C. americana,* Brown Creeper; LVII; pp. 49, 51 n.1, 57, 60 n.3, 105 n.13)

[73]   278. *Sitta aculeata,* Cassin.—Slender-billed Nuthatch. (*Sitta carolinensis aculeata,* White-breasted Nuthatch; pp. 145, 146 n.18, 151)

[74]   282. *Polioptila caerulea,* Sclat.—Blue-gray Gnatcatcher. (LV)

[75]   287. *Lophophanes inornatus,* Cassin.—Gray Titmouse. (*Parus inornatus,* Plain Titmouse; LIV)

[76]   294. *Parus montanus,* Gambel.—Mountain Titmouse. (*P. gambelii,* Mountain Chickadee; LIII)

[77]   298. *Psaltriparus minimus,* Bonap.—Least Tit. (Common Bushtit; LII, LXVIII)

[78]   302. *Eremophila cornuta,* Boie.—Sky Lark. (*E. alpestris,* Horned Lark; XXXIV; CXXIX)

[79]   306. *Carpodacus californicus,* Baird.—Western Purple Finch. (*C. purpureus californicus,* Purple Finch; XXXVI)

[80]   307. *Carpodacus cassinii,* Baird.—Cassin's Purple Finch. (Cassin's Finch; XXXVII; pp. 52, 153–54 n.1, 215 n.3)

[81]   308. *Carpodacus frontalis,* Gray.—House Finch. *C. mexicanus frontalis,* House Finch; XXXII; pp. 11, 22 n.50, 49, 51 n.2, 52, 56 n.10, 145, 146 n.19, 152)

[82]   314. *Chrysomitris psaltria,* Bonap.—Arkansas Finch. (*Carduelis psaltria,* Lesser Goldfinch; XLII, XLVI)

[83]   316. *Chrysomitris lawrencii,* Bonap.—Lawrence's Goldfinch. (*Carduelis lawrencei;* XXXV, XLIV; pp. 145, 146 n.20)

[84]   317. *Chrysomitris pinus,* Bonap.—Pine Finch. (*Carduelis pinus,* Pine Siskin; LXII; pp. 61 n.6, 152)

[85]   335. *Passerculus alaudinus,* Bonap.—Lark Sparrow. (*P. sandwichensis alaudinus,* Savannah Sparrow)

[86]   344. *Chondestes grammaca,* Bonap.—Lark Finch. (Lark Sparrow; CLIV)

[87]   346. *Zonotrichia gambelii,* Gambel.—Gambel's Finch. (*Z. leucophrys gambelii,* White-crowned Sparrow; XXXIII; pp. 104–5 n.9, 134, 145)

[81]   347. *Zonotrichia coronata,* Baird.—Golden-crowned Sparrow. (*Z. atricapilla coronata;* pp. 134, 138 n.2, 144)

[89]   352. *Junco oregonus,* Sclat.—Oregon Snow Bird. (*J. hyemalis oregonus,* Dark-eyed Junco; XLV; pp. 101, 105 n.15)

[90]   359. *Spizella socialis,* Bonap.—Chipping Sparrow. (*S. passerina;* pp. 145, 146 n.22)

[91]   364. *Melospiza hermanni,* Baird.—Heermann's Song Sparrow. (*M. melodia heermanni,* Song Sparrow)

[92]   366. *Melospiza rufina,* Baird.—Rusty Song Sparrow. (*M. melodia rufina,* Song Sparrow)

[93]   376. *Melospiza fallax,* Baird.—Mountain Song Sparrow. (*M. melodia fallax,* Song Sparrow)

[94]   368. *Melospiza lincolnii,* Baird.—Lincoln's Finch. (Lincoln's Sparrow; XXXIX; pp. 56 n.8, 62 n.7, 145, 146 n.21)

[95]   372. *Peucaea ruficeps,* Baird.—Brown-headed Finch. (*Aimophila ruficeps,* Rufous-crowned Sparrow; LXIV; p. 62 n.8)

[96]   375. *Passerella townsendii,* Nutt.—Oregon Finch. (*P. iliaca townsendii,* Fox Sparrow; XXXVII; pp. 55, 134, 138 n.4, 144, 146 n.16, 152, 163)

[97]   376. *Passerella schistacea,* Baird.—Slate-colored Sparrow. (*P. iliaca shistacea,* Fox Sparrow; XXXVII; pp. 55, 134, 138 n.4, 144, 146 n.16, 152, 163)

[98]   381. *Guiraca melancephala,* Sw.—Black-headed Grosbeak. (*Pheucticus melanocephalus;* XXIX; pp. 133, 133 n.4)

[99]   382. *Guiraca caerulea,* Sw.—Blue Grosbeak. (pp. 146 n.9, 152, 154 n.2)

[100] 386. *Cyanospiza amoena,* Baird.—Lazuli Finch. (*Passerina amoena,* Lazuli Bunting; XIX)

[101] 394. *Pipilo megalonyx,* Baird.—Spurred Towhee. (*P. erythrophthalmus megalonyx,* Rufous-sided Towhee; pp. 100, 104 n.8, 134, 154)

[102] 396. *Pipilo fuscus,* Sw.—Brown Towhee. (pp. 143, 144, 146 n.8, 152)

[103] 401. *Agelaius phoeniceus,* Vieill.?—Red-winged Blackbird. (pp. 132, 133 n.2)

[104] 403. *Agelaius tricolor,* Bonaparte.—Red and White-shouldered Blackbird. (Tricolored Blackbird)

[105] 404. *Xanthocephalus icterocephalus.*—Yellow-headed Blackbird. (*Xanthocephalus xanthocephalus;* LXXX)

[106] 407. *Sturnella neglecta,* Aud.—Western Lark. (Western Meadowlark; XXXIII; pp. 80, 82 n.10)

[107] 416. *Icterus bullockii,* Bonap.—Bullock's Oriole. (*I. galbula bullockii,* Northern "Bullock's" Oriole; LXXVII; pp. 134, 138 n.11, 140–41, 144, 151)

[108] 418. *Scolecophagus cyanocephalus.*—Brewer's Blackbird. (*Euphagus cyanocephalus*)

[109] 423. *Corvus carnivorus,* Bartram.—American Raven. (*Corvus corax,* Common Raven; LXXXIX; pp. 145, 146 n.26, 169)

[110] 430. *Picicorvus columbianus,* Bonap.—Clark's Crow. (*Nucifraga columbiana,* Clark's Nutcracker; pp. 142, 145 n.5, 147)

[111] 435. *Cyanura stelleri,* Sw.—Steller's Jay. (*Cyanocitta stelleri;* XVIII; pp. 100, 103, 143)

[112] 437. *Cyanocitta californica,* Strick.—California Jay. (*Aphelocoma coerulescens californica,* Scrub Jay; XVII; pp. 45 n.12, 134, 138 n.12, 214 n.3)

[113] 445. *Columba fasciata,* Say.—Band-tailed Pigeon. (LXXXIV)

[114] 451. *Zenaidura carolinensis,* Bonap.—Common Dove. (*Zenaida macroura,* Mourning Dove)

[115] 473. *Oreortyx pictus*, Baird.—Mountain Quail. (CXXIII; pp. 53, 56, 102–3, 105)

[116] 474. *Lophortyx californicus*, Bonap.—California Quail. (*Callipepla californica*; LXXXVII; pp. 102, 105 n.17)

[117] 485. *Garzetta candidissima*, Bonap.—Snowy Heron. (*Egretta thula*, Snowy Egret; pp. 137, 138 n.15)

[118] 486a. *Herodias egretta*, v. *californica.*—California Egret. (*Casmerodius albus*, Common or Great Egret; pp. 11, 22 n.56, 137, 138 n.15, 147)

[119] 493. *Butorides virescens*, Bonap.—Green Heron. (*B. striatus virescens*, Green-backed Heron)

[120] 495. *Nyctiardea gardeni*, Baird.—Night Heron. (*Nycticorax nycticorax*, Black-crowned Night Heron; CXLVI)

[121] 500. *Ibis ordii*, Bonaparte.—Glossy Ibis. (*Plegadis chihi*, White-faced Ibis; CLIII; pp. 129, 142, 131 n.10, 142)

[122] 504. *Aegialitis vociferus*, Cassin.—Kildeer. (*Charadrius vociferus*; XCIV, CXLI; pp. 145, 146 n.25)

[123] 517. *Recurvirostra americana*, Gm.—American Avoset. (American Avocet; pp. 11, 132, 133 n.1)

[124] 518. *Himantopus nigricollis*, Vieillot.—Black-necked Stilt. (*H. mexicanus*; CXLVII; pp. 142, 146 n.7, 182)

[125] 523. *Gallinago wilsonii*, Bonap.—English Snipe. (*Gallinago gallinago*, Common Snipe)

[126] 525. *Machrohamphus scolopaceus*, La.—Greater Longbeak. (*Limnodromus scolopaceus*, Long-billed Dowitcher)

[127] 532. *Tringa wilsonii*, Nuttall.—Least Sandpiper. (*Calidris minutilla*)

[128] 535. *Ereunetes petricatus*, Ill.—Western Sandpiper. (*Calidris mauri*)

[129] 539. *Gambetta melanoleuca*, Bonap.—Tell-tale; Stone Snipe. (*Tringa melanoleuca*, Greater Yellowlegs)

[130] 543. *Tringoides macularius*, Gray.—Spotted Sandpiper. (*Actitis macularia*)

[131] 554. *Rallus virginianus*, Linn.—Virginia Rail. (*R. limicola*)

[132] 559. *Fulica americana*, Gmelin.—Coot. (American Coot; CXLIV)

[133] 575. *Dendrocygna fulva*, Burm.—Brown Tree-duck. (*D. bicolor*, Fulvous Whistling-Duck; pp. 142, 146 n.6, 215 n.3)

[134] 576. *Anas boschas*, Linn.—Mallard. (*A. platyrhynchos*; CXLII)

[135] 578. *Dafila acuta*, Jenyns.—Sprig-tail; Pin-tail. (*Anas acuta*, Northern Pintail; CXXI)

[136] 579. *Nettion carolinensis*, Baird.—Green-winged Teal. (*Anas crecca carolinensis*; CXIX)

[137] 582. *Querquedula cyanopterus*, Cassin.—Red-breasted Teal. (*Anas cyanoptera*, Cinnamon Teal; CXXXIV; pp. 113, 116 n.2, 142)

[138] 583. *Spatula clypeata,* Boie.—Shoveller. (*Anas clypeata,* Northern Shoveler; CXX)

[139] 585. *Marca americana,* Stephens.—Baldpate. (*Anas americana,* American Wigeon)

[140] 591. *Aythya americana,* Bonap.—Red-head. (Redhead; CXXXIX; pp. 129, 131 n.11, 147)

[141] 595. *Bucephala albeola,* Baird.—Butter Ball. (Bufflehead; CXLIII)

[142] 609. *Erismatura rubida,* Bonap.—Ruddy-Duck. (*Oxyura jamaicensis rubida,* Ruddy Duck)

[143] 663. *Larus californicus,* Lawr.—California Gull.

[144] 698. *Colymbus torquatus,* Brunn.—Loon. (*Gavia immer,* Common Loon)

Bibliography

Academy of Natural Sciences of Philadelphia. 1857. "Donations to the Museum." *Proceedings of the Academy of Natural Sciences of Philadelphia* 9:i–viii.

———. 1856. "Annual Report for 1856." *Proceedings of the Academy of Natural Sciences of Philadelphia* 8:323–27.

Agnew, Duncan Carr, and Kerry E. Sieh. "A Documentary Study of the Felt Effects of the Great California Earthquake of 1857." *Bulletin of the Seismological Society of America* 68 (6):1717–29.

Bache, Alexander. 1852. "Report of the Superintendent of the Coast Survey." *Senate Executive Document No. 64*, 33rd Congress, 2nd Session, 1852–53. Washington, D. C.: A. Boyd Hamilton. [Serial Set 681]

Baird, Spencer F. 1856. "Report of the Assistant Secretary." *Annual Report of the Board of Regents of the Smithsonian Institution, Showing the Operations, Expenditures, and Condition of the Institution for the Year 1855.* Washington, D. C.: A. O. P. Nicholson, Printer.

———. 1857. "Report of the Assistant Secretary." *Annual Report of the Board of Regents of the Smithsonian Institution, Showing the Operations, Expenditures, and Condition of the Institution for the Year 1856.* Washington, D. C.: A. O. P. Nicholson, Printer.

———. 1858a. "Description of new genera and species of North American lizards in the museum of the Smithsonian Institution." *Proceedings of the Academy of Natural Sciences of Philadelphia* 10:253–356.

———. 1858b. "General Report upon the Zoology of the Several Pacific Railroad Routes (Birds)." U. S. War Department. *Reports of Explorations and Surveys, to Ascertain the Most Practicable and Economical Route for a Railroad from the Mississippi River to the Pacific Ocean 1853–1856.* Vol. 8. *Senate Executive Document No. 78*, 33rd Congress, 2nd Session, 1855. Washington, D. C.: Beverly Tucker, Printer. [Serial Set 766]

———. 1858c. "General Report upon the Zoology of the Several Pacific Railroad Routes. Part III. Reptiles." U. S. War Department. *Reports of Explorations and Surveys, to Ascertain the Most Practicable and Economical Route for a Railroad from the Mississippi River to the Pacific Ocean 1853–1856.* Vol. 9. *Senate Executive Document No. 78,* 33rd Congress, 2nd Session, 1855. Washington, D. C.: Beverly Tucker, Printer. [Serial Set 766]

————. 1858d. "General Report upon the Zoology of the Several Pacific Railroad Routes. Mammals." U. S. War Department. *Reports of Explorations and Surveys, to Ascertain the Most Practicable and Economical Route for a Railroad from the Mississippi River to the Pacific Ocean 1853–1856.* Vol. 8. *Senate Executive Document No. 78,* 33rd Congress, 2nd Session, 1855. Washington, D. C.: Beverly Tucker, Printer. [Serial Set 765]

————. 1860 "Report of the Assistant Secretary." *Annual Report of the Board of Regents of the Smithsonian Institution, Showing the Operations, Expenditures, and Condition of the Institution for the Year 1859.* Washington, D. C.: William A. Harris, Printer.

————. 1861. Ibid., *1860.* Washington, D. C.: George W. Bowman, Printer.

————. 1862. Ibid., *1861.* Washington, D. C.: Government Printing Office.

————. 1866. "Review of American Birds in the Museum of the Smithsonian Institution." *Smithsonian Miscellaneous Collections XII* (181). Washington, D. C.: Government Printing Office.

————. 1872. "Report of the Assistant Secretary." *Annual Report of the Board of Regents of the Smithsonian Institution, Showing the Operations, Expenditures, and Condition of the Institution for the Year 1863.* Washington, D. C.: Government Printing Office.

————, Thomas M. Brewer, and Robert R. Ridgway. 1905. *A History of North American Land Birds.* 3 vols. Boston: Little Brown and Co.

Bancroft, Hubert H. 1884–90. *History of California.* 7 vols. San Francisco: The History Company.

Barsness, Richard W. 1967. "Los Angeles' Quest for Improved Transportation, 1846–1861." *California Hstorical Society Quarterly* 46 (4):291–306.

Beale, Edward Fitzgerald. 1858. "Report of the Secretary of War, Communicating, In answer to a resolution of the Senate, a report of E. F. Beale of his exploration for a wagon road from Fort Defiance, in New Mexico, to the western borders of California." *Senate Executive Document No. 43,* 35th Congress, 1st Session, 1857–58. Washington, D. C.: William A. Harris, Printer. [Serial Set 929]

Blake, William P. 1857. "Report of Explorations in California for Railroad Routes to Connect with the Routes near the 35th and 32d Parallels of North Latitude. Part II. Geological Report." *Explorations and Surveys, to Ascertain the Most Practicable and Economical Route for a Railroad Route from the Mississippi River to the Pacific Ocean,* Vol. 5. *Senate Executive Document No. 78,* 33rd Congress, 2nd Session, 1853–54. Washington, D. C.: Beverly Tucker, Printer. [Serial Set 762]

Bolton, Herbert H. 1931. "In the South San Joaquin Ahead of Garcés." *California Historical Society Quarterly* 10:211–19.

Brewer, Thomas M. 1859. "North American Oology." *Smithsonian Contributions to Knowledge* 11(2):1–132. Washington, D. C.: Smithsonian Institution.

Brodhead, Michael J. 1973. *A Soldier-Scientist in the American Southwest, Being a Narrative of the Travels of Brevet Captain Elliott Coues.* Tucson: Arizona Historical Society. Historical Monograph No. 1.

Browne, J. R. 1869. *Adventures in Apache Country.* New York: Harper & Brothers.

Buchanan, President James. 1860. "Message of the President of the United States Communicating, In Compliance with a Resolution of the Senate, information in relation to The Massacre at Mountain Meadows, and other Massacres in Utah Territory, May 4, 1860." *Senate Executive Document No. 42,* 36th Congress, 1st Session, 1859–60. Washington, D. C.: George W. Bowman, Printer. [Serial Set 1033]

Burt, William H., and Richard P. Grossenheider. 1976. *A Field Guide to the Mammals.* Boston: Houghton Mifflin Company.

Calvin, Ross, ed. 1951. *Lieutenant Emory Reports.* Norman: University of Oklahoma Press.

Camp, Charles L., ed. 1828–29. "An Irishman in the Gold Rush. The Journal of Thomas Kerr." *California Historical Society Quarterly* 7:205–27, 395–404; 8:167–82, 262–77.

Carleton, James H. 1850. "Table of Distances." *Stryukers American Register and Magazine.*

Cassin, John. 1856. *Illustrations of the Birds of California, Texas, Oregon, British, and Russian America.* Philadelphia, J. P. Lippincott & Co.

Chickering, Allen L. 1938. "Bandits, Borax and Bears. A Trip to Searles Lake in 1874." Translated from the French of Edmon Leuba. *California Historical Society Quarterly* 17:99–117.

Clarke, N. S. "Letters. Report of the Secretary of War." *House Executive Document No. 2,* 35th Congress, 2nd Session, 1858–59, pp. 343–44. Washington, D. C.: James B. Steedman, Printer. [Serial Set 998]

Cleland, Robert Glass. 1922. *A History of California: The American Period.* New York: The Macmillan Company.

Cooke, Philip St. George. 1857. *Scenes and Adventures in the Army; or the Romance of Military Life.* Philadelphia: Lindsay & Blakiston.

———. 1878. *The Conquest of New Mexico and California.* New York: G. P. Putnam's Sons.

Cope, E. D. 1867. "A review of the species of the Amblystomidae." *Proceedings of the Academy of Natural Sciences of Philadelphia* 19:166–211.

Coues, Elliott. 1877. *Birds of the North-West: A Hand-book of American Ornithology, Containing Accounts of All the Birds Inhabiting the Great Missouri Valley, and Many Others, Together Representing a Large Majority of Birds of North America, with Copious Biographical Details from Personal Observation, and an Extensive Synonymy.* Boston: Estes and Lauriat.

———. 1878. *Birds of the Colorado Valley.* Washington, D. C.: Government Printing Office.

Crowe, Earle. 1957. *Men of El Tejon.* Los Angeles: Ward Ritchie Press.

Cullimore, Clarence. 1949. *Old Adobes of Forgotten Fort Tejon.* Bakersfield, California: Kern County Historical Society.

Cutright, Paul Russell, and Michael J. Brodhead. *Elliott Coues.* Urbana: University of Illinois Press, 1981.

Dall, William H. 1915. *Spencer Fullerton Baird, A Biography.* Philadelphia & London: J. B. Lippincott Company.

Davis, A. C. 1932. "A list of the *Coleoptera* of Fort Tejon, California." *Bulletin of the Southern California Academy* 31:75–87.

Davis, W. N., Jr. 1973. "Research Uses of County Court Records, 1850–1879. And Incidental Intimate Glimpses of California Life and Society. Part I." *California Historical Society Quarterly* 52:241–66.

Deiss, William A. 1980. "Spencer F. Baird and his Collectors." *Journal of the Society for the Bibliography of Natural History* 9 (4):635–45.

Denburgh, John Van. 1895. "The species of the genus *Xantusia.*" *Proceedings of the California Academy of Sciences* 5 (series 2):523–34.

———. 1916. "Four species of salamanders new to the state of California, with a description of *Plethodon elongatus,* a new species, and notes on other salamanders." *Proceedings of the California Academy of Sciences* (series 4)6: 215–21.

Edgar, Dr. William F. 1893. "Historical Notes of Old Landmarks in California." *Historical Society of Southern California* 3:22–30.

Emory, William H. 1848. "Notes of a Military Reconnoissance from Fort Leavenworth," in *Missouri, to San Diego, in California, Including Parts of the Arkansas, Del Norte, and Gila Rivers. House Executive Document No. 41, 31st Congress, 1st Session, 1849–50.* Washington, D. C.: Wm. M. Belt, 1850. [Serial Set 562]

———. 1857. *Report on the United States and Mexican Boundary. House Executive Document No. 135,* 34th Congress, 1st Session, 1855–56. Washington, D. C.: Cornelius Wendell, Printer. [Serial Set 861]

Essig, E. O. 1965. *A History of Entomology.* New York: Hafner Publishing Company.

Farquhar, Francis P., ed. 1932. "The Topographical Reports of Lieutenant George H. Derby." *California Historical Society Quarterly* 11:247–65.

Feilner, John. 1872. "Exploration in Upper California in 1860, under the Auspices of the Smithsonian Institution." *Annual Report of the Board of Regents of the Smithsonian Institution for 1864,* pp. 421–30. Washington, D. C.: Government Printing Office

Frazer, Robert W., ed. 1963. *Mansfield on the Condition of the Western Forts 1853–54.* Norman: University of Oklahoma Press.

Fujino, Yozo, and Alfred H-S. Ang. 1981. "Estimation of Seismic Response of Long-Period Structures by Fault Dislocation Theory, Part 1: 1857 Fort Tejon Earthquake—Strike-Slip Faulting." In *Proceedings of US.-Japan Cooperative Re-*

search on Seismic Risk Analysis and Its Application to Reliability-Based Design of Lifetime Systems, edited by K. Kubo and M. Shinozuka. Tokyo:Oh-Okayama, Meguroku.

Gates, Paul W. 1977. "Carpetbaggers Join the Rush for California Land." *California Historical Society Quarterly* 56:98–127.

Gray, A. A. 1940. "Camels in California." *California Historical Society Quarterly* 9:299–317.

Gray, Asa. 1859–61. "List of a collection of dried plants made by L. J. Xantus, at Fort Tejon, and vicinity, California, near lat. 35°, and long. 119°, 1857–8." *Proceedings of the Boston Society of Natural History* 7:145–49.

———. 1875–76. "Miscellaneous botanical contributions." *Proceedings of the American Academy* 11:71–104.

Green, James. 1860. "On Filling Barometer Tubes." *Smithsonian Annual Report to the Board of Regents of the Smithsonian Institution, Showing the Operations, Expenditures, and Condition of the Institution for the Year 1859.* Washington: Thomas H. Ford, Printer.

Griffin, Helen S., and Arthur Woodward. 1942. *The Story of El Tejon.* Los Angeles: Dawson's Bookshop.

Grinnell, Joseph. 1905. "Old Fort Tejon." *The Condor* 7:9–13.

———. 1938. "California's Grizzly Bears." *Sierra Club Bulletin* 23:70–81

———, J. S. Dixon, and J. M. Linsdale. 1937. *Fur-bearing Mammals of California; Their Natural History, Systematic Status, and Relations to Man.* Berkeley: University of California Press.

Gudde, Erwin G., ed. and trans. 1933. "The Memoirs of Theodor Cordua. The Pioneer of New Mecklenburg in the Sacramento Valley." *California Historical Society Quarterly* 12:279–311.

Hall, E. R., and K. R. Kelson. 1959. *The Mammals of North America.* New York: Ronald Press.

Hallowell, Edward. 1856. "Notes of a Collection of Reptiles from Kansas and Nebraska, presented to the Academy of Natural Sciences, By Dr. Hammond, U.S.A." *Proceedings of the Academy of Natural Sciences of Philadelphia* 8:238–53.

———. 1859. "No. 2. Report upon Reptiles Collected on the Survey." *In* "Report of Explorations for a Railroad Route near the 32nd Parallel of North Latitude, lying between Dona Ana, on the Rio Grande, and Pimas Villages, on the Gila, by Lieutenant John G. Parke, Corps of Topographical Engineers." *Reports of Explorations and Surveys, to Ascertain the Most Practicable and Economical Route for a Railroad from the Mississippi River to the Pacific Ocean 1853–1856.* Vol. 10. *Senate Executive Document No. 78,* 33rd Congress, 2nd Session, 1855. Washington, D. C.: Beverly Tucker, Printer. [Serial Set 767]

Hamersly, Thomas H. S. 1880. *Complete Regular Army Register of the United States: For One Hundred Years, (1779–1879).* Washington: T. H. S. Hamersly.

Heitman, Francis B. 1903. *Historical Register and Dictionary of the United States*

Army, from Its Organization, September 29, 1789, to March 2, 1903. House Executive Document No. 446, 55th Congress, 2nd Session, 1902–3. Washington, D. C.: Government Printing Office, 1903. [Serial Set 4535]

Herber, Elmer C., collector and editor. 1936. *Correspondence between Spencer Fullerton Baird and Louis Agassiz: Two Pioneer American Naturalists.* Washington, D. C.: Smithsonian Institution.

History of Carroll County. 1881. St. Louis: The Missouri Historical Company.

Hume, Edgar E. 1942. *Ornithologists of the United States Army Medical Corps; Thirty-six Biographies.* Baltimore: The Johns Hopkins Press.

Hussey, John Adam. 1950. "Kit Carson at Cajon—Not Tejon." *California Historical Society Quarterly* 29:29–38.

Jackson, W. Turrentine. 1966. "A New Look at Wells Fargo, Stagecoaches and The Pony Express." *California Historical Society Quarterly* 45:291–324.

Kemble, John Haskell. 1934. "The Genesis of the Pacific Mail Steamship Co." *California Historical Society Quarterly* 13:240–54, 386–408.

———. 1937. "The 'Senator,' The Biography of a Pioneer Steamship." *California Historical Society Quarterly* 16:61–78.

Kip, William Ingraham. 1922. *A California Pilgrimage, Being an Account of the 65th Anniversary of Bishop Kip's First Missionary Journey through the San Joaquin Valley, together with Bishop Kip's Own Story of the Events Commemorated,* Louis C. Sanford, ed. Fresno, California.

Lawson, Thomas. 1839. "Statistical Report on the Sickness and Mortality in the Army of the United States. *House Executive Document No. 2,* 26th Congress, 1st Session, 1847–48. Washington, D. C.: Gales and Seaton. [Serial Set 363]

———. 1857. "Report of the Surgeon General." *House Executive Document No. 1,* 34th Congress, 2nd Session, 1858–60. Washington, D. C.: Cornelius Wendell, Printer, 1857. [Serial Set 976]

Layne, J. Gregg. 1934. "Annals of Los Angeles. Part II. From the American Conquest to the Civil War. The American Conquest." *California Historical Society Quarterly* 13:300–54.

Leavitt, Francis Hale. 1943. "Steam Navigation on the Colorado River." *California Historical Society Quarterly* 22:1–25.

Le Conte, John L. 1858. "Notes on the species of *Eleodes* found within the United States." *Proceedings of the Academy of Natural Sciences of Philadelphia* 10:180–88.

———. 1859a. "Catalogue of the Coleoptera of Fort Tejon, California." *Proceedings of the Academy of Natural Sciences of Philadelphia* 11:69–90.

———. 1861. "New species of Coleoptera inhabiting the Pacific district of the United States." *Proceedings of the Academy of Natural Sciences of Philadelphia* 13:338–59.

———. 1861–1862. "Classification of Coleoptera of North America." *Smithsonian Miscellaneous Collections* 3 (136):1–208, 208–78. Washington, D. C.: Smithsonian Institution.

———. 1866. "Additions to the coleopterous fauna of the United States. No. 1." *Proceedings of the Academy of Natural Sciences of Philadelphia* 18:361–94.

Madden, Henry Miller. 1949a. *Xantus, Hungarian Naturalist in the Pioneer West.* Linz, Austria: Oberosterreichischer Landesverlag.

———, ed. 1949b. "California for Hungarian Readers, Letters of Janos Xantus, 1857 and 1859." *California Historical Society Quarterly* 28:125–42.

Marcy, R. B. 1853. *Exploration of the Red River of Louisiana, in the Year 1852.* Senate Executive Document No. 54, 32nd Congress, 2nd Session, 1851–52. Washington, D. C.: Robert Armstrong, Public Printer. [Serial Set 666]

Meisling, Kristan E., and Kerry E. Sieh. 1980. "Disturbance of Trees by the 1857 Fort Tejon Earthquake, California." *Journal of Geophysical Research* 85:3225–38.

Merriam, C. H. 1914. "Descriptions of thirty apparently new grizzly and brown bears from North America." *Proceedings of the Biological Society of Washington* 27:173–96.

Möllhausen, Heinrich Balduin. 1858. *Tagebuch einer Resie vom Mississippi nach den Kusten der Sudsee.* Leipzig: H. Mendelssohn.

———. 1858. *Diary of a Journey from the Mississippi to the Coasts of the Pacific, with a United States Government Expedition.* London: Longmans, Brown, Green & Longmans. [New York: Johnson Reprint House, 1969].

———. 1861. *Reisen in die Felsengebirge Nord-Amerikas bis zum Hoch-plateau von Neu-Mexico.* Leipzig: H. Costenoble.

Nostrand, Jeanne Skinner Van. 1943. "The American Occupations of Rancho Santa Margarita y Las Flores." *California Historical Society Quarterly* 22:175–77.

Peterson, Roger Tory. 1961. *A Field Guide to Western Birds.* Boston: Houghton Mifflin Company.

Poole, Arthur J., and Viola S. Schantz. 1942. "Catalog of the Type Specimens in the United States National Museum, Including the Biological Surveys Collection." *United States National Museum Bulletin 178.* Washington, D. C.: Smithsonian Institution.

Rickey, Don Jr. 1981. *Forty Miles a Day on Beans and Hay.* Norman: University of Oklahoma Press.

Ridgway, Robert (and Herbert Friedman). 1901–50. *The Birds of North and Middle America. A Descriptive Catalogue of the Higher Groups, Genera, Species, and Subspecies of Birds Known to Occur in North America, from the Arctic Land to the Isthmus of Panama, the West Indies and other Islands of the Caribbean Sea, and the Galapagos Archipelago.* 12 vols. *United States National Museum Bulletin No. 50.* Washington D. C.: Smithsonian Institution.

Russell, R. J. 1919? "Land Forms of San Gorgonio Pass, Southern California." *University of California Publications in Geography* 6:23–121.

Ryan, William Redmond. 1973. *Personal Adventures in Upper and Lower California.* New York: Arno Press.

Scammel, J. M. 1950. "Military Units in Southern California, 1853–1862." *California Historical Society Quarterly* 29:229–49.

Sherzer, Karl Ritter von, and Moritz Wagner. 1856. *Die Republik Casta Rica in Central-Amerika.* Leipzig: Arnoldische Buchhandlung.

Simpson, J. H. 1850. *Report of the Secretary of War, Communicating the Report of Lieutenant J. H. Simpson of an Expedition into the Navajo Country in 1849. Senate Executive Document No. 64,* 31st Congress, 1st Session, 1849–50. Washington, D. C.: Wm. M. Belt. [Serial Set 562].

Sitgreaves, Lorenzo. 1853. "Report of an Expedition down the Zuni and Colorado rivers." *Senate Executive Document No. 59,* 32nd Congress, 2nd Session, 1851–52. Washington, D. C.: Robert Armstrong, Public Printer. [Serial Set 668]

Stansbury, Howard. 1852. *Exploration and Survey of the Valley of the Great Salt Lake of Utah, Including a Reconnaisance of a New Route through the Rocky Mountains.* Philadelphia: J. B. Lippincott.

Steptoe, Edward J. 1859. Letters, *in* "Report of the Secretary of War." *House Executive Document No. 2,* 35th Congress, 2nd Session, 1858–59. Washington, D. C.: James B. Steedman, Printer. [Serial Set 998]

Trask, John B. 1858–62. "Earthquakes in California during 1858. Earthquakes during 1859." *Proceedings of the California Academy of Natural Sciences* 2:38–39.

———. 1864. "Earthquakes in California from 1800 to 1864." *Proceedings of the California Academy of Natural Sciences* (first series) 3(2):130–53.

Treutlein, Theodore E. 1972. "Fages as Explorer, 1769–1772. Journal from March 20, 1772 to November 2, 1773." *California Historical Society Quarterly* 51:338–56.

True, F. W. 1894. "Diagnoses of some undescribed wood rats (genus *Neotoma*) in the Naional Museum." *Proceedings of the United States National Museum* 17:353–55.

U. S. Patent Office. 1857. "Report of the Commissioner of Patents for the Year 1856. Agriculture. *House Executive Document No. 65,* 34th Congress, 3rd Session, 1856–57. Washington, D. C.: Cornelius Wendell, Printer. [Serial Set 905]

U. S. Postmaster General. 1860. "Report of the Postmaster General." *Senate Executive Document No. 1,* 35th Congress, 2nd Session, 1861–62. Washington, D. C.: U. S. Government Printing Office. [Serial Set 1119]

U. S. Secretary of the Interior. 1862. *Register of Officers and Agents, Civil, Military, and Naval, in the Service of the United States, The Thirtieth September, 1861.* Washington, D. C.: Government Printing Office.

U. S. Secretary of the Navy and the Postmaster General. 1852. "Communicating, in Compliance with a Resolution of the Senate, Information in Relation to the Contracts for the Transportation of the Mails by Steamships between New York and California." *Senate Executive Document No. 50,* 32nd Congress,

1st Session, 1851–52. Washington, D. C.: A. Boyd Hamilton, 1852. [Serial Set 619]

U. S. Secretary of War. 1858. *Reports of Explorations and Surveys, to Ascertain the Most Practicable and Economical Route for a Railroad from the Mississippi River to the Pacific Ocean, 1853–6.* 10 vols. *Senate Executive Document No. 78,* 33rd Congress, 2nd Session, 1855. Washington: Beverly Tucker, Printer, 1858. [Serial Sets 760–767]

Whipple, Lieut. A. W. 1856. "The Report of Lieutenant A. W. Whipple, Corps of Topographical Engineers, upon the Route near the Thirty-fifth Parallel." *Reports of Explorations and Surveys, to Ascertain the Most Practicable and Economical Route for a Railroad from the Mississippi River to the Pacific Ocean, 1853–6.* Vol. 3. *Senate Executive Document No. 78,* 33rd Congress, 2nd Session, 1853–54. Washington, D. C.: Beverly Tucker, Printer. [Serial Set 760]

Wilke, Philip J., and Harper W. Lawton. n.d. "The Expedition of Captain J. W. Davidson from Fort Tejon to the Owens Valley in 1859." Socorro, New Mexico: Ballena Press.

Wilkes, Charles. 1852–74. *United States Exploring Expedition 1844–1874.* 24 vols. (of which 20 published). Washington, D. C.: Government Printing Office.

Williamson, Robert S. 1856. "Routes in California to Connect with the Routes near the 35th and 32d Parallels, Explored by Lieut. R. S. Williamson, Corps of Topographical Engineers, in 1853." *Reports of Explorations and Surveys, to Ascertain the Most Practicable and Economical Route for a Railroad from the Mississippi River to the Pacific Ocean, 1853–6.* Vol. 5. *Senate Executive Document No. 78,* 33rd Congress, 2nd Session, 1853–54. Washington, D. C.: Beverly Tucker, Printer, 1856. [Serial Set 762]

Wilson, Alexander. 1853. *Wilson's American Ornithology; with notes by Jardine; to Which Is Added a Synopsis of American Birds including those described by Bonaparte, Audubon, Nuttall, and Richardson: by T. M. Brewer.* New York: H. S. Samuels.

Wood, H. C. 1862–63. "On the *Chilopoda* of North America, with a catalogue of all the specimens in the collection of the Smithsonian Institution." *Journal of the Academy of Natural Sciences of Philadelphia* 5(series 2):5–52.

Württemberg, Duke Paul. 1828. *Erste Reise nach dem nordlichen America in den Jahren 1822 bis 1824.* Stuttgart; J. G. Cotta.

Xantus, John. 1858a. "Descriptions of two new species of birds from the vicinity of Fort Tejon, California." *Proceedings of the Academy of Natural Sciences of Philadelphia 10:117.*

———. 1858b. *Xantus Janos levelei Ejszakamerikabol.* Pest, Hungary: Lauffer and Stolp.

———. 1859. "Catalogue of birds collected in the vicinity of Fort Tejon, California, with a description of a new species of *Syrnium.*" *Proceedings of the Academy of Natural Sciences of Philadelphia* 11:189–93.

———. 1860. *Utazas Kalifornia deli reszeiben.* Pest: Lauffer and Stolp.

———. 1975. *Letters from North America,* translated and edited by Theodore

Schoenman and Helen Benedek Schoenman. Detroit: Wayne State University Press.

———. 1976. *Travel in Southern Parts of California,* translated and edited by Theodore Schoenman and Helen Benedek Schoenman. Detroit: Wayne State University Press.

Yarrow, H. C. 1883. *Check List of North American Reptilia and Batrachia, with Catalogue of Specimens in U. S. National Museum. United States National Museum Bulletin No. 24.* Washington: Smithsonian Institution.

Zwinger, Ann. 1985. *The Letters of John Xantus from Cabo San Lucas, 1859–1861.* Los Angeles: Dawson's Bookshop [in press].

Index

GR = General Register entry

Africa, 84
Agassiz, Louis, xi, 158, 161 n.7, 189 n.1
Alamos Rancho, 185
Alexander, George, 185, 186 n.1
Amsterdam, 76
Ant(s), 39, 86, 92 n.9
Antelope, Pronghorn (*Antilocapra americana*), 9, 18 n.14, 23, 53, 169, 197, 198 n.3
Anthus. See Pipit
Archibuteo, 206. *See* Hawk
Ardea. See Egret
Arizona, 28 n.34, 117 n.7, 150 n.6, 155 n.1
Asia, x, 72
Aspinwall, 5, 6 n.3
Atlantic & Pacific Steam Navigation Co., 115
Audubon, John James, *A Synopsis of the Birds of North America*, 19 n.29, 21 n.48, 34, 37 n.7, 39, 41, 42, 49, 52, 57, 86, 88, 102, 105 n.12, 129; 142, 154
Auratus. See Flicker
Austria/Austrian government, x, 72, 74 n.6
Avocet, 11; American (*Recurvirostra americana*), 132, 133 n.1

Bache, Alexander, 166–67 n.2
Badger (*Meles labrodoria*, now *Taxidea taxus*), 9, 12 n.1, 18 n.21, 23, 26 n.8, 29, 30, 143, 147, 164; spoiled specimens, 124, 143
Bahamas, 136, 147

Baird, Spencer F., vii, ix–x, xii–xxiv, 3 n.2, 26 n.1; agreement with Xántus, xviii–xix, 70–71, 95–98, 99 n.3, 101; birds named after, 71, 74 n.4, 106; collecting for, xii, 27 n.28; "General Report upon the Zoology of the Several Pacific Railroad Routes (Birds)," xx, 42, 95, 99 n.3, 99–100, 106, 113, 125, 128, 143, 153, 154, 162, 182, 186, 200; "General Report upon the Zoology of the Several Pacific Railroad Routes. Mammals," 34, 37 n.9, 39, 42–43 n.1, 46, 47, 50, 108, 182, 186; "General Report upon the Zoology of the Several Pacific Railroad Routes. Part III. Reptiles," 189 n.1, 200, 201 n.3; letter to Agassiz, 161 n.7, 189 n.1; letter to Archbishop of New York, 174 n.6; letter to Coolidge, 143; letter to Forbes, 17 n.5; letter to Mrs. Gardiner, x; letter to Ten Broeck, xiii, 20–21 n.37; letters, xiii, xviii, xxiii, xxvi. *See also* Baird, letters to Xántus
Baird, letters to Xántus: March 11, 1857, 22; June 1, 1857, 6 n.4; July 16, 1857, 19 n.31, 21 n.44, 22 n.55, 32, 36 n.2, 39, 42–43 n.1; September 18, 1857, 63, 187; October 3, 1857, 63, 67 nn.1 and 2; October 17, 1857, xiii, xix, 17 n.5, 18 n.24, 36 n.3, 37 nn.6 and 7, 38 nn.11, 15, and 16, 42 n.1, 75; November 2, 1857, 32 n.9, 84, 90–91 n.1, 130 n.1; November 10, 1857, 18–19 n.29, 19 n.33, 45 n.13, 92 n.7; November 16, 1857, 43 n.3, 74 n.3, 84; December 3, 1857, 54 n.6, 56 n.8, 68 n.7, 99 n.3; December 15, 1857,